First World War
and Army of Occupation
War Diary
France, Belgium and Germany

2 DIVISION
Divisional Troops
Divisional Trench Mortar Batteries
27 May 1916 - 31 December 1918

WO95/1329

The Naval & Military Press Ltd
www.nmarchive.com
Published in association with The National Archives

Published by

The Naval & Military Press Ltd

Unit 10 Ridgewood Industrial Park,
Uckfield, East Sussex,
TN22 5QE England
Tel: +44 (0) 1825 749494

www.naval-military-press.com

www.nmarchive.com

This diary has been reprinted in facsimile from the original. Any imperfections are inevitably reproduced and the quality may fall short of modern type and cartographic standards.

© Crown Copyright
Images reproduced by permission of The National Archives, London, England, 2015.

Contents

Document type	Place/Title	Date From	Date To
Heading	2 Division Troops Division Trench Mortar Batteries 1916 May To 1918 Dec.		
Heading	2nd Division Divl Artillery		
Heading	V/2 Heavy Trench Mortar Battery May To September. (27.5.16 to 7.9.16) 1916		
War Diary	Gauchin-Legal	27/05/1916	27/05/1916
War Diary	St. Venant	27/05/1916	07/09/1916
Heading	2nd Divisional Artillery V/2. Trench Mortar Battery September To December 1916		
War Diary	Colincamps	08/09/1916	31/10/1916
War Diary	Serre Sector	01/11/1916	17/11/1916
War Diary	Sarton	18/11/1916	31/12/1916
War Diary	2nd Divisional Artillery Y/2 Trench Mortar Battery September To December 1916		
War Diary	Hebuterne Area	01/09/1916	01/10/1916
War Diary	Serre Front	02/10/1916	31/10/1916
War Diary	Sarton	01/10/1916	02/10/1916
War Diary	Amplier	03/10/1916	03/10/1916
War Diary	Maizicourt	05/10/1916	06/10/1916
War Diary	St Acheul	06/10/1916	31/10/1916
War Diary	Sarton	01/11/1916	30/11/1916
Heading	2nd Divisional Artillery Z/2 Trench Mortar Battery September To December 1916.		
War Diary	La Signy Farm Serre Sector	26/08/1916	03/09/1916
War Diary	Serre	04/09/1916	04/09/1916
War Diary	Beaumont Hamel Serre	05/09/1916	30/09/1916
War Diary	La Signy Farm Serre Sector	01/10/1916	31/10/1916
War Diary	Bertrancourt	01/11/1916	01/11/1916
War Diary	Sarton	02/11/1916	06/11/1916
War Diary	Colincamps	07/11/1916	14/11/1916
War Diary	Bertrancourt	15/11/1916	20/11/1916
War Diary	Sarton	21/11/1916	02/12/1916
War Diary	Amplier	03/12/1916	03/12/1916
War Diary	Maizicourt	05/12/1916	05/12/1916
War Diary	St Acheul	06/12/1916	31/12/1916
War Diary	2nd Divisional Artillery X/2. Trench Mortar Battery September To December 1916		
War Diary	In The Field	02/09/1916	04/11/1916
War Diary	Serre Sector	01/11/1916	08/11/1916
War Diary	Sarton	09/11/1916	01/12/1916
War Diary	Amplier	02/12/1916	02/12/1916
War Diary	Maizicourt	03/12/1916	03/12/1916
War Diary	St Acheul	05/12/1916	27/12/1916
Heading	Trench Mortar Batteries Jan-Dec 1917		
Heading	2nd Divisional Artillery V/2 Trench Mortar Battery January 1917		
War Diary		01/01/1917	31/01/1917
War Diary	2nd Divisional Artillery X/2 Trench Mortar Battery : January 1917		
War Diary	St Acheul	01/01/1917	02/01/1917

War Diary	Occoches	02/01/1917	02/01/1917
War Diary	Marieux	03/02/1917	03/02/1917
War Diary	Senlis	04/09/1917	09/09/1917
War Diary	Bouzincourt	30/09/1917	30/09/1917
Heading	2nd Divisional Artillery. Y/2 Trench Mortar Battery : January 1917		
War Diary	St Acheul Occoches	02/01/1917	02/01/1917
War Diary	Marieux	03/01/1917	03/01/1917
War Diary	Senlis	04/01/1917	04/01/1917
War Diary	Bouzincourt	09/01/1917	09/01/1917
War Diary	Senlis	05/01/1917	05/01/1917
War Diary	Bouzincourt	14/01/1917	28/01/1917
Heading	2nd Divisional Artillery Z/2 Trench Mortar Battery : January 1917		
War Diary	St Acheul	02/01/1917	02/01/1917
War Diary	Occoches	02/01/1917	02/01/1917
War Diary	Marieux	03/01/1917	03/01/1917
War Diary	Senlis	04/01/1917	09/01/1917
War Diary	Bouzincourt	09/01/1917	31/01/1917
Heading	2nd Divisional Artillery V: X: Y & Z Trench Mortar Batteries February 1917		
War Diary	Bouzincourt	01/02/1917	19/02/1917
War Diary	Albert	20/02/1917	28/02/1917
War Diary	Bouzincourt	01/02/1917	18/02/1917
War Diary	Albert	19/02/1917	28/02/1917
War Diary	Bouzincourt	01/02/1917	18/02/1917
War Diary	Albert	19/02/1917	28/02/1917
War Diary	Bouzincourt	01/02/1917	18/02/1917
War Diary	Albert	19/02/1917	28/02/1917
Heading	2nd Trench Mortar Brigade 2nd Divisional Artillery V: X: Y & Z. Trench Mortar Batteries March 1917.		
War Diary	Albert	01/03/1917	08/03/1917
War Diary	Mondicourt	09/03/1917	10/03/1917
War Diary	Arras	11/03/1917	31/03/1917
War Diary	Albert	01/03/1917	31/03/1917
War Diary	Albert	01/03/1917	08/03/1917
War Diary	Mondecourt & Frevyn Capelle Arras	09/03/1917	31/03/1917
War Diary	Albert	01/03/1917	08/03/1917
War Diary	Mondicourt	08/03/1917	09/03/1917
War Diary	Frevyn Capelle	09/03/1917	10/03/1917
War Diary	Arras	10/03/1917	31/03/1917
War Diary	Albert	01/03/1917	07/03/1917
War Diary	Mondicourt	08/03/1917	08/03/1917
War Diary	Arras	09/03/1917	31/03/1917
Heading	Trench Mortar Brigade 2nd Divisional Artillery V: X: Y: & Z. Trench Mortar Batteries April 1917.		
War Diary	Arras (Roclincourt Sector)	01/04/1917	14/04/1917
War Diary	Arras	15/04/1917	30/04/1917
War Diary	Arras	01/04/1917	08/04/1917
War Diary	Arras	09/04/1917	30/04/1917
Heading	Trench Mortar Brigade 2nd Divisional Artillery V: X: Y & Z. Trench Mortar Batteries May 1917.		
War Diary	Arras (Roclincourt)	01/05/1917	31/05/1917
War Diary	Arras	01/05/1917	31/05/1917
War Diary	Roclincourt	04/05/1917	28/05/1917
War Diary	Arras	01/05/1917	03/05/1917

War Diary	Roclincourt	04/05/1917	31/05/1917
War Diary	Trench Mortar Brigade 2nd Divisional Artillery V: X: Y & Z. Trench Mortar Batteries June 1917		
War Diary	Roclincourt	06/06/1917	27/06/1917
War Diary	Roclincourt	01/06/1917	02/06/1917
War Diary	Oppy	03/06/1917	30/06/1917
War Diary	Roclincourt	01/06/1917	01/06/1917
War Diary	Ploegsteert	02/06/1917	06/06/1917
War Diary	Le Romarin	07/06/1917	15/06/1917
War Diary	Roclincourt	16/06/1917	30/06/1917
Heading	Trench Mortar Brigade 2nd Divisional Artillery V: X: Y & Z Trench Mortar Batteries July 1917.		
War Diary	Roclincourt	01/07/1917	01/07/1917
War Diary	Bethune	02/07/1917	03/07/1917
War Diary	Annequin	04/07/1917	31/07/1917
War Diary	Roclincourt	01/07/1917	01/07/1917
War Diary	Bethune	02/07/1917	02/07/1917
War Diary	Annequin	04/07/1917	30/07/1917
War Diary	Roclincourt	01/07/1917	01/07/1917
War Diary	Bethune	02/07/1917	02/07/1917
War Diary	Annequin	04/07/1917	28/07/1917
War Diary		01/07/1917	20/07/1917
War Diary	Givenchy La Bassee	20/07/1917	31/08/1917
Heading	Trench Mortar Brigade 2nd Divisional Artillery V: X: Y & Z. Trench Mortar Batteries August 1917.		
War Diary	Givenchy Canal Cambrin	01/08/1917	31/08/1917
War Diary	Annequin	01/08/1917	27/08/1917
War Diary	Annequin	01/08/1917	01/08/1917
War Diary	Beuvry	16/08/1917	31/08/1917
War Diary	Givenchy La Bassee	01/08/1917	30/08/1917
Heading	Trench Mortar Brigade 2nd Divisional Artillery V: X: Y & Z. Trench Mortar Batteries September 1917.		
War Diary	Stoney Castle Camp Brookwood	28/06/1918	30/06/1918
Heading	Confidential. War Diary of 41st Light Trench Mortar Battery From: 1st July 1918 To 31st July 1918 Volume II		
War Diary	Stoney Castle Camp Brookwood	01/07/1918	02/07/1918
War Diary	Folkestone	03/07/1918	03/07/1918
War Diary	Ostrone Camp Boulogne	04/07/1918	06/07/1918
War Diary	Loquinhem	07/07/1918	07/07/1918
War Diary	Laronville	08/07/1918	14/07/1918
War Diary	Lecosthol	14/07/1918	31/07/1918
Heading	Confidential. War Diary of 41st Trench Mortar Battery. From: 1st August, 1918. To: 31st August, 1918 Volume III.		
War Diary	Lecosthol	01/08/1918	11/08/1918
War Diary	St Jan-Ter-Biezen	19/08/1918	19/08/1918
War Diary	Brake Camp	27/08/1918	28/08/1918
War Diary	Appendix I Condition of Battery Before Leaving England	02/07/1918	02/07/1918
War Diary	Appx II		
Heading	Confidential. War Diary of 41st Trench Mortar Battery (Light). From: 1st September, 1918. To: 30th September, 1918.		
War Diary	Givenchy Canal Cambrin	01/09/1917	30/09/1917
War Diary	La Basse	01/09/1917	01/10/1917

War Diary	Beuvry	01/09/1917	30/09/1917
War Diary	Givenchy Lez La Bassee	01/09/1917	30/09/1917
Heading	Trench Mortar Brigade 2nd Divisional Artillery V: X: Y: & Z. Trench Mortar Batteries October 1917.		
War Diary	Canal Givenchy Cambrin	01/10/1917	08/10/1917
War Diary	Ames	09/10/1917	10/10/1917
War Diary	Steenbecque	17/10/1917	17/10/1917
War Diary	Godewaersvelde	18/10/1917	18/10/1917
War Diary	Siege Camp	19/10/1917	31/10/1917
War Diary	La Bassee	01/10/1917	08/10/1917
War Diary	Arras	09/10/1917	18/10/1917
War Diary	Seige Camp Nr. Vlamertinghe	19/10/1917	30/10/1917
War Diary	Cambrin	01/10/1917	07/10/1917
War Diary	Beuvry	08/10/1917	08/10/1917
War Diary	Ames	09/10/1917	13/10/1917
War Diary	Steinbecque	17/10/1917	17/10/1917
War Diary	Godewaersvelde	18/10/1917	18/10/1917
War Diary	Godewaersvelde & Siege Camp	19/10/1917	19/10/1917
War Diary	Siege Camp	22/10/1917	30/10/1917
War Diary	Givenchy Lez La Bassee	01/10/1917	08/10/1917
War Diary	Ames	09/10/1917	15/10/1917
War Diary	Steenbecque	17/10/1917	17/10/1917
War Diary	Godwaersvelde	18/10/1917	18/10/1917
War Diary	Vlamertinghe	19/10/1917	31/10/1917
Heading	Trench Mortar Brigade 2nd Divisional Artillery "V" Battery Disbanded 19.11.17. V: X: Y & Z. Trench Mortar Batteries. November 1917.		
War Diary	Siege Camp	01/11/1917	20/11/1917
War Diary	St Lawrence	20/11/1917	24/11/1917
War Diary	Haplincourt	23/11/1917	23/11/1917
War Diary	Royaulcourt	27/11/1917	27/11/1917
War Diary	Hermies	29/11/1917	30/11/1917
War Diary	Vlamatinghe	01/11/1917	19/11/1917
War Diary	St Lawrence	20/11/1917	20/11/1917
War Diary	Esquelbesques	24/11/1917	24/11/1917
War Diary	Happlincourt	24/11/1917	25/11/1917
War Diary	Royaulcourt	27/11/1917	27/11/1917
War Diary	Hermies	29/11/1917	29/11/1917
War Diary	Vlamertinghe	01/11/1917	19/11/1917
War Diary	St Laurent	20/11/1917	20/11/1917
War Diary	Esquelbecq	24/11/1917	24/11/1917
War Diary	Bapaume	25/11/1917	25/11/1917
War Diary	Haplincourt	26/11/1917	29/11/1917
Heading	Trench Mortar Brigade 2nd Divisional Artillery. X: Y: Z. Trench Mortar Batteries December 1917.		
War Diary	Hermies	01/12/1917	04/12/1917
War Diary	Ruyalcourt	04/12/1917	17/12/1917
War Diary	Stag Heap	17/12/1917	31/12/1917
War Diary	Hermies	01/01/1918	03/01/1918
War Diary	Royaulcourt	04/01/1918	17/01/1918
War Diary	Hermies	01/12/1917	02/12/1917
War Diary	Ruyaulcourt	03/12/1917	05/12/1917
War Diary	Canal du Nord	08/12/1917	17/12/1917
War Diary	Canal du Nord (Hermies)	18/12/1917	31/12/1917
Heading	2nd Division Divl. Artillery 'X', 'Y' & 'Z' Trench Mortar Batteries, Jan-Dec 1918.		

Heading	2nd Divisional Artillery. X: Y: & Z: Trench Mortar Batteries January 1918.		
War Diary	Ruyaulcourt	01/01/1918	04/01/1918
War Diary	Haplincourt	05/01/1918	23/01/1918
War Diary	Metz	30/01/1918	30/01/1918
War Diary	Royaulcourt	01/01/1918	04/01/1918
War Diary	Happlincourt	05/01/1918	21/01/1918
War Diary	Metz en Couture	23/01/1918	31/01/1918
War Diary	Canal Du Nord (Hermies)	01/01/1918	03/01/1918
War Diary	Haplincourt	04/01/1918	22/01/1918
War Diary	Metz en Couture	23/01/1918	31/01/1918
Heading	2nd Divisional Artillery. X & Y Trench Mortar Batteries : February 1918		
War Diary	Metz	01/02/1918	28/02/1918
Heading	2nd Divisional Artillery. "X"/2nd Divisional Trench Mortars. March 1918		
War Diary		01/03/1918	31/03/1918
Heading	2nd Divisional Artillery. X/2 Trench Mortar Battery April 1918		
War Diary	Varennes	01/04/1918	05/04/1918
War Diary	Bont de Pres	06/04/1918	06/04/1918
War Diary	Berlencourt	07/04/1918	09/04/1918
War Diary	Capelle-Fremont	11/04/1918	11/04/1918
War Diary	Anzin S.A.	12/04/1918	14/04/1918
War Diary	Anzin St Aubyn	05/04/1918	30/04/1918
Heading	2nd Divisional Artillery. "Y"/2nd Divisional Trench Mortars March 1918		
War Diary	Metz-en-Couture	01/03/1918	27/03/1918
War Diary	Verennes	28/03/1918	30/03/1918
Heading	2nd Divisional Artillery. Y/2 Trench Mortar Battery April 1918		
War Diary	Varennes	01/04/1918	03/04/1918
War Diary	Varennes-Grouches	05/04/1918	05/04/1918
War Diary	Grouches-Berlencourt	06/04/1918	08/04/1918
War Diary	Berlencourt Capelle-Fermont	09/04/1918	09/04/1918
War Diary	Capelle-Fermont-Anzin	11/04/1918	11/04/1918
War Diary	Anzin	12/04/1918	30/04/1918
Heading	2nd Divisional Artillery. X & Y Trench Mortar Batteries : May 1918		
War Diary	Anzin St Aubin	01/05/1918	31/05/1918
War Diary	2nd Divisional Artillery X & Y Trench Mortar Batteries : June 1918		
War Diary	Anzin St Aubin	01/06/1918	21/06/1918
War Diary	St Amand	22/06/1918	25/06/1918
War Diary	Berles-Aubois	26/06/1918	30/06/1918
War Diary	Anzin St Aubin	01/06/1918	20/06/1918
War Diary	Anzin St Aubin-St Amand	22/06/1918	22/06/1918
War Diary	St Amand	24/06/1918	25/06/1918
War Diary	St Amand-Berles-Au-Bois and Monchy-Au-Bois	26/06/1918	26/06/1918
War Diary	Monchy-Au-Bois	27/06/1918	30/06/1918
Heading	2nd Divisional Artillery. X & Y Trench Mortar Batteries : July 1918		
War Diary	Berles-au-Bois	01/07/1918	16/07/1918
War Diary	Pommier	16/07/1918	31/07/1918
War Diary	Monchy-Au Bois	01/07/1918	07/07/1918
War Diary	Rotten Ravine F.2.d.08.25.	08/07/1918	31/07/1918

Heading	2nd Divisional Artillery X & Y Trench Mortar Batteries : August 1918		
War Diary	Pommier	01/08/1918	31/08/1918
War Diary	Rotten Ravine F.2.d.08.25.	01/08/1918	21/08/1918
War Diary	Pommier	22/08/1918	31/08/1918
Heading	2nd Divisional Artillery. X & Y Trench Mortar Batteries : September 1918		
War Diary	Pommier	01/09/1918	09/09/1918
War Diary	Morchies	10/09/1918	27/09/1918
War Diary	Hermies	28/09/1918	30/09/1918
War Diary	Pommier	01/09/1918	10/09/1918
War Diary	Morchies	11/09/1918	27/09/1918
War Diary	Hermies	28/09/1918	30/09/1918
War Diary	Lock 7 Canal du Nord	30/09/1918	30/09/1918
Heading	2nd Divisional Artillery. X & Y Trench Mortar Batteries : October 1918.		
War Diary	Lock 7 Canal du Nord	01/10/1918	05/10/1918
War Diary	Flesquieres	06/10/1918	11/10/1918
War Diary	Noyelles	13/10/1918	17/10/1918
War Diary	Estourmel	18/10/1918	22/10/1918
War Diary	St Vaast	23/10/1918	23/10/1918
War Diary	St Python	24/10/1918	31/10/1918
War Diary	Lock 7 Canal du Nord	01/10/1918	02/10/1918
War Diary	Alesquieres	03/10/1918	10/10/1918
War Diary	Noyelles	11/10/1918	17/10/1918
War Diary	Estourmel	18/10/1918	21/10/1918
War Diary	St Vaast	22/10/1918	23/10/1918
War Diary	St Python	24/10/1918	31/10/1918
Heading	2nd Divisional Artillery. X & Y Trench Mortar Batteries : November 1918.		
War Diary	St Python	01/11/1918	04/11/1918
War Diary	Ruesnes	05/11/1918	09/11/1918
War Diary	Villers-Pol	10/11/1918	15/11/1918
War Diary	St Python	16/11/1918	26/11/1918
War Diary	St Python	01/11/1918	05/11/1918
War Diary	Ruenes	06/11/1918	09/11/1918
War Diary	Villers-Pol	10/11/1918	16/11/1918
War Diary	St Python	17/11/1918	30/11/1918
Heading	2nd Divisional Artillery. X & Y Trench Mortar Batteries : December 1918		
War Diary	St Python	01/12/1918	31/12/1918
War Diary	St Python	01/01/1919	30/01/1919
War Diary	Ypres Sector	01/09/1918	05/09/1918
War Diary	Night	05/09/1918	12/09/1918
War Diary	Ypres Sector	17/09/1918	19/09/1918
War Diary	Night	19/09/1918	30/09/1918
Heading	Confidential. War Diary of 41st Trench Mortar Battery (Light) From: 1st October, 1918. To: 31st October, 1918.Volume V.		
War Diary	Medoc Farm	01/10/1918	01/10/1918
War Diary	Messines	02/10/1918	05/10/1918
War Diary	P26.C. 30.95.	06/10/1918	11/10/1918
War Diary	P26.C. 30.95.	12/10/1918	14/10/1918
War Diary	Night	15/10/1918	15/10/1918
War Diary	Wulverghem	16/10/1918	17/10/1918
War Diary	Comines	18/10/1918	18/10/1918

War Diary	Roncq	19/10/1918	19/10/1918
War Diary	Herseaux	20/10/1918	31/10/1918
Heading	Confidential. War Diary of 41st Trench Mortar Battery (Light). From: 1st November, 1918 To: 30th November, 1918.		
War Diary	Dottignes	01/11/1918	16/11/1918
War Diary	Bondues	18/11/1918	25/11/1918
Heading	Confidential. War Diary of 41st Light Trench Mortar Battery. From: 1st December, 1918. To: 31st December, 1918.		
War Diary	Bondues	01/12/1918	31/12/1918
Heading	Stray/WO/95/U		

2 DIVISION. TROOPS.
DIVISION TRENCH MORTAR
BATTERIES.
1916 MAY TO 1918 DEC.

1329

2 DIVISION. TROOPS.
DIVISION TRENCH MORTAR BATTERIES.
1916 MAY TO 1918 DEC.

2ND DIVISION
DIVL ARTILLERY

V-2 HEAVY TRENCH MORTAR BATTERY
        MAY - DEC 1916
X-2 HEAVY T.M.B.
        SEP - DEC 1916
Y-2 HEAVY T.M.B.
        SEP - DEC 1916
Z-2 HEAVY T.M.B.
        SEP - DEC 1916

2nd Div.

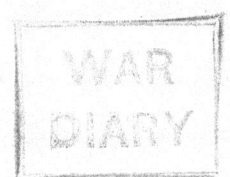

V/2 HEAVY TRENCH MORTAR BATTERY.

MAY TO SEPTEMBER.

(27.5.16 to 7.9.16)

1 9 1 6

Vol I. 2 Army For C/218

WAR DIARY or INTELLIGENCE SUMMARY.

V/2 Heavy T.M. Battery

(Erase heading not required.)

Place	Date	Hour	Summary of Events and Information	Remarks and references to Appendices
GAUCHIN-	27/5/16		Battery was formed Present being drawn from surplus of Col. 44th Howr Bde. and 2nd D.A.C. Officer i/c H.W. Stubbs Lt. R.F.A. T.P. Wolcott R.F.A.	
LEGAL.				
ST. VENANT	27/5/16		Bty underwent course of instruction at First Army T.M. School.	
	9/6/16		Fired 2 rounds on range on last day of course.	
	10/6		Joined 2nd D.A.C. at CAUCOURT.	
	12/6		Bty moved to VILLERS-AU-BOIS from V/1 Battery.	
	14/6		Fired 3 rounds in retaliation to enemy Minenwerfer took over 1 hour in action on VIMY RIDGE from V/1 Battery	
	18/6		" 10 " " " " " " and trench	
			Hours not of action at night. Lt. H.W. Stubbs admitted to Casly from 26/6/16	
	22/6		Bty moved to GOUY-SERVINS, and with 35 O.R's attached from 2nd D.A.C. worked under C.R.E. 4th Corps on buried cable system on LORETTE RIDGE	
	4/7/16		Bty was complimented by GOC 4th Corps for work done.	
	21/7/16		"Capt. H.W. Stubbs admitted to Hospital Lt. P. Wolcott assumed command.	
	22/7		Bty entrained for AMIENS.	
			Marched to DAOURS bivouac in woods for 3 nights	

contd

H.W.Stubbs Capt R.F.A.
Comdg V/2 Bty
7/9/16

Army Form C. 2118.

WAR DIARY or INTELLIGENCE SUMMARY.
(Erase heading not required.)

1/2 T.M. Battery 2/

Instructions regarding War Diaries and Intelligence Summaries are contained in F. S. Regs., Part II. and the Staff Manual respectively. Title pages will be prepared in manuscript.

Place	Date	Hour	Summary of Events and Information	Remarks and references to Appendices
	25/7/16		Marched to BOIS-DES-TAILLES	
	26/7		Marched to CARNOY and took over 1 Hour from 1/9 Bty.	
	27/7		Fired 2 rounds. Gun then put out of action by enemy fire. Sgt Croxdale Wounded, Br Hallam and Br Lowles to Hospital with shell-shock.	
	2/8/16		Took over 1 Hour from 1/3 Bty	
	7/8		Bty marched to MAULTE	
	20/8		Handed over 1 Hour to 1/3 Bty	2nd Lt A.D. Chalmers attd from 2nd D.A.C.
	21/8		Bty moved to COIGNEUX Lt - Capt Westcott to Hosp (Dysentry)	
	27/8		Bty " to COLINCAMPS and took over 4 news Hours (British make) Bty not in action and 1 French Hour in action at CHASSEURS HEDGE from 1/Guards Bty.	
	30/8		Capt A.W. Stubb rejoined Lt. P.C. Head joined from Base	
	1/9/16		Working on new positions near MATTHEW COPSE.	
	3/9/16		Fired 5 rounds in retaliation to enemy's T.M.s	
	3 to 7 d		One Hour in action remainder of Bty working on new emplacements.	

T2134. Wt. W708—776. 500000. 4/15. Sr J. C. & S.

2nd Divisional Artillery.

V/2. TRENCH MORTAR BATTERY

SEPTEMBER TO DECEMBER 1916.

WAR DIARY
or
INTELLIGENCE SUMMARY.
(Erase heading not required.)

September 1916   Army Form C. 2118.
1/2 T.M. Battery   No 3

Place	Date	Hour	Summary of Events and Information	Remarks and references to Appendices
COLINCAMPS	8/9/16			
	9th		No firing, working on new emplacement near MATTHEW COPSE. O.o. L. Davis, D' Bray, D' Barker killed by Minenwerfer near new position.	
	11th		Fired 2 rounds from No 2 retaliation 1 round fell in our lines probably due to defective charge. How itzer in action near MATTHEW COPSE (No 1)	
	12th		Fired 6 rounds retaliation (No 2) Lt. J.B. slightly gassed from 6" gas	
	14th		Discovered a badly made How" position near CHASSEURS HEDGE and commenced work on it. Fired 2 rounds from No 1 and 4 from No 2 in co-operation with Infantry raids. (12 mid-night)	
	16th		Took over another How.	
	18th		No 1 fired 2 rounds retaliation	
	19th		No 1 fired 4 rounds "Slaying"	
	21st		No 1 fired 2 rounds retaliation. Third gun put in action (No 3)	
	23rd		No 1 fired 3 rounds registration. No 2 fired 1 round retaliation	
			2 Rounds from No 1 were air bursts	

WAR DIARY
or
INTELLIGENCE SUMMARY.
(Erase heading not required.)

Army Form C. 2118.

September 1916

Hotchkiss Battery
Emery r/o T.M. 13/5
8/10/16

Place	Date	Hour	Summary of Events and Information	Remarks and references to Appendices
	24/9/16		No 1 out of action awaiting for repairs to pile damage caused by firing yesterday. No 2 fired 2 rounds "Sleeping"	
	25"		No 2 fired 3 rounds } Co-operation with Left Group R.A. retaliation scheme No 3 fired 3 rounds }	
	26"		Dr Culshaw slightly wounded by Shrapnel. All three Hows fired in co-operation with Left Group R.A. bombardment, 32 rounds. Fire very effective. No 2 had 1 short round and No 3 had 2 short rounds doing no damage to our own line. "Huns" fired a few rounds near each gun but did no damage, on the whole retaliation was very slight.	
	27"		No 3 fired 4 rounds retaliation	
	28"		No 3 fired 1 round } retaliation No 2 fired 1 round }	
	29/30"		No firing. Commenced work on a new position on HEBUTERNE – SERRE road. Note: Diary from 1st to 7th sent to Base on 9" Sept.	

T2134. Wt. W708—776. 500000. 4/15. Sr J. C. & S.

Army Form C. 2118.

1/2 4TM Bty

Vol 6

WAR DIARY
or
INTELLIGENCE SUMMARY.
(Erase heading not required.)

Instructions regarding War Diaries and Intelligence Summaries are contained in F. S. Regs., Part II. and the Staff Manual respectively. Title pages will be prepared in manuscript.

Place	Date	Hour	Summary of Events and Information	Remarks and references to Appendices
Colincamps	1/11/16		No firing owing to lack of ammunition in Div. Working on new position.	
	2nd		Working on new position.	
	3rd		No firing ordered to cease working on position near Hebuterne, and take charge of 2" T.M. ammunition for 2nd and 3rd 18th Lahore 63rd R.N.D. 1st and 2nd Canadians Divisions.	
	4th		Ordered to find 2 positions and put in Howitzers to fire at the Quadrilateral. Officers and men still assisting in supply of 2" T.M. Ammunition.	
	5th		Commenced work on one position at K34 central (No 1. gun)	
	6th		Continued work on new No 1 and commenced work on new position at K34 B 15-65- (No 2 gun) Handed over old No 2 to V/51. Continued to assist supply of 2" T.M. Bombs	

WAR DIARY
or
INTELLIGENCE SUMMARY

Army Form C. 2118.

Place	Date	Hour	Summary of Events and Information	Remarks and references to Appendices
Colincamps	7/10/16		Work on new positions	
	8th		Handed over old No 3 gun to 51st Div. Work on new positions	
	9th		Handed over old No 1. to 63rd R.N.D. V/11 attached and selected 2 positions for them to commence work at once off Rouen Road	
	10th		Continued work on positions with help of RND Engineers. Continued work on positions and supply of bombs to 2" T.M.s at night took 2 Howitzers into line and 40 rounds to each	
	11th		Continued work on position	
	12th		Continued work on position. 11 H.T.M.s took one Howitzer and 20 rounds into the line.	
	13th		Continued work on position. Cp. Jurisolton slightly wounded in leg. Received 1 Howitzer from 19th Div. in very bad condition & many stores difficult & supply of T.M. bombs	
	14,15,16,17,18		Work on positions	
	19th		Work on positions	
	20th		No 2 gun in action. Work on positions	
	21st		No 1 gun in action continued work on positions. Another gun for V/11	

WAR DIARY

3

Colincamps

22/10/16. Continued work on positions.

23rd Ordered to fire from 10 a.m till 5 p.m but too misty for observation until 11.30 a.m. Fired 50 rounds from 4 guns V/11 firing 32 and our own guns firing 9 each. Enemy retaliated heavily. Dr Cox slightly wounded. Firing was on Q undertaken and appeared to be very effective.

24th N° 7 wing detachment withdrawn from the line.

Operations postponed owing to bad weather.

25th Nothing done. Bad weather.
26th do do do
27th do do do
28th do do do. att 2.30 p.m. a 4.2 shell hit our billet bursting in mess and officer. Some very narrow escapes. 2Lt Thead + slight cuts on the head otherwise very little damage.

29th N° 2 position damaged by shell fire
30th Work on repairing N° 2 position.
31st Work on repairing N° 2 position.

H W Webb Lt
for Major O.C. 85
January 2/11/16

WAR DIARY or INTELLIGENCE SUMMARY

Army Form C. 2118.

V⁺ T.M. Battery

Vol 7

(Erase heading not required.)

Place	Date	Hour	Summary of Events and Information	Remarks and references to Appendices
SERRE SECTOR	1/16		Continued work on repairing No. 2 position Lr. Wyler & Sr. Read wounded at the Pillets.	
	2/16		C.A.R.E's helping us to repair No. 2 pit.	
	3/16		Do.	
	4/16		Do.	
	5/16		Do.	
	6/16		Do.	
	7/16		Do. Dr. Hudspeth returns.	
	8/16		Captain Stults & Corporal Jamieson go to V Army Trench Mortar School of Instruction. Lt. Roberts takes command. 2ⁿᵈ Lt. A. D. Chalmers slightly wounded in left leg.	
	9/16		Working Party repairing No. I.	
	10/16		Lt Roberts to be Temporary Captain while in command.	
	11/16		"X day" Working parties and detachments at both guns - cleaning guns - cleaning pits, ammunition, and generally making all ready for "Y Day" bombardment. New telephone No. 2 position chilled between 03 43.30 Mm with a dozen H.2 in. Direct hit on bomb store, burying 4 bombs beyond recovery. Gunners Hamilton, Adamson, Lance Stephen wounded in Colincamps. Y/11. H.T.M. Bty. reports:- "We have been repairing our positions all day & are now ready to fire. We were cont)	

2449 Wt. W14957/M90 750,000 1/16 J.B.C. & A. Forms/C.2118/12.

WAR DIARY or INTELLIGENCE SUMMARY

Army Form C. 2118.

Place	Date	Hour	Summary of Events and Information	Remarks and references to Appendices
SERRE SECTOR	11/11/16		"X day" Cont. unable to lay fresh wire to Green St. as trenches all filled up, & I was obliged to withdraw Telephonist as Boche M.G. Fire brought to bear on us. Our O.P. is wiped out, however I propose to run a fresh wire to an O.P. close to old one, just before we fire.	
	12/11/16		"Y day". No 1. Gun fired 30 rounds on the Chord of the QUADRILATERAL; only one very short. Effect of the great majority very good. No 2. Gun fired 24 rounds on the Chord & Northern face. Two very short. Effect very good. Practically no retaliation. Heavy Guns were bombarding along the whole front during the shoot. Shooting area from 10 a/m. to 12 noon and 1. to 2 p/m. Two Gunners wounded from "nerves" after the shoot, but quickly recovered. V/11. H.T.M. Bty. reports:— "We fired remaining 149 rounds to day, no casualties. Good bursts + much damage observed in enemy's lines.	
	13/11/16		"Z day". Very misty. Infantry attacked at dawn. Battery remained in Colincamps which was rather heavily shelled during the evening.	
	14/11/16		Party of 20 under Captain Roberts taken up to "Old German" second line to relieve the wounded. Parade at midnight; return at 6 a/m. Carried its Succurie.	
	15/11/16		Moved to Bertrancourt. Party of 11 under 2 Lts. Chalmers + Lindley carried wounded from Old German 2 L. to White City. Paraded 5.30 p/m. Returned 4 a/m.	

WAR DIARY
or
INTELLIGENCE SUMMARY.

(Erase heading not required.)

Army Form C. 2118.

Place	Date	Hour	Summary of Events and Information	Remarks and references to Appendices
	16/10/16		Party of 20 under 2.Lt Head carried wounded from Quadrilateral to Souveniv. Paraded 4 p/m returned 11 p/m.	
	17/10/16		Party of 13 lent to Z.2. Battery to assist in extracting Medium Guns from line, under Lt Vaisey. Paraded 1.30 p/m returned 8.30 p/m.	
SARTON	18/10/16		Battery moved to SARTON. Only two G.S. Wagons were provided so the stores had to be left in Bertrancourt in charge of Z.2. Billets in SARTON all overcrowded but packed in for 1 night with the help of X.2. + Y.2. accommodation.	
	19/10/16		Changed billets in SARTON. Bombardier Mayhew proceeded to V Army School of Mortars for a course of instruction.	
	20-24/10/16		Daily Parade for Instruction + Drill.	
	25/10/16		Party went up + cleaned all four guns. Reported No 2. left Gun damaged by shell fire, principally as to elevating axis + lifting rings. As for 20 - 24/10/16.	
	26/10/16			
	27/10/16		Standed over two right guns to V/39. H.T.M.Bty. all gun stores included.	
	28/10/16		Handed over two left guns to V/39 H.T.M.Bty. all gun stores included.	
	29-30/10/16		Parades for Inspection + Drill.	

WAR DIARY or INTELLIGENCE SUMMARY

V. L T M Bty 2 A Vol 8

Army Form C. 2118.

Place	Date	Hour	Summary of Events and Information	Remarks and references to Appendices
SARTON	1/10		Battery paraded at full strength at 5.50 a/m to reload 18 br. Ammunition at A.R.P. on Puchevillers - Acheux Road. Returned 4 p/m.	
	2/10		2/Lt A.D. Chalmers on leave. 10 G.S. wagons, 60 mules, 2 horses and attendant personnel attached to V: on behalf of 2nd Divisional Trench Mortar Batteries. 5 Reinforcements joined from 2nd D.A.C.	
	3/10		Marched to AMPLIER and stayed there for the night.	
	4/10		Marched to MAIZICOURT.	
	5/10		Rested in MAIZICOURT.	
	6/10		Marched to ST ACHEUL and settled down in good billets for the Rear. 9 wagons, 54 mules, 2 horses and attendant personnel returned to 2nd D.A.C. one wagon team (6 mules) and three drivers being retained as supply wagon. 5 Reinforcements sent to V. Army School of Mortars for Instruction. 5 horses and 2 drivers lent by 36th Brigade for use of T.M. Officers. Drills and Inspections.	
	7/10		Br. Mayhew returned from Course of Instruction. 3 horses and 2 drivers lent by 36th Brigade for use of T.M. Officers. Drills and Inspections.	

V: N T M Bty

Army Form C. 2118.

WAR DIARY
or
INTELLIGENCE SUMMARY.
(Erase heading not required.)

Instructions regarding War Diaries and Intelligence Summaries are contained in F. S. Regs., Part II. and the Staff Manual respectively. Title pages will be prepared in manuscript.

Place	Date	Hour	Summary of Events and Information	Remarks and references to Appendices
	8/12/16		2/Lt. J.B. Lindley on leave.	
	14/12/16		2/Lt. A.D. Chalmers returned from leave.	
	9-15/12/16		Parades, Drills & Inspections daily.	
	16/12/16		2/Lt. P.B. Head + 1 other rank proceeded on leave to England.	
			Usual Parades & Drills.	
	17-24/12/16		Daily Parades, Inspections + Drills.	
	25/12/16		Church Parade at 9 a.m. No subsequent Parades.	
	26-30/12/16		Daily Parades, Inspections + Drills	
	29/12/16		2/Lt. P.C. Head returned from leave	
	30/12/16		Horses returned to 36th Brigade.	
			Capt. Roberts proceeded on leave to England	
	31/12/16		4 Reinforcements joined Battery from 2nd D.A.C.	

2nd Divisional Artillery.

Y/2 TRENCH MORTAR BATTERY

SEPTEMBER TO DECEMBER 1916.

WAR DIARY 1/2 T.M.B.

INTELLIGENCE SUMMARY September 1916

Army Form C. 2118

Place	Date	Hour	Summary of Events and Information	Remarks and references to Appendices
HÉBUTERNE area.	Sept 1.		Work continued on dug out in JEAN BART trench. Gun emplacements started in DENT STREET. No rounds fired.	
	Sept. 2. - Sept. 7.		Infantry object to guns in CHASSEURS HEDGE being fired. No firing. Work continued on dug out and the two gun emplacements in DENT STREET.	
	Sept. 7.		Lt. G. SCOTT, R.F.A. relinquished Command of the battery on being transferred to the 16th Batt. R.F.A. 2/Lt. G.C.SMITH took over Command of the battery. Dug out completed.	
	Sept.7-10.		No firing. Work still continued on gun emplacements.	
	Sept. 10.		New 1 gun position was found in front of LABOUR AVENUE, turning off PASTEUR at K.17.C.2.½. This position had been used as a latrine by the infantry but it was decided to dig it out.	
	Sept. 11		2/Lt. C.P. McIlquham. R.F.A. joined the battery from the 61st Div. A working party of 11 men joined the	

WAR DIARY or **INTELLIGENCE SUMMARY**

Army Form C. 2118

Y/2 T.M.B. September 1916

Place	Date	Hour	Summary of Events and Information	Remarks and references to Appendices
HÉBUTERNE	Sept. 12.		The two guns (Nos. 1&2) in CHASSEURS HEDGE were registered on enemy front line; 8 rounds fired.	
	Sept. 13.		Wire cutting continued on DENT STREET position. Wire cutting started by Nos. 1 & 2 guns on front of enemy line at the "POINT", K.23.6.6.0. Coffee firing 27 rounds & having cut a gap in the wire, the position was shelled by 5.9's. No. 2 gun was completely buried with two direct hits and the passage leading to No. 1 gun was blown in. JEAN BART trench was filled in for nearly 20 yds.	
	Sept. 14.		The new position near LABOUR AVENUE completed (No. 5 gun). During the night 11 rounds were fired from this gun and 12 rounds from No. 1. Young was ordered	

WAR DIARY 1/2 T.M.B.

or

INTELLIGENCE SUMMARY September 1916

Army Form C. 2118

Place	Date	Hour	Summary of Events and Information	Remarks and references to Appendices
HÉBUTERNE Area.	Sept 14		by the infantry as part of a scheme for a night raid.	
	Sept. 15		Work still continued on DENT STREET emplacements. We made a gun attack a our front. During the night in an infantry raid we fired 10 rounds from No. 1 gun. It was decided not to put No. 2 gun back in its former position.	
	Sept. 16.		Gun pits started in DENT STREET. The work was then taken over by the R.E.'s, working parties being supplied from the battery. D.A.C. and 21st Bde R.F.A.	
	Sept. 16-19		Work continued. 12 rounds fired in retaliation.	
	Sept. 20		Next position found near No. 3 gun at K.17.c.2½.1. The front was reconnoitred up to "16 Poplars" K.17.a.5.9. for new positions but none were found within range of enemy front line.	
	Sept. 21.		During a night libd 37 rounds were fired from No. 1 & 3 guns	

WAR DIARY or INTELLIGENCE SUMMARY

Army Form C. 2118

Nr. T.M.B. September 1916

Place	Date	Hour	Summary of Events and Information	Remarks and references to Appendices
HÉBUTERNE Area	Sept. 22 -24		Work continued on all positions. No. 4 position was slowly completed & found of No. 3 position was rebuilt.	
	Sept 24 25		During a night raid 22 rounds were fired. 40 rounds fired by night. Passage to No. 1 gun again flown in by a 5.9 shell "mountain" carried	
	26		Dull night in preparation for wire cutting. Wire cutting carried by No. 3 & 4 guns — 90 rounds fired on wire at K.23.t.2.9. A good gap was cut. A combined scheme of retaliation was brought in — all mortars & field guns to fire during a certain time at wire, front line, & "Minnie" emplacements	
	Sept 27. 28		58 rounds fired in wire cutting and 14 in retaliation. Work still continued on trenches.	
	Sept. 28 -30		Tent Street was blown in twice by our heavy mortars falling short. Work delayed by mistakes	

Army Form C. 2118.

WAR DIARY
or
INTELLIGENCE SUMMARY 1/2 T.M.B. September 1916

(Erase heading not required.)

Place	Date	Hour	Summary of Events and Information	Remarks and references to Appendices
HEBUTERNE	Sept. 28	-30th	made by the RE's in digging shafts to gun pits. The whole front was reconnoitred for positions for 20 extra 2" guns. 36 rounds were fired in retaliation.	

G.C. Smith 2nd
O.C. 1/2 T.M.B.

3/10/16

Army Form C. 2118.
TRENCH MORTAR
BATTERY.

No.................
Date................

WAR DIARY or INTELLIGENCE SUMMARY

of Y/2 T.M.B. for October. Vol 2

(Erase heading not required.)

Place	Date	Hour	Summary of Events and Information	Remarks and references to Appendices
HEBUTERNE area.	1st		Handed over positions to the 184 Division. Our battery moved in to the Centre Brigade front & started digging in all four guns.	
	2nd 3rd		Work continued on gun positions. Four guns were finally ready for action – two in ROB ROY trench, one in a disused trench a few yards in front of ROB ROY & the other in a communication trench, LE CATEAU.	
	4th		Opened fire with 2nd. 394 gun. 32 rounds were fired – all a wire cutting	
	5th 6th		60 rounds were fired – position heavily shelled. 23 rounds were fired. Gnr. TIGHE 2nd DOWLING were killed in action by a premature at No. 3 gun. the bomb exploding on the parapet.	
	7th		40 rounds were fired. Positions were again shelled while guns were in action.	

WAR DIARY

4th T.M.B
INTELLIGENCE SUMMARY for October

Army Form C. 2118.

Y/2 TRENCH MORTAR BATTERY.

Place	Date	Hour	Summary of Events and Information	Remarks and references to Appendices
Somme Front.	9th		The battery moved in to the right Brigade Front + took over positions from the 63rd Division. The battery from whom we took over had only two guns in action neither of which was in range of enemy wire. There was no ammunition handed over to us.	
	10th / 11th		Time was occupied in digging positions. One gun was dug in in the frontline, another in WOLF trench and disused positions were found + cleared out in CHATHAM & TOM FOY trenches	
	12th — 16th		372 rounds were fired on enemy front line wire. Batteries were shelled daily owing to shortage of men, work was stopped at the CHATHAM position & we concentrated on TOM FOY position.	

Army Form C. 2118.

WAR DIARY
or
INTELLIGENCE SUMMARY

of Y/2 T.M.B.

(Erase heading not required.)

TRENCH MORTAR BATTERY.	Y/2
No.	for October

Instructions regarding War Diaries and Intelligence Summaries are contained in F. S. Regs., Part II. and the Staff Manual respectively. Title Pages will be prepared in manuscript.

Place	Date	Hour	Summary of Events and Information	Remarks and references to Appendices
Serre Front.	17th		Position in WOLF trench and front line had to be improved. The gun beds were put in afresh.	
	18th		29 rounds were fired. Weather was extremely bad — rain nearly every day — Great difficulty was experienced with the gun beds. The gun in the front line was fast out of action.	
	19th		Weather was very bad. 32 rounds were fired on enemy wire. O.P. in CHEEROTH trench was heavily shelled.	
	20th / 21st		126 rounds fired on enemy wire. Good gaps had previously been made by our fire & these were enlarged.	
	22nd		TOM POY gun was registered. The charges were very bad but bands falling back into the gun pit. Minimud position was heavily shelled by the enemy.	

2449 Wt. W14957/M90 750,000 1/16 J.B.C. & A. Forms/C.2118/12.

Army Form C. 2118.

WAR DIARY of **Y/2 T.M.B.**

INTELLIGENCE SUMMARY for **October**

Y/2 TRENCH MORTAR BATTERY.

Place	Date	Hour	Summary of Events and Information	Remarks and references to Appendices
Serre front.	23rd		40 rounds were fired. T.M. Pt position was completely smashed in by enemy trench mortars; it was impossible to recognise the position or where it had been. 46 gas bombs were brought up to the gun positions.	
	24th		Position in front line again knocked out. 29 rounds were fired.	
	25th		Bomb store at the Wolf trench position was blown in — some gas bombs were hit & began to leak. These were buried by it was considered unsafe to fire the gun at that position.	
	26th		Front line completely filled in by enemy shell fire. It was then impossible to reach this gun in daylight.	

Army Form C. 2118.

WAR DIARY or INTELLIGENCE SUMMARY

of Y/h T.M.B Army Form
for October

(Erase heading not required.)

TRENCH MORTAR BATTERY. Y/2

Place	Date	Hour	Summary of Events and Information	Remarks and references to Appendices
Serre front.	27th		Weather was again extremely bad – It was almost impossible to fire guns owing to heavy rain. Took over two guns from X/h battery in BURROW Trench.	
	28th	7.15	29 rounds were fired – both gun beds shifted considerably & had to be dug in afresh. 26 jam bombs were fired off in a gas attack at 11pm. More could have been fired but the infantry carrying party to bring up bombs failed to arrive.	
	29th 30th		Weather extremely bad. 30 rounds were fired. Owing to the bad state of trenches it was impossible to carry the bombs to send positions.	
	31st		Our battery moved back to BERTRANCOURT. G.C. Smith Lt. O.C. Y/h T.M.	

Army Form C. 2118.

WAR DIARY of Y/2 T.M.B.
INTELLIGENCE SUMMARY
(Erase heading not required.)

Vol 4

Place	Date	Hour	Summary of Events and Information	Remarks and references to Appendices
SARTON	1st		Billets, stores, etc. Cleaned up preparatory to moving.	
SARTON	2nd		Marched to AMPLIER.	
AMPLIER	3rd		Marched to MAIZICOURT.	
MAIZICOURT	5th		Marched to ST. ACHEUL. Bdr. BELTON proceeded to V Army T.M. School for course of instruction. Gnr. WILSON. A.E. joined the Battery	
ST. ACHEUL to	6th to		Battery remained at rest. Daily parades & inspections were carried out. Instruction was given in the telephone & Morse Code. Firing instruction was given to the last joined men.	
	31st		On the 6th Cpl. PEMBERTON & Bdr. NOYLAND rejoined from V Army T.M. School. On the 24th 2/Lt L.W. GILL & R.T.O. BARRATT joined the Battery. G.C. Smith Lt. O.C. Y/2 Bty	

WAR DIARY or **INTELLIGENCE SUMMARY** of Y/½ T.M.B. for NOVEMBER.

Army Form C. 2118.

Place	Date	Hour	Summary of Events and Information	Remarks and references to Appendices
SARTON	Nov.1. to Nov.30.		The battery moved to SARTON. During this month the battery was out of action. Inspections were carried out daily. Foot drill, rifle drill, physical training, note trenches and lectures on the field telephone etc. were also carried out. On the 8th Bdr. NOYLAND went to V Army T.M. School as instructor. On 19th CPL. PEMBERTON proceeded to T.M. School for a course of instruction.	Vol 3

C.C. Smith
1/12/16 O.C. Y/½ T.M.B.

2nd Divisional Artillery.

Z/2 TRENCH MORTAR BATTERY

SEPTEMBER TO DECEMBER 1916.

Army Form C. 2118.

2/2 T.M.B.
September 1916

Vol 1

WAR DIARY or INTELLIGENCE SUMMARY

(Erase heading not required.)

Place	Date	Hour	Summary of Events and Information	Remarks and references to Appendices
LA PLUS FARM, SERRE SECTOR.	26/8/16	5.30 P.M.	Took over from Yeomanry T.M.B. 2 no guns in action on NORTH MONK STREET – K.29.C.35.50. Right gun gave two hits immediately F.L. at K.29.D.25.50, left gun at K.29.B.10.00. 20 bombs at gun.	
		8 P.M.	Fired 5 rounds from No. 1 gun in retaliation for machine gun on Y/840. 479. 17 & 90 zero. Moved from F.L. first left of GREY. First approximately correct, range & height long.	
		10 P.M.	About 10 began 4.20 full push on front of position.	
	27/8/16	9 P.M.	Enemy set brush afire. Detachment carried bombs from store at K.29.A.35.50 to guns.	
		10.30 P.M.	Received orders to cut wire.	
		11 P.M.	Detachment at East British Infantry working parties 35 carrying bombs from K.29.A.35.10 to guns and Lightbat bombs K. from K.26.C.30.20 to guns. Total complete bombs at guns at end of day – 170.	
			Fired 7 rounds from No. 2 gun in retaliation for machine gun. Placed wounds box & both guns to stand pull of twist for elevating. F.L. Oldham Chapel at K.29.C.80.75 and K.29.C.80.60 about	

Army Form C. 2118.

2nd/1 M Bty
September 1916

WAR DIARY
or
INTELLIGENCE SUMMARY

(Erase heading not required.)

Place	Date	Hour	Summary of Events and Information	Remarks and references to Appendices
	27/8/16		Quiet night with rain. Shoots from guns.	
	28/8/16		Everything set ready for firing at dawn, and in GREY an answer to F.L.O.P., when heavy thunderstorm fell in GREY a few yards from Left O.P., smashing telephone wire and bogging it in Clips Ships. Felt nothing in the way of return could be done until check. Observed fire from Gate Battery O.P. on TAUPIN along Right Battalion wire. Fired 40 rounds from No. 2 gun, howitzer was shot considerably. Very high percentage of shorts, our firing most especially so to deflection, and the range could not be got quite true enough owing to dust-cover on gun dial thermal parts felt in enemy F.L. trenches, throwing up earth timber and causing a fire. Fired 13 rounds from No. 1 gun, but observation of F.L. in this line impossible. Good observation for support line, however. Position shelled by 4.20, something from heavy trench mortars in two places. Close to Gun throughout. Lieut Stone and Vaughan with gun. 2nd Lt G.C. Smith took 2 pairs N.5 battery & duty here in the Beaumont Hamel sector. Work at 42246 unsupporting on aiming trench, digging out trench above	

WAR DIARY or INTELLIGENCE SUMMARY

Army Form C. 2118.

2nd T.M. Bty.

September 1916

Place	Date	Hour	Summary of Events and Information	Remarks and references to Appendices
	2/3 P.M.		Sent No.1 gun out in enlarging No.3 that so as to get greater stability and shorter range. Work completed by 6 P.M., but No.2 gun had to again be relaid on a dead-cow support somewhat rightward being obstinate, necessitating gun being removed & put forward to clear.	
	3/4 P.M.		Parados shelled with 5.9s and H.E. shrapnel. No damage, shells falling behind guns.	
	4.30 P.M.			
30/8/16	9 P.M.		Both guns ready for action, but a heavy thunderstorm during night shook foundations. Gun in Beaumont Hamel Redan dug in.	
			Notified Right Battalion that firing would commence at 10 a.m., but was requested by Bn. Commander to postpone shooting until completion of Relief (about 7 P.M.). Inspected 3 Infantry O.Ps. and Snipers posts, but these were found to be nowhere from our point of view. The firing cannot cut away to ? Relief not being completed until after dark.	

WAR DIARY or INTELLIGENCE SUMMARY

2/⁴ T.M. By Army Form C. 2118.
September 1916

Date	Hour	Summary of Events and Information
31/8/16		Very bad weather. No firing. Work on gun positions, front and rear gun-emplacements in about entrances of this country.
1/9/16		Sunk in Beaumont Hamel left, floored & dismounted E.N. Ammunition brought up during night. Morning spent on front position and gun cleaning, laying of telephone wires, etc. Reconnoitred Left Battalion Front for positions.
	5 p.m.	Registration carried out. No. 2 gun shooting with considerable enfilade enfilation, but accurate shooting. After 6 rounds, a shrapnel from the field firing from about K.35.D.10.60 in retaliation for our shooting. 13th Bty. R.F.A. was directed on to the target by Major B. Cameron who subsequently reported position to Howitzer Bty. during this and gun position was very heavily shelled not heavy oil, with front trap cradled (approx 8"). The gun turret, No. 2 position and the left entrance to the dug-out were all completely covered. No. 76939 Dvr. H. SWINNERTON was buried, his legs being so jammed by beams & planks that it took 1½

2449 Wt. W14957/M90 750,000 1/16 J.B.C. & A. Forms/C.2118/12.

WAR DIARY or INTELLIGENCE SUMMARY

Army Form C. 2118.

2nd/1st M.Sy.Bty.

September 1916

Place	Date	Hour	Summary of Events and Information	Remarks and references to Appendices
	2/9/16	11 p.m.	Horses hand over by the personnel of the Battery and a party of 6 men from the Right Battalion under the Stables disinfection of Major CARTER, M.C., to contribute the trophy. Beaumont Hamel - Beds changed - fires refastened. 6 rounds fired from SWINNERTON thrown on British Cemetery at X.26.D.00.50 by Revd. MURRAY. Battery Commander & 3 men attended.	
		3 p.m.	Reconnoitred Left Battalion Front for positions with D.T.M.O.	
		8.30 p.m.	Received orders to abandon position. Dug out 20 a-gun with great difficulty, cleaned and stored all ordnance and equipment, sent Lewis Gun's personnel after 8 days tour.	
	3/9/16		Beaumont Hamel. More ammunition brought up. Nipihi an rear support carried up Right Battalion in COLIN CAMPS.	
		5 a.m. to 8 a.m.	Beaumont Hamel. Tailing bomb all night. Had very fine shooting. Firing at front line support & wire Difficulty with shifting of hide & minefire. Fire ZZ 130 rounds.	

Army Form C. 2118.

2/3rd Bhy.
September 1916

WAR DIARY or INTELLIGENCE SUMMARY

(Erase heading not required.)

Place	Date	Hour	Summary of Events and Information	Remarks and references to Appendices
Serre	1/9/16.		Eve its plans for new position at K.29.c.w.5.85. with officers of 2nd Anglian Field Co. R.E.	
Beaumont Hamel Serre	2/9/16	8 p.m.	½ Battery + guns brought out + taken to Colincamps by 2 lots F.C. Smith.	
	3/9/16		Commence work on new position.	
	6/9/16		Endeavour to find positions for two guns on left Batt- level, but find it is all too much overlooked by Enemy. 2nd F.C. Smith takes forward 9/½ B.L.	
	7/9/16		Continue work on new position. Progress slow owing to the fact that two stairways have first to be made and which only a very few men can be employed. Enfilading warnings of impending operations. Position is in the Zone that direct two Minnenwerfer. Three men killed. Borrowed for work from 1/2 B.by. killed last overnight.	
	13/9/16		Position in Grey Trench.	
	14/9/16	7 p.m.	On receiving instructions to coöperate in Raid undertaken by 1/B + the King's Rif. Prepare no 1 gun for action, kept in to stand in an emergency position + carried in parapet in front March 31 about K.29.c.25.7. Slight shelling of trench by Enemy during digging operations. Position completed + one burst fired to verify. No return from Enemy. Parapet to fall on Enemy parapet at K.29.0.2.8.	

Army Form C. 2118.

2nd T.M. S&y 7

September 1916

WAR DIARY
or
INTELLIGENCE SUMMARY

(Erase heading not required.)

Instructions regarding War Diaries and Intelligence Summaries are contained in F.S. Regs., Part II. and the Staff Manual respectively. Title Pages will be prepared in manuscript.

Place	Date	Hour	Summary of Events and Information	Remarks and references to Appendices
	16/9/16 Cont.	12.35 P.M.	Bombardment start. Fire was resumed & an attempting recover fired. Rifle McLaren was badly wet & wore. Try new mackintosh sheet before putting it in Depot. Stores were freed, but at new position continued.	
	17/9/16			
	17/9/16	9 P.M.	Very heavy enemy bombardment. Some 800 heavy machine gun being sent in about the front line from K.29.B.8.8 to K.29.B.5.0. in half an hour. Guns could not be fired owing to teams being all working on new positions. Arrange to have these seen at 2.00 a.m. & 2 guns to that firing may be possible if required. 2nd Lt. Lamb have posted to Battery temporarily during absence of Lt. M. Roberts M.C. on leave.	
	18/9/16			
	19/9/16	9.30 P.M.	Fire 16 rounds during enemy's bombardment of enemy front overlapping trench. New position still firing on temporary still working on new position.	
	20/9/16		Allies out billet from men as old one was damaged by a 5.9 in shell.	
	21/9/16			
	22/9/16			
	23/9/16		New position (continued)	

WAR DIARY or INTELLIGENCE SUMMARY

Army Form C. 2118.

2" T.M.By
September 1916

Place	Date	Hour	Summary of Events and Information	Remarks and references to Appendices
	24/9/16	4 P.M.	Organised Bombardment on enemy front & support lines. Fire 19 rounds. Difficulty with firing mechanisms.	
	25/9/16		Work on new positions as usual. Stander from Bombardment on 2.6.	
	26/9/16		Go to Headquarters of 17" Derby & Notts & obtain party of 7 Infantry Men at 12 midnight. Heavy bomb. between midnight & 7 A.M. carry up 250 bombs. The proper number of component parts do not arrive. so have only 7 complete charges available.	
		12.50 P.M. to 7.30 P.M.	Bombardment during which 70 bombs are fired from Nos. 1 & 5 guns. No 2 gun works bore after firing 30 rounds & had to be cut up again. About six dumb minenwerfer fired in retaliation into our front line.	
	27/9/16	10 A.M.	Carrying party at Euston Dump to carry component only 13 men turn up.	
		3 P.M.	Rifisit both Nos 1 & guns which have both been deep in afrad. one round from each gun.	
		11 P.M.	Get another party from the 17" Watts & Derby. carry two boxes of component from Euston Dump to the Sam place stores.	

WAR DIARY or INTELLIGENCE SUMMARY

Army Form C. 2118.

2nd T.M. Bty.
T.M. Battery

Place	Date	Hour	Summary of Events and Information	Remarks and references to Appendices
	28/9/16	10 a.m.	Left Euston Dump with shall party to bury all traces of our work not yet carried up to derived fire pit. Arrange that each party working on new positions shall carry home an heavy machine minenwerfer bomb each way.	
		6 p.m.	After few an heavy machine minenwerfer bombs per position.	
	29/9/16		Work on new positions.	
	30/9/16		Receive instructions to prepare for extensive scale. Chose positions for wire cutting & behind new position not yet completed. Thus jobs have for two have fire behind new position elsewhere as cover for the men. Laid observing positions in K.28.B.4.8. & arrange for wire to be from there to all guns on following day.	

2449 Wt. W14957/Mgo 750,000 1/16 J.B.C. & A. Forms/C.2118/12.

WAR DIARY or INTELLIGENCE SUMMARY

Army Form C. 2118.

22 TMB 16 Vol 2

Place	Date	Hour	Summary of Events and Information	Remarks and references to Appendices
LA SIGNY FARM. SERRE SECTOR	1/10/16	10 a.m.	Receive orders to haul wire cutting with all available guns at once. No 1 gun at K29c 25.55. has to be relaid on a new line. So leaving a detachment to dig in this gun open fire with the 2 guns from K29c 20.60. Telephone lines not yet laid out to observe from K28d 95.85. corrected by means of runners. Gun shooting very erratically, difference variations of over 50 yards being noticed at a range of 475 yards. Luckily our new line about our second for this. Fire 40 rounds without drawing any severe enemy retaliation. Cut a lane about 8-10 yards wide at K29d 2.7 + 8.	
		12 noon		
	2/10/16	2 p.m.	Two detachments commence digging two guns in at K29 c 8.19 Gun then lay out wires from O.P. at K28d 2.8 to gun positions.	
		7 p.m.		
	2/10/16	7 a.m.	Start partly digging in the two new positions.	
		8 a.m.	Very wet. Can start shooting with the 1 + 2 guns. Only fire 15 rounds as observation very difficult.	
		5 p.m.	Get new guns in to correct line.	
	3/10/16	11 a.m.	Open fire with all four guns. Firing 50 rounds. Enemy call	

Army Form C. 2118.

WAR DIARY
or
INTELLIGENCE SUMMARY

(Erase heading not required.)

Date	Hour	Summary of Events and Information	Remarks and references to Appendices
3/10/16 (cont'd)		firing erratically. Heavy enemy retaliation with 5.9 in. & 4.2 in. fire on No 1 M.G. gun pit blown in - two direct hits on huts, dug out at that pier.	
4/10/16	3 p.m.	Resumed wire from No 1 & 2 pieces. Open fire with Nos 3 & 4. Fire 29 rounds. Enemy retaliation heavily on my 1→ pun H.	
	9 p.m.	Co to Staff Capre to meet carrying party of 150 men. 30 men here up two hours late. Col 20 men per pier, this Battery, this owing to bad condition of trenches thus arly for two journeys.	
5/10/16	5 a.m.	Fire from Nos 2.3 & 4. Enemy retaliation on Nos 3-4. Fire 28 rounds.	
	5 p.m.	Fire again, that off 23 rounds, making 51 rounds in all. Enemy shooting rather more heavily. Probably owing to the ammunition brought from guns removed have been exhausted.	
	9 p.m.	Go to Staff Capre to meet carrying party of 100 men. Some arrived. So returned to dug out at 1.30 a.m.	
6/10/16	12.30 p.m.	Fire Nos 2.3 & 4. Col off 50 rounds in pieces of fairly heavy enemy retaliation. Cut lane at K.29.d 2-9.	
	7 p.m.	Go to Staff Capre to meet carrying party. E.1.2.5 men to be de Thur / Beebeeny ?	

WAR DIARY or INTELLIGENCE SUMMARY

Army Form C. 2118.

Date	Hour	Summary of Events and Information	Remarks and references to Appendices
1/10/16	12 noon	Open fire with No's 2.3 & 4. Fire 62 rounds with excellent results. Heavy enemy retaliation especially on old No's 1 pm & on No's. No's 2 felt direct hit. Gunners Kemp & Collier both killed outright, & Mr Reid man - Sr. Cuthbert slightly wounded in thigh -	
	2 a.m.	Gas out at K29 d-2-8 & K29 d-2-9. After returning from survey up the two fingers who were killed received report that large enemy working party had been seen in the moonlight repairing wire. No apparent attempt had been made to disperse them with machine gun fire ascertain that they lay by this time from back sidons but to fire using to Infantry Relief.	
2/10/16	11 a.m.	Met working party. 50 men here up 3 hours tack for four batteries.	
	12 pm	Start work moving No's 1 & 2 guns. Selest new positions in Ret Roy at K 29 C 5.9. start work there at once	
	9 pm	Men carrying party at Staff Copse. Carry bombs till 2 a.m.	

WAR DIARY or INTELLIGENCE SUMMARY

Army Form C. 2118.

Place: TRESCAULT

Date	Hour	Summary of Events and Information	Remarks and references to Appendices
9/10/16	9 am	Receive orders to take over from 2/1/3 Battery our right hand position. Find nothing in rear view pin above, only about one dozen rounds at the guns. Telephoned to position in which want to be started at once. Carried two O.P.'s. Attached found carrying party continued work all night.	
10/10/16		Look for further position without success. Continue work on new positions. Lay wire from O.P. to guns. Carry food.	
11/10/16		Got two guns in readiness for firing – Carry Food. Shell Shot at 10/1 pm – Make small shells at 40/1 pm.	
12/10/16 12 am		Fire 36 rounds 10/1 pm at K 34 b 3.6. Firing on beer at K 35 a 4.3 fire 11 rounds 10/2 pm at K 29 c 2.2 firing on Wind K 35 a 6.3. Fire 25 rounds. Many retaliation especially on No.1 gun on F.P. at K 35 a 1.8. Telephonic communication always about at times. Guns shot being erratically no' crew at 4.50 were hit accidentally but not much damage. Put out to pull stores in. Fift hesitation broken. Gun not put out of action.	

WAR DIARY or INTELLIGENCE SUMMARY

Army Form C. 2118.

(Erase heading not required.)

TRENCH MORTAR 2/1 HIGHLAND

Date	Hour	Summary of Events and Information	Remarks and references to Appendices
13/10/16	11am	Fire 20 rounds from stokes gun. Great trouble experienced with Rifle Mechanisms. Three being broken whilst firing 20 rounds. Wire damaged at K29a 6.3. but so far cut. Ranging still inaccurate. One round falling behind own wavefront. Then the next at the same elevation falling beyond Enemy wire.	
14/10/16	11am	Fired 6-9 rounds from stokes 1" + 2-pdr. Wire at K35a 6.3 at K35d 4.3 considerably damaged but no gap visible. Even rather too inaccurate but still bad. Slant work on new emplacement at 19, K35a 15.80.	
15/10/16	2pm	Fire 15 rounds from two guns. Shooting erratic + retaliation heavy. to one broken. Look on new position stopped by enemy shelling.	
16/10/16	3pm	Fire 83 rounds from stokes 1"+2. Fairly successful shooting — Wire badly cut about at K35a 5.3. but no gap visible. New position blown in — as the beds of both stokes mortar have to be relaid. Leave his position for a day.	

WAR DIARY or INTELLIGENCE SUMMARY

Army Form C. 2118.

Date	Hour	Summary of Events and Information	Remarks and references to Appendices
17/9/16		Preparing an account of Infantry Relief. Heavy enemy shelling.	
	11 pm to 11 am	Start relief and new position which came only to close of night. Got all ready for carrying his in morning.	
18/9/16	2 pm	Fired 63 rounds 15 from No 1 & 48 from No 2 - wire again much knocked about, but no gaps visible. Heavy enemy retaliation & telephone communication impossible to keep up. Both guns buried during previous night, but in action after 2 hours work. New positions occupied.	
19/9/16	10 am	Fire 18 rounds from No 2 gun. No 1 gun carried up fresh ammo & heavy hostile bombardment. Wire Cut & the gun covering the approaches missing to Trench being blown in. The gun buried after 15 rounds. New position also blown in. Weather very bad. Had hard work firing difficult. The camp of the 2 gun nearly 1/2 covered by such ming. Kelep B/B wire damaged & trough cart been in a/c [illegible] — 1 officer & 10 NCOs and

WAR DIARY or INTELLIGENCE SUMMARY

Army Form C. 2118.

Place	Date	Hour	Summary of Events and Information	Remarks and references to Appendices
	2[?]/[?]	11am	Fired 119 rounds from No.1 & 2 – were much damaged at K35a5.3 – K35a3.3 – gap at [Fresnoy?] reference. Gun at new position (No 3) mis fired repeatedly & was finally dismounted the next of T.O.M. after shooting. Enemy retaliation heavily especially on No.6 gun – pit & near this gun recognized by men & on one entrance completely closed, Gun Trench completely closed.	
		2pm	Take advantage of our artillery fire & get off 52 rounds from Nos 1 & 2 gun. Try before 3 gun but April 1st misfires owing to dampness of new gun. Damages were considerably at K35a 45.55. No 2 gun out of action owing to striking of No 2 etc. gun also required bed taking up. This I proceeded to do.	
	2[?]/[?]	11am	Fire Nos 1 & 3. Get off 614 rounds. Were much damaged. Both fired again taking up – No 1 only lasting for 15 rounds [?]	

WAR DIARY or INTELLIGENCE SUMMARY

Army Form C. 2118.

Place	Date	Hour	Summary of Events and Information	Remarks and references to Appendices
	23/4/16 cont'd	7 P.M.	Meet carrying party at Eustan. Take up 50 pr. 5 bombs, 25 A ch 2 & 25 b ch 3.	
	25/4/16		Fire 33 rounds. Observation very bad owing to screen. M/ Gun had clips after 15 rounds. No 3 pin bench blown in close to a front. Fire put cleaning (?) relaying carried on with during the day wherever possible.	
	24/4/16	1 P.M.	Fired 35 rounds. Observation again impossible. Enemy retaliation on our No 2 Gun Structures one pr bomb, many the trenches - most of the men in attending their Jas helmets & emerged from the dug out, none casualties. Gun opened up. Enemy's own trench severely affected.	
		3 P.M.	Bomb carrying under fresh heavy fire - owing to state of trench, truck can not be crankled right up to front, so to rear it is necessary to 10 pr from distance in light of trying weather condition this will not lead to more than 15 trucks in a fortnight being placed.	

Army Form C. 2118.

WAR DIARY
or
INTELLIGENCE SUMMARY

(Erase heading not required.)

Place	Date	Hour	Summary of Events and Information	Remarks and references to Appendices
	25/10/16	9am	Still following positions. No 3 gun blown in. Fire 3 rounds from No 2. Heavy enemy retaliation on all guns. No. one ceased danger from the gun found cease firing & shore the burn about 150 to 3 gun under cover of splinter proof shelter. Several found buried near gun position. There are obvious on the interior of the two gun pits.	
	26/10/16	11am	Fire 26 rounds from Nos. 1 & 2 guns. After 10 rounds from No 1 the two recovers machine & after 16 rounds from No 2 the same thing happens. Spend the rest of the day digging in the kids.	
	27/10/16		Received orders to hand over to the 37 Div: 7, N^{s} Bring the battery back to no 1 billet in Fosseux carryup.	

Army Form C. 2118.

WAR DIARY
or
INTELLIGENCE SUMMARY

(Erase heading not required.)

Date	Hour	Summary of Events and Information	Remarks and references to Appendices
28/10/16		Marched the battery to res billets at Bertrancourt.	
29/10/16 to 31/10/16		In rest at Bertrancourt. Parados built & inspection carried out daily.	

Army Form C. 2118.

20.

Vol 3

Z/2 TRENCH MORTAR BATTERY.

WAR DIARY
or
INTELLIGENCE SUMMARY
(Erase heading not required.)

Place	Date	Hour	Summary of Events and Information	Remarks and references to Appendices
BERTRANCOURT	1/11/16		Marched from Bertrancourt to Sarton – Go into Reg'l. Billets.	
SARTON	2/11/16 to 6/11/16		Parades – Drills & Inspections as usual.	
Colincamps	7/11/16		March to Colincamps & take over Billets from X/2 T.M.B. there. Very wet.	
	8/11/16		Take working party up to take the pieces from Chatham Trench K34 d 60.85, where X/2 T.M.B. had been in action, to a dug out in Eiver Strut, where they could be cleaned & stores. Owing to the very bad state of the Trenches, particularly Vallade Trench & Egg Trench which were almost impassable being 3ft. deep in mud, the pieces were with great difficulty carried to a dug out in Egg Strut – cleaned & left there. K34 d 78. All the Challis men rendered assistance in getting them? The men'cl. Lt. H. N. Roberts kept the battery to take command of X/2 T.M.B. the command of this battery being taken over by 2nd Lt. R. M. Varey.	

2449 Wt. W14957/M90 750,000 1/16 J.B.C. & A. Forms/C.2118/12.

WAR DIARY
or
INTELLIGENCE SUMMARY

(Erase heading not required.)

Army Form C. 2118.

2/-

Z/2 TRENCH MORTAR BATTERY.

No............
Date............

Place	Date	Hour	Summary of Events and Information	Remarks and references to Appendices
	9/1/16		Received instructions from B.J. H.Q. to dig in a bed in the vicinity of Colincamps for experimental purposes. Sited a position in an old shell hole at J.36.b.95 & made arrangements to secure the necessary timber.	
	10/1/16		Started work on Experimental Bed, sinking upright supports down about 1½ ft on a foundation- kind shell party of three men to Talbot Ave. 2" for bomb buried in the trenches. On position locating "marks" the Bn. could not be reached owing to the mud being impassable. The Trenches considerably blown about.	
	11/1/16		Found an experimental bed continued- The bed being bone to th supports already driven in.	
	12/1/16		Tried Experimental bed & received 50 bombs Fir 12 rounds at 3 p.m. Bed satisfactory so far, 10 fuses proved experienced with erratic shooting manifacture. The latter being particularly noticeable with the cartridges of the Birmingham Metal Company.	

2449 Wt. W1457/M90 750,000 1/16 J.B.C. & A. Forms/C.2118/12.

WAR DIARY
or
INTELLIGENCE SUMMARY

(Erase heading not required.)

Army Form C. 2118.

Z/2 TRENCH MORTAR BATTERY.

Place	Date	Hour	Summary of Events and Information	Remarks and references to Appendices
	13/11/16		Again fire 11 rounds from Experimental bed. The results being practically the same as before.	
	14/11/16		Fire 27 rounds. Rounds somewhat little. Length fuse still too inaccurate. Line fairly good when frown weights with sand bags.	
		11.30 p.m.	Volunteer asked for to bring in stretchers from newly captured trenches. All battery volunteer. One N.C.O. + 1 sent up. All return safely.	
Beaucourt	15/11/16	9 am	March to Red Billets in Bertrancourt.	
	16/11/16	9 am	Volunteers again asked for, all the men + N.C.O.'s not up the previous night volunteer.	
		3 p.m.	The men up farm shelter having on the 14th go up again – Remainder rest in billets.	
	17/11/16	11 a.m.	Take left battery to Egg Trench dug out to bring out guns left there on the 8th inst. Meet in Egg Trench Holland. Very heavy – Enemy open heavy fire on Hollands Trench, necessitating a halt in a dugout for shelter.	

Army Form C. 2118.

WAR DIARY
or
INTELLIGENCE SUMMARY
(Erase heading not required.)

Z/2 TRENCH MORTAR BATTERY.

Place	Date	Hour	Summary of Events and Information	Remarks and references to Appendices
	17/11/16 (cont.)	7.30 P.M.	Enemy fire still heavy, & no progress will now likely be so slow, they are kept in dugout at K.3 d 36 & only taken quickly through zone of enemy's fire. Rest in billets & improvement.	
	18/11/16			
	19/11/16		Piers & elevating frames brought from Vallali Trench Beutrancourt, & all stores of X/2 & Y/2 7. M. Battery from Leune - colincamps to Beat soncourt in 2 G.S. Wagons. Rest in Billets at Beutrancourt.	
	20/11/16			
STAFFTEN	21/11/16 to 27/11/16		March to Rest Billet in Sarton.	
	28/11/16		Parades, Drills & Inspections as usual.	

WAR DIARY of 2/2 T.M.B.

INTELLIGENCE SUMMARY

(Erase heading not required.)

Army Form C. 2118.

Vol 4

Place	Date	Hour	Summary of Events and Information	Remarks and references to Appendices
SARTON.	1st		Billets, stores etc. cleaned up in preparation for moving	
SARTON.	2nd		Marched to AMPLIER.	
AMPLIER.	3rd		Marched to MAIZICOURT.	
MAIZICOURT	5th		Marched to ST. ACHEUL. Gn. Wilson & Gn. Whitehouse went to V Army T.M. School for course of instruction.	
ST. ACHEUL.	6th to 31st		Battery remained at rest. Daily parades & inspections were carried out. Instruction was given in Telephone & Morse Code. Firing instruction was given to the last joined men. On the 24th 2/Lts H. Greatwood & E.W. Vellas joined the Battery.	

H. Greatwood 2nd Lt.
for O.C. 2/2 T.M.B.

2nd Divisional Artillery.

X/2. TRENCH MORTAR BATTERY

SEPTEMBER TO DECEMBER 1916.

WAR DIARY or INTELLIGENCE SUMMARY

Army Form C. 2118

X2 TM Bty

Place	Date	Hour	Summary of Events and Information	Remarks and references to Appendices
In the field	2/9/16		Some trench M.B. activity. Fired 5 or 6 rounds in retaliation. Lt. Banbury B.C. wounded in both feet & thighs with H.E. while at work on the gun.	
	3/9/16		Nothing of importance. Enemy shelled village twice today. About 10 rounds each time. Believed to be 5.9". Few casualties.	
	4/9/16		Enemy aeroplanes active, but was driven back by our A.A. Aircraft guns.	
	5/9/16		Great deal of trench M.B. activity. Enemy heavily shelled the village in the evening & serious casualties. Killed.	
	6/9/16		Artillery & trench M.B. activity. Fired several rounds in retaliation. Nothing of importance to report.	
	7/9/16		Enemy trench M.B. showed considerable activity. Village slightly shelled at intervals during day.	
	8/9/16		Some trench M.B. activity. Fired several rounds in retaliation.	
	10/9/16		Enemy artillery quiet.	
	12/9/16		C.P. 12/3083 Lieut. E.J. Edge (4th Section 2nd D.T.M.) admitted into Hosp. 78630 W. Dadley reported sick returned to 2nd D.A.C.	
	13/9/16		Nothing of importance. Enemy artillery very quiet.	
	15/9/16		Two L. T. M. fired. Forwarded to I.O.M. 2nd Div. for afternoon & repair. Shelling quiet. Enemy efforts activity at intervals.	
	16/9/16		58446 Gnr. Tonkinson admitted to hospital sick.	
	17/9/16		Village shelled at intervals during day. Enemy M.B. quiet.	

WAR DIARY or INTELLIGENCE SUMMARY

Army Form C. 2118

Place	Date	Hour	Summary of Events and Information	Remarks and references to Appendices
In the Field	18/9/16		Enemy Aeroplanes showed some activity but were repelled by our a/c. guns. Enemy Artillery quiet.	
	19/9/16		Enemy trench mortars displayed some activity in evening.	
	20/9/16		P. 11958. 2362 M. Williams R. admitted to hospital. S.84.06. Pte Londwood discharged from hospital. Several a/c activity. Fired several rounds in retaliation.	
	21/9/16		Enemy shelled village during day. C/P. 42917 Pte Williams B. 13th section 2nd D.C.C.) killed. C/P. 4604 Cpl Sparks (3rd section 2nd D.C.C.) admitted to hosp. Sept. Three enemy trench mortars to X & M.H.B.	
	22/9/16		C/P. 41916 D. Hayes & 3rd section 2nd D.C.C.) admitted to Hospital. 11076 " Reynolds J. 3rd " " " Sick. Enemy shelled village. Les Cavaliers. Enemy Artillery & trench M. quiet. Les Cavaliers.	
	23/9/16		Fired 48 rounds at enemy's first line were the enemy say oct. 23" Lancers in retaliation to our fire.	
	24/9/16		2/Lt pounds fired etc C/P. of thiereco on our front etc. He thereon was taken by enemy's fire & we were killed in reply. Their clearing of the afternoon. Nine were took place for account of relief.	
	25/9/16		Infantry twice continued throughout the afternoon.	
	26/9/16		40 pounds fired 86. C/P. of thiereco. or our force 18. 2nd H.B. concentrated our fire on the some Jalonnes 20th with good effect. Men. Cavaliers are 20 g 3.05. 2nd Sero C.C. Lanciers wounded 1 Sero Lanciers Hospital.	

1875 Wt. W 503/826 1,000,000 4/15 J.B.C. & A. A.D.S.S./Forms/C. 2118.

WAR DIARY or INTELLIGENCE SUMMARY

Army Form C. 2118

Place	Date	Hour	Summary of Events and Information	Remarks and references to Appendices
In the field	26/9/16		Batt. with Bruce & one sect. Lahore. All four guns were silenced. The Pothum line & pothum line by 5.9 shells the northern two [guns?] being cleared but are now being cleared well in. Afraid that the two northern positions were caused no before the subsequence. Two casualties were caused on Station position by 5.9 splinter or loaded gun. The next two or three rounds into the position was destroyed by shinter from Rennie. Southern position. Will take shelter from three guns & make position suitable for firing.	
	27/9/16		By orders from R.A. X 2 X LdB was withdrawn from the line temporarily in order to take up new positions.	
	28/9/16		Kent Booth transfered to the D.A.C. y. command of Battery taken over by Lieut. Brown. Lebared Gnr. Rouse. 9. discharged from hospital to duty. Rejoined Bn. Bttry.	
			Posted to X2 X LdB. No 47637 Cpl. Mack. L No 14-9130 Gnr Davey W. " 74146 " Hardwick " 118083 " Brown " 127974 " Wright W. " 45937 " Copeland W.g " 43406 Dge L.	
			Lieut Booth to R.F.G.? D.A.C. Munt R. Stephens RFA	
			Guns Reverd to	

J Bram Lieutn
L. H. Bty
X.LdMB.

WAR DIARY or INTELLIGENCE SUMMARY

Army Form C. 2118

Place	Date	Hour	Summary of Events and Information	Remarks and references to Appendices
In the Field	28/9/16		Contd. Work on new entrenchments in Hop Avenue continued.	
	29/9/16		Lieut. R. Lupton joined the Battery. Dept. entrenchment in Avenue.	
	30/9/16		Carrying parties supplied to 328th Coy R.E. for work on new position. Entrance to new dug-out blown in by officers.	
	31/9/16		Capt. and 2nd D.M.C. together with two other officers, two men, Dvrs. of Squad. Motor arrived. Early at 1st Squadron. Another gone. Another left position. Moved all horses from left section. Dvrs. on Hop Avenue. Wagon on new position could be handed over line to 1st Squadron as new wheeler.	
	1/10/16		Moved forward new positions all day for new guns. Started work on same.	
	2/10/16		Continued work on new positions. Carried up guns to new position.	
	3/10/16		Guns nearly two fairly bright today. Fired 8 rounds for registration purposes.	

WAR DIARY
or
INTELLIGENCE SUMMARY — N/2 TMB 1-7

Army Form C. 2118

Vol 2

Place	Date	Hour	Summary of Events and Information	Remarks and references to Appendices
In the Field	4/10/16		Fired 8 rounds. Low visibility. Rain & mist.	
	5/10/16		No. of rds fired 43. A good deal of wire cut but no definite gaps visible. K.29.6.1-2.	
	6/10/16		No. of rds fired 37. Wire cut in 3 places. All guns put out of action 3/10. Seriously damaged. Enemy retaliated with 77.cm 4.2 & "Onions". Detachments relieved. No casualties.	
	7/10/16		No of rds fired 51. Two good gaps cut at K.29, L.33, K.29.b.22. Enemy retaliated with guns of all calibres. Met working party at night. 9 carried up bombs. Met working parties, carried up ammunition. Received orders not to fire to day and to hand over to 63rd Division.	
	8/10/16		Handed over 3 guns and 4 beds to 63rd Dn & tools complete. Took over 2 guns and 2 beds 9 tools from 63 Dn. Found a lot of work was needed on new emplacements. Carried up 30 rds of ammunition. 2Lt FOULSHAM re-joined Battery (from 2/2)	
	9/10/16		Work on new positions finished. Telephone system laid out & completed. 2Lt FOULSHAM went to Rest Camp at KORTEPYP.	
	10/10/16		Carried up 130 rounds of ammunition.	J Bromfield Capt OC 1/2 TMB

WAR DIARY or INTELLIGENCE SUMMARY   X/2 T.M.B.

Army Form C. 2118

Place	Date	Hour	Summary of Events and Information	Remarks and references to Appendices
In the Field	11/10/16		Completed Bomb Store and Component Part Store. Finished a third Gun position. Carried up more ammunition.	
	12/10/16		No of rds fired 41. Cut one good gap in front-line wire of Granulated. About 6 yds broad. Detachment relieved. Enemy retaliation heavy with guns of all calibres. 2/Lt FOULSHAM Sick. Gunner BROWN Sick.	
	13/10/16		No of rds fired 69. More wire cut. Wire getting much thinner. 6 D.A.C. men returned to 3 & 4 Sec D.A.C. Sergt BYRANT ROGERSON retained on Detachment withdrawn in view of TMO. Sgr FARBRACE [Nachville Dump].	
	14/10/16		Turned Gun position fired at all day. Supposed to be due to word of a "Spy". Description of suspicious person given to Batt HQ Row St. Gnr HOWARD [?] Bn HQ Bow St. Gnr HOWARD hit. Bomb store blown up.	
	15/10/16		Fired 30 rds. Bdr WILLIAMS Killed in Action. Gnr ROUSE buried but was dug out alive, took him to I.A.P. breakdown with Shock. Gnr BUCKLEY Sick. Retaliation light.	
	16/10/16		No of rds fired 109. Very good results, two good gaps. Retaliation light.	
	17/10/16		No firing to day by order of C.R.A. Enemy very active to day. Started work on new position in [Colt Pit?]. Heavy rain. Gnrs STIRZAKER, COLES, BIDDLECOMBE "Posted".	
	18/10/16		No of rds fired 93. Enemy retaliated with 4.2s. Detachments had to take [cover?] 3 times. No 1 gun flown in.	

F. Brownfullwood X/2 T.M.B

WAR DIARY or INTELLIGENCE SUMMARY

X/2 TMB5

Army Form C. 2118

(Erase heading not required.)

Place	Date	Hour	Summary of Events and Information	Remarks and references to Appendices
In the field	19/10/16		Abandoned "AT Pt" position. Tunnell not safe. Very heavy rain. No of rds fired 76 with good effect. A great deal of wire cut. Heavy retaliation on our guns, detachments were driven to ground on 3 different occasions. Started work on 2 new positions, present ones untenable.	
	20/10/16.		No 2 position ready to fire. No 1 position nearly completed.	
	21/10/16.		No of rds fired 14. Positions heavily shelled. Had a good deal of difficulty getting Infantry Carrying party near little guns at all, the left is short of ammunition. 2/Lt YOULSHAM Rejoined.	
	22/10/16.		Church Parade. Carried up 50 "Special Bombs at night. No of rds fired 60. Two Pioneers attached for Duty with "Special Bombs" Gnr Fairhurst Hospital.	
	23/10/16.		No of rds fired 37. Had to stop after each 10 rds to replace "Beds" very wet. very muddy and could not observe.	
	24/10/16.		No of rds fired 57. Fired on Registered points & could only just observe "Burst" in enemies wire. Retaliation heavy. More trouble with "Beds". "Shook" Retaliation Light.	
	25/10/16		No of rds fired 22. Corp Mack wounded. Gnr Ballantyne "Shook" Retaliation Light.	
	26/10/16.		No of rds fired 25. 6 No 1 gun put out of action. More trouble with kedow not proved.	
	27/10/16		Heavy rain. Handed over to Y/2 6 battleaxe Battery. 2/Lt Foulsham & 2/Lt Staples, Sergt Roberson 3 Gunners left for BERTRANCOURT. Gnr Wright admitted to Hospital. Moved remainder of Battery to BERTRANCOURT.	

J. Campbell Major T. M.

Army Form C. 2118

WAR DIARY
or
INTELLIGENCE SUMMARY X/2 T.M.B.
(Erase heading not required.)

Place	Date	Hour	Summary of Events and Information	Remarks and references to Appendices
In the Field	29/10/16		Revellie 7 a.m. Breakfast 8 a.m. Roll call 9.45, Dinner 1 p.m. Clear Parade 2 p.m. Roll 8.30 p.m.	
	30/10/16		– Ditto – – Ditto – – Gas Helmets, Respirators 10.15 – Dinner 1 p.m. – Ditto –	
	31/10/16		Bdr Smith promoted Corporal. Gunner Farbrace promoted Bomb. Both from 25/10/11. Left BERTRANCOURT 10.40. Arr COLINCAMPS 11.45. Left COLINCAMPS 1 p.m. Arrived in trenches 3 p.m. Took over from 3/2. Worked on positions which were under water. Heavy rain. Positions under water. Worked on positions + finished 3 position	
	1/11/16		N° of rds fired 26, 1 beds being under water, had to be replaced twice.	
	2/11/16		N° of rds fired 37. Wire cut. Enemy lines never damaged and appear to be very wet. Each shell or bomb sending up a good deal of water. Carried up	
	3/11/16		N° of rds fired 15. Kept next. Enemy retaliated. Carried up 89 rds from Euston. Company party fired on, also in danger of "Prematures" from our own guns.	
	4/11/16		Total N° of rds fired during month 860 Fired on 19 different days. Average per firing day — — — 45 Most fired in one day 109 out of 2 guns	

WAR DIARY or INTELLIGENCE SUMMARY

Army Form C. 2118

X¹ T.M. Battery November 1916 Vol 3

(Erase heading not required.)

Place	Date	Hour	Summary of Events and Information	Remarks and references to Appendices
SERRE SECTOR	1st Novr 1916.		The battery continued working on the gun positions taken over from Y2, & the third position in Roman Road was completed. Heavy rain fell during the night & the gun positions were under water.	
	2nd Novr	"	The huts all sank as the result of the heavy rain, & had to be replaced twice. Fired 26 rounds.	
	3rd "	"	Wire was cut at 35c 4.6.4.8. Fired 37	
	4th "	"	Fired 15 rounds at wire around 35c 4.6.4.8 & were still further damaged. Carried up 89 bombs to gun positions, the carrying party being heavily shelled, the trenches being knocked down & the northing exposed to enemy observation.	
	5th "	"	Carried up 42 bombs to the guns. Guns placed in dug out under charge of two gunners & the rest of the detachments withdrawn by order of the D.T.M.O. & taken back to Colincamps.	
	6th "	"	Yesterdays orders cancelled detachments returned to trenches & guns &c were replaced & ammunition carried up ready for firing.	
	7th "	"	Fired 21 rounds under very bad conditions — Heavy rain, & beds under water made beds sink & further firing impossible. The battery was withdrawn & moved at 1.35 p.m. to Sailow. From this date till the end of the month the battery were at Sailow in billets. Parades were carried out systematically, including arms & foot drill & physical training, N.C.O's & gunners being practised in words of command &c. They all showed considerable improvement, & acting Sergt Hunters	

1875 Wt. W593/826 1,000,000 4/15 J.B.C. & A. A.D.S.S./Forms/C. 2118.

Army Form C. 2118

WAR DIARY
or
INTELLIGENCE SUMMARY
(Erase heading not required.)

Instructions regarding War Diaries and Intelligence Summaries are contained in F. S. Regs., Part II. and the Staff Manual respectively. Title Pages will be prepared in manuscript.

Place	Date	Hour	Summary of Events and Information	Remarks and references to Appendices
Sailly	9th Nov 1916		Lower B command was especially satisfactory. Batteries were regular, & into battery & practise football matches were arranged. Instruction was given on the telephone & in wire laying. Standing orders were issued with reference to general conduct of the men in town & billets & the smart turn out of the men made them an object of remark in the village. Two services were held, & the Communion was administered once during the month. One church parade was held on R.Co. The battery was also photographed while out at rest.	
"	12th "		Church Parade for R.Co at 2.45 pm. Football match v X2 T.M.B. Those who did not play went & shouted.	
"	25th "		Battery photographed.	
"	30th "		Gnr Sutherland went on leave.	
			Gnr Tarney went on leave.	

C.G. McIlpham
2nd Lt R.F.A.
O.C. X 2 T.M.B.

WAR DIARY
or
INTELLIGENCE SUMMARY

X 2 T.M. Battery Vol 4

During the month of December this battery was out of action till the 5th, when they moved into rest at St Acheul. While the battery was out of action at Sarton fatigues were carried out at Acheux Dump, when they moved into rest there were the usual morning parades, while instructions were also given in the telephone service, laying, "buzzing", classes were started & instruction was given in the use of the hose respirator. A practical course of firing with "dud" bombs was carried out, special attention being paid to those gunners who had seen none or little actual firing in the trenches. Instruction was also given to new men in the correct laying of bedsoe. The battery had two 'feeds' on Xmas day, one at midday the other at 6 p.m., two hundred odd francs

WAR DIARY
or
INTELLIGENCE SUMMARY

Army Form C. 2118

Place	Date	Hour	Summary of Events and Information	Remarks and references to Appendices
Saxton	1 Dec 1916		being available, & the battery spent a really merry Xmas.	
Amplier	2 "		Fatigues at Acheux Dump.	
	3 "		Battery left Saxton for Amplier.	
Inaysecourt	" "		" " Inaysecourt	
St Acheul	5 "		" " St Acheul. Bdr Fairbrace proceeded to 5-15 Army School of Instrs.	
	" "		" " Wakefield posted to battery & also proceeded to School.	
	6 "		Gunners Ward & Wakefield posted to battery & also proceeded to School.	
	" "		Lt J. Bum- Callender posted to 5.0-1st Battery — 2nd Lt C. P. McMahon to command	
	7 "		2nd Lt K. T. Stephen rejoined battery from 5-1st Army School, also Bombr Tomlinson.	
	" "		Sergt Roycroon also rejoined battery from 3rd Army School, where he had been acting	
			Sergt Major.	
	12 "		Billets inspected by C.R.A.	

WAR DIARY
or
INTELLIGENCE SUMMARY

(Erase heading not required.)

Army Form C. 2118

Instructions regarding War Diaries and Intelligence Summaries are contained in F.S. Regs., Part II. and the Staff Manual respectively. Title Pages will be prepared in manuscript.

Place	Date	Hour	Summary of Events and Information	Remarks and references to Appendices
St Acheul	16 Dec 1916		Football match at Naugecourt v 36th Bde, who won 2 – 0. Concert in the evening	
	17		Church parade	
	18		School opened	
	25		Xmas Day. Church Parade 7am — Holy Communion 7.30 am. "Feed" midday & 6 pm, 2/11 francs available.	
	27		Practical instruction in firing to gunners who had seen little trench work	

Clinton J. McAlpham
2nd Lt. R.F.A
O.C
X2 T.M.B.

2ND DIVISION
ROYAL ARTILLERY

TRENCH MORTAR BATTERIES

JAN-DEC 1917

2nd Divisional Artillery.

V/2 TRENCH MORTAR BATTERY ::: JANUARY 1917.

Army Form C. 2118.

V/2 T.M. Battery
January 1917
Vol 9

WAR DIARY
INTELLIGENCE SUMMARY.
(Erase heading not required.)

Instructions regarding War Diaries and Intelligence Summaries are contained in F.S. Regs., Part II. and the Staff Manual respectively. Title pages will be prepared in manuscript.

Place	Date	Hour	Summary of Events and Information	Remarks and references to Appendices
	1/1/17		9 wagons complete attached from D.A.C. for move. 2 N.C.O. and 18 men reported to 41st Brigade for duty with 51st Division.	
	2/1/17		Marched to OOODCHES for one night.	
	3/1/17		Marched to MARIEUX, men in huts.	
	4/1/17		Marched to SENLIS.	
	5/1/17		1 N.C.O. and six men to Trench Mortar School.	
	6/1/17		One N.C.O. and one man returned from leave. Two O.R's proceeded on leave. Bombardier George and 4 men returned from working party.	
	night 6.7.17		Fire in Pallet in Bouzincourt extensive damage done.	
	7/1/17		1 Sergeant and 23 O.R's reported to 41st Brigade for duty on gun pits &c.. 2 O.R's went to Dump with Lt Varcey.	
	8/1/17		Moved to BOUZINCOURT. 8 wagons complete rejoined D.A.C.	
	9/1/17		Court of Inquiry on fire.	
	10/1/17		Daily Parades and Inspections.	
	12/1/17		Capt. T.W. Roberts M.C. returned from leave. 4 O.R's attached to 41st Brigade for duty under Lt Varcey.	
	13/1/17		Pr. Young, Pr. George & Pr. Humphries on leave to England. Cpl Emery promoted Sergeant vice B.Q.M. Hughes.	

Army Form C. 2118.

WAR DIARY
— or —
INTELLIGENCE SUMMARY
(Erase heading not required.)

Instructions regarding War Diaries and Intelligence Summaries are contained in F. S. Regs., Part II. and the Staff Manual respectively. Title pages will be prepared in manuscript.

Place	Date	Hour	Summary of Events and Information	Remarks and references to Appendices
	14/7		Capt Estridge to Hospital - sick.	
	16/7		4 O.R's attached to 41st Brigade under Lt Vousey. Dr Allies proceeded on leave to England. Lt Inglis & Dr Cox returned from leave to England.	
	16/7		2 O.R's attached to 41st Brigade. Capt. E. Bailey returned from leave to England.	
	19/7		Lieut Argent & Lt Wrey rejoined from leave to England. E. Brown to Hospital.	
	20/7		2/Lt Head on course of instruction with new Box Respirator. 2/Lt Head and 17 O.R's had a practical tour of Drill and Instruction in Smoke Bomb and Lachrymatory Gas Test with new Box Respirator, a short period being spent in Gas Chamber. All Box Respirators proved an efficient protection against Gas. Capt J. W. Roberts, M.C. 2nd Division Traffic Manager.	
	25/7		2/Lt J. B. Hindley to assist Capt J. W. Roberts M.C. as Traffic Manager.	
	27/7		2/Lt Head to Pozieres.	
	28/7		Bombardiers Laving, George & Dr. Humphries rejoined Unit from leave to England.	
	30/7		Capt J. W. Roberts M.C. rejoined Unit.	

WAR DIARY or INTELLIGENCE SUMMARY.

Army Form C. 2118.

(Erase heading not required.)

Place	Date	Hour	Summary of Events and Information	Remarks and references to Appendices
	31/7		Position. All Officers, N.C.Os and men are at work on Dumps, Gun pits, Dug-outs, Railway Construction, Loading and similar duties, with the exception of Capt. Roberts, 2/Lt Shalaum, Sgt Emery, Far. Gordon and 10 men who remain on various duties in Bouzincourt. Advance working parties are under Lt Vousey of Z/2.T.M. Battery, and all (including Medium Batteries) advanced working parties are relieved by V/2. 21. T.M. Bty. One wagon, six mules and three drivers are attached for this purpose.	

2nd Divisional Artillery.

X/2 TRENCH MORTAR BATTERY :::: JANUARY 1917.

Army Form C. 2118

Vol C

WAR DIARY
or
INTELLIGENCE SUMMARY
(Erase heading not required.)

January 1917.

X/2 T.M. Battery

Place	Date	Hour	Summary of Events and Information	Remarks and references to Appendices
St Acheul	1-2 Jan 1917.		The battery moved out of rest at St Acheul on 2nd January 1917, billetting in Occoches	
Occoches Marieux	2nd " " 3rd " "		that night, and proceeding to Marieux the next day, reaching Senlis on the	
Senlis	4th–9th " "		4th. This unit moved from Senlis on the 9th to Bouzincourt.	
Bouzincourt	9th – 31st " "		The nature of this divisional front has prevented the use of this battery in action, and in consequence they have been transferred by attachment to Brigades for fatigues, or have been on courses, or at work on tramways and R.A.R.E dumps. Gunners Ballantyne, Bishop, Cole, Davy, Gray, Sutherland and Watt proceeded on courses to the 5th Army School of Mortars; and 2nd Lt K.T. Stephen, Corporal Hunter and Bombardier Fairbrace attended the Divisional Gas School at Bouzincourt. Subsequently lectures were given with especial reference to the use and care of Gas respirators, the treatment of gassed men, and the construction of dug outs with regard to Gas attacks. Corporal Hunter, Bombardier Freeman, and Gunners Clarke and Logan proceeded on leave during the month.	

Clinton S. McIlpham
Lt. R.F.A
O.C. X/2 T.M.B.

2nd Divisional Artillery.

Y/2 TRENCH MORTAR BATTERY   :::   JANUARY   1917.

Army Form C. 2118.

WAR DIARY January 1917 1/2 Y/I Bty
or
INTELLIGENCE SUMMARY
(Erase heading not required.)

Instructions regarding War Diaries and Intelligence Summaries are contained in F. S. Regs., Part II. and the Staff Manual respectively. Title pages will be prepared in manuscript.

Place	Date	Hour	Summary of Events and Information	Remarks and references to Appendices
ST. ACHEUL	2.1.17		The Battery move up from rest on the 2nd Jan from ST ACHEUL. Programme granted was as follows:-	
OEUF OCHES	"			
MARIEUX	3.1.17		At Senlis practically all the remaining men went away on fatigues, leaving only 2 men & 4 N.C.O's to look after & clean the guns.	
SENLIS	4.1.17 to 9.1.17			
BOUZINCOURT	9.1.17		Conditions were such that the battery could not go into action on the front, so all the time has been spent on doing fatigues & courses at T.M. School & gas lectures.	
SENLIS	5.1.17		2nd Lt Barrett, & 2nd Lts H. Collier R, Collier R, Evans went to T.M. School V Army.	
Bouzincourt	14.1.17		Lt SMITH. M.C. & 2nd Lt MALLOY proceeded on leave	
"	15.1.17		G. Collier R sent to C.C.R.S. Megaucourt from T.M. School	
"	17.1.17		Cpl ELLIOTT sent on 3 day Gas Course	
"	22.1.17		G. COXON on leave	
"	23.1.17		D. ALLEN sent to T.M. School also Lt SMITH M.C. unable to return from leave to Edward School.	
"	24.1.17		B. Ferguson on 3 day Gas course	
"	25.1.17		D. Moore sent to Hospital from R.E. dump	
"	27.1.17		Lecture on Gas defence etc available N.C.O's & men by 2nd Lt Stephen X.T.M.Bty	
"	28.1.17		Cpl Pemberton wounded at R.E. dump	

Leonard W. [signature] 2 Lt. O.C.3/4
to O.C. 1/2 T.M. Bty
1.2.17

2nd Divisional Artillery

Z/2 TRENCH MORTAR BATTERY ::: JANUARY 1917.

WAR DIARY or INTELLIGENCE SUMMARY

Army Form C. 2118.

(Erase heading not required.)

Place	Date	Hour	Summary of Events and Information	Remarks and references to Appendices
[Place]	2/Sep 1917		The battery moved from St Rychal where we had been & just arrived 19th having through WK Becogne & moving to Moncint through Bay.	
[Place]	2/Sep		Sends the following day. The Battery arrived from Sunda to Boyardstown	
[Place]	3/Sep			
[Place]	4 Sept & 5 Sept		The grates of the divisional front have been tied to the rear of this Batty who as we have key transferred to Brigade for Supply & have remained & boards of have been at work in trainings, RA, RE & shoots. 2/Lt E. le Plac, & 2/Lt Gretwood both of 15th, the 5 Hewy School of Gunnery & lea Dos Grent Highmon, futter with lcd to 5 Hewy School of Mortars 9 Octr. 2/Lt F.E. Eatory attended the Divisional Gas School, Lithne was given on the use & care of gas respirators, & the treatment of gassed men. Lieut the Hon G Johnstone, 2/Lt Eatough, at Doll Gro Hunt & 2/Lt W.F. Whitmore proceed on leave.	

Lt Col Cdr 27 T M B
for O.C. 2. T.M.B

2nd Divisional Artillry

V: X: Y & Z TRENCH MORTAR BATTERIES

FEBRUARY 1917.

Army Form C. 2118.

V/2 T.M. Battery

JM 5

WAR DIARY
or
INTELLIGENCE SUMMARY.
(Erase heading not required.)

Instructions regarding War Diaries and Intelligence Summaries are contained in F.S. Regs, Part II. and the Staff Manual respectively. Title pages will be prepared in manuscript.

Place	Date	Hour	Summary of Events and Information	Remarks and references to Appendices
BUZINCOURT.	FEBRUARY 1917.			
	1.		2 N.C.O. & 2 men proceed on leave to England.	
	2.		2 men exchanged for 2 other men from D.A.C.	
	3.		1 man returned from leave.	
	4.		2 men sent up to join working parties under Lt. VOISEY of 3/ T.M.B.	
			Lt. CHALMERS & Servant gone on do. do. do.	
	5/6		1 N.C.O. & 3 men return from leave. Normal Routine.	
	6.		Capt. Roberts & 2 N.C.O. attend Special Gas Lecture in SENLIS.	
	7.		Gnr. CAHILL to T.M. School.	
	8.		Gnr. HALL do. do. do.	
	9.		5 men passed through gas chamber in BUZINCOURT. All small box respirators efficient.	
	10.		4 men into camp ready for leave 9/2/17 returned for work under Lt. VOISEY, leave having been cancelled.	
	11.		Capt. Roberts & 2 N.C.O. attend Special Gas Lecture in SENLIS. Normal Routine.	
	12.		Sgt. Helliwell returns from leave.	
	13.		Sgt. Helliwell to Brigade Gun for work under Lt. VOISEY.	
	14.		1 N.C.O. & 1 man returned from leave.	
	15.			

Army Form C. 2118.

WAR DIARY
or
INTELLIGENCE SUMMARY.
(Erase heading not required.)

Instructions regarding War Diaries and Intelligence Summaries are contained in F. S. Regs., Part II. and the Staff Manual respectively. Title pages will be prepared in manuscript.

Place	Date	Hour	Summary of Events and Information	Remarks and references to Appendices
	FEBRUARY, 1917.			
BOUZINCOURT	16		1 Pro and 1 Pro to Bouzincourt area for work under Lt. VAISEY.	
	17/18		Normal Routine.	
	19		Moved to Billets in ALBERT.	
	20		Normal Routine.	
ALBERT	21		Capt. ROBERTS took over the duties of Lt. VAISEY at Bouzincourt area, the latter being accidentally injured.	
	22/23		Normal Routine.	
	24		2nd Lt. MARTIN rejoined from leave & Hospital in England. 2nd Lt. CAPHIE & HAPER rejoined from II Army School of Bombers. 1 Pro to Bouzincourt area for work under Capt. ROBERTS.	
	25		Normal Routine.	
	25/28			

Townsend Roberts
Capt.
Comdg. ½ H.T.M.B.

WAR DIARY

INTELLIGENCE SUMMARY

Army Form C. 2118

X/2 T.M Battery

Place	Date	Hour	Summary of Events and Information	Remarks and references to Appendices
Bouzincourt	1st	18th	February 1917. Battery was billeted at Bouzincourt	
Albert	19th	20th	On the 19th the Battery moved to Albert where it has remained since. The battery has not been in action owing to the nature of the Divisional front which prevented its use. The men at work on tramways & R.A. & R.E. dumps last month remained so during this month, being accommodated in Nissen huts by Instp. Well Comn. The major portion of the battery was so employed. Newton 6" gas drill was carried out with the men at the battery & then reported to tests at the Divisional Gas school	
	22nd		2/Lt. A. K. Stephen was attached temporarily to the 50th Battery R.F.A	
	24th		on the 24th.	
			During the month Q.L. Smith & Br. Tomlinson proceeded on leave.	

Clinton
Lieut. McWyndham
2/Lt R.F.A

O.C. X/2 T.M.B.

Army Form C. 2118.

WAR DIARY
INTELLIGENCE SUMMARY
Y 2 T.M. Battery
(Erase heading not required.)

Place	Date	Hour	Summary of Events and Information	Remarks and references to Appendices
Bouzincourt	February 1917 7 to 18		During this period the battery billeted in Bouzincourt. Lt. L. White & Gnr. Carson proceeded to I Army Trench Mortar School	
Albert	19 to 28		On 19th the Battery moved into billets in Albert, have remained since. Lt. L. Gill & Gnr. Carson return from Trench Mortar School. Lt. R. Barrett Temporarily attached 48th Battery. The nature of the Divisional Front being such that it was not possible for the battery to go into action the personnel of the battery summer have been so was the case last month temporarily attached to R.A. & R.E. Dumps, Light Railways etc with the exception of those men who were in charge of the battery stores. Lt. R.B. Barrett attached to the 48th Battery in the 24th. Instruction was on the use of the Box Respirator was carried out from time to time when available and Gas Respirators tested at the Div. Gas School. Both May cancer proceeded on leave during the month.	

W.M. Foukham
O.C. Y2 T.M.B.

Army Form C. 2118.

WAR DIARY of 2/2 T.M.B.
INTELLIGENCE SUMMARY
(Erase heading not required.)

Instructions regarding War Diaries and Intelligence Summaries are contained in F. S. Regs., Part II. and the Staff Manual respectively. Title Pages will be prepared in manuscript.

Place	Date	Hour	Summary of Events and Information	Remarks and references to Appendices
Bouzincourt	February 1917		Battery was billeted at Bouzincourt.	
Albert	19th Feb		On the 19th the battery moved to Albert where it has remained since. The battery has not been in action owing to the nature of the front which prevented its use. The men transferred for work on tramways & R.A. & R.E. dumps last month remained so during this month. Gas drill was carried out with the men at the battery, & then respirators tested at the Divisional Gas school. During the month Ln. Northwood proceeded on leave.	

J. Greenwood 2nd Lt
for O/C 2/2 T.M.B.

2nd Trench Mortar Brigade
2nd Divisional Artillery.

V: X: Y & Z. TRENCH MORTAR BATTERIES

MARCH 1917.

Army Form C. 2118.

V/2 T.M. Battery
March 1917

WAR DIARY
or
INTELLIGENCE SUMMARY.
(Erase heading not required.)

Instructions regarding War Diaries and Intelligence Summaries are contained in F. S. Regs., Part II. and the Staff Manual respectively. Title pages will be prepared in manuscript.

Place	Date	Hour	Summary of Events and Information	Remarks and references to Appendices
ALBERT	March 1917 1.		1 O.R. reported from Hospital	
	3.		1 O.R. to Hospital	
	7.		Do. Do. 1 N.C.O. & 5 O.Rs joined from 2nd D.A.C. 2 Lt Chalmers rejoined from MEAULTE and detached men except those remaining under Capt R. Blanc rejoin Bty. at ALBERT	
	8.		Battery complete moved by Motor Lorries to MONDICOURT. She paraded from POZIERS and ALBERT joining up there	
MONDICOURT	9.		Await orders from 7th Corps. 3rd Army to which the Bty is attached for action. Gun drill and Route Parades	
	10.		Received orders from 14th Div, to which Bty has been attached for action, to move to ARRAS. Left MONDICOURT with 4 guns (finished w/o Blank) 11.30 p.m. Reached ARRAS, Rs & 1 Lorry which could not be extricated from mud, at 5 a.m. 11/3/17	
ARRAS	11.		Settled into Billets in ARRAS	
	12.		Officers and N.C.Os. reconnoitring gun positions situated P,Q,T,U and V. Commenced work on P,Q,T and V in evening. 1 O.R. to Hospital	
	13.		Day and night work on P,Q,T,&V. 1 O.R. to Hospital	
	14.		Do. Do.	
	15.		Attached 56th Div. for action. Subs & other gun positions. Gun in action V/It to continue manning gun positions (innumerated) P,1,R,3,T,V. No 3 with	
	16.		Day work on P&R. Night work on P,Q,T,&V Nightwork on ?	
	17.		Do. Do.	
	18.		Seize over gun points and ammunition 13rds at gun + 13 at GROUPE DES MAISONS from V/It + forts 1 N.C.O. + 1 O.R. to leave with another after gun. Enemy retired rendering gun pits out of range.	
	19.		Work on old pits abandoned after morning. Slight 1 O.R. to Hospital gun Drill, gun cleaning and Routine work	
	20.		3 N.C.Os + 14 men at work on gun pits (15 pdr) Bty 281st "Bele" R.F.A. 1 N.C.O. + 4 O.Rs. joined from 2nd D.A.C. 2 O.Rs. rejoined from Hospital	

Army Form C. 2118.

WAR DIARY
or
INTELLIGENCE SUMMARY.
(Erase heading not required.)

Place	Date	Hour	Summary of Events and Information	Remarks and references to Appendices
ARRAS	MARCH 1917			
	21		1 N.C.O. and 16 men at work on 2/c positions - gun emb - 1 man to hospital	
	22		2 N.C.O. " 16 men " " " 2/c " Attached to 17th Coy's	
	23		Attached 34th Divn. Capt. R Stoetz reconnoitred positions and took over positions Nos 6, 7, 8 and 9 on 34th Divl. front. Night working parties	
	24		Continuous work on positions	
	25		Capt. Rice & gun visited on mag. Day & Night work on all positions. Bowr South and Coninnet Park carrying at night one man hosp [?] to X.7.TT.113 and one man to hospital	
	26		Day & night work on positions 1 gun complete taken to Irnad & 40 light [?] to No 7. 1 man reported from Hospital	
	27		Heavy parts & gun carried to No 7 & light parts & another gun carried to No 6. Had over one gun complete in ARRAS to V/34 H.T.M.B. Lt Chalmers & hospital.	
	28		Day & night work on positions. 1 gun complete taken & tunnel & fight parts carried up to 8. 1 man reported from Hospital	
	29		Day and night work on positions. Heavy parts & gun carried into tunnel. 1 man to hospital 1 N.C.O. to hospital 1 man reported from hospital.	
	30		Do. Beds # 6 & 7 laid. 1 + 9 Bcn. relieved	
	31		Do. Do carrying. 2Lt Chalmers reported from Hospital	

V/2 HEAVY TRENCH MORTAR BATTERY

O.R.Chalmers 2Lt RGA
for O.C. V/2 H.T.M.B.S.

Army Form C. 2118

WAR DIARY
or
INTELLIGENCE SUMMARY
(Erase heading not required.)

X/2 T.M. Battery

Instructions regarding War Diaries and Intelligence Summaries are contained in F.S. Regs., Part II. and the Staff Manual respectively. Title Pages will be prepared in manuscript.

Place	Date	Hour	Summary of Events and Information	Remarks and references to Appendices
Albert	1917 March			
	8.3.17		Battery engaged in fatigue work in neighbourhood of Dyke Valley and on Pozieres Dump	
	10.3.17		Moved to Mushroom dump to dump	
	15.3.17		Arrived at Arras – Battery attached to 14th Div.	
	16th/17th/18th/19th/20th		Reconnaissance inspect battery positions from Beaurains skating above 20 km until day wounded to allotted ones – took to RESPs	
	20.3.17		No instructions received. Instructed to recce impact new battery	
			attached 56th Div. Instructed with RE & recce – inclue batt.	
			positions – one 30 – influence every round – guns approach	
	25.3.17		Gun positions – when completed every round – guns approach	
			in Velaines RES instead.	
	26.3.17		No further instructions	
	27.3.17		Moved from 34th Div – endeavoured to two – endeavoured kept	
	27.3.17		A difficult gun relative but failed –	
			Moved inspect positions – did so & reported them – gave advice to	
	28.3.17		recce them suggest allotted but put to finally –	
			Have been suffering for some delay involved approx positions	
	29.3.17		yards to two – found on serious delay involved approx positions	
			Have to be abrupt suspend & to finally was Manin	
	30.3.17		Got to return allotted but exact gone indifferent – Clarke morning	
	31.3.17		Van Lieu	

Continued writing from positions

WAR DIARY
INTELLIGENCE SUMMARY
(Erase heading not required.)

Army Form C. 2118.

Y/2 T.M. Battery

Place	Date	Hour	Summary of Events and Information	Remarks and references to Appendices
Albert	March 7th	8th	During the first week the Battery remained out of action at Albert & the same fatigues were carried out on Rations Dumps & Light Rly as during the previous month. On the 8th the Battery moved off	
Montecourt	8	9	to carry out Relief orders. Realisation at that time unknown and reached Montecourt the same day were quarters there for the night left next morning for Serre Park at Savy from here they were	
Serre Capella &	9th	8.30	attd. to the H.Q. 50 Dn D.A.C. to shelter we were attacked reached Hae came night. The following evening we left Serre Capelle for Roclincourt where we left our guns & the Personnel proceeded to Arras & were billeted H.Q. on the 13th Left of the Battery with 21 H.M. Trench [Mortar] went up line & relief of Battery dug in commence firing same afternoon as were glad to be out for a rest which took place on the 17th During the raid two guns were in action from one to two hours by a premature along the fuse of gun about half an hour made it impossible to continue firing. Gun & Position owing to the Pits being in frames. Permanent positions were they allotted to us within the lep of Infantry	
Arras.				

Army Form C. 2118.

WAR DIARY
or
INTELLIGENCE SUMMARY.
(Erase heading not required.)

Place	Date	Hour	Summary of Events and Information	Remarks and references to Appendices
Arras			Working parties at night to our men during the day fortified were improved as much as was possible in such a short time as was allowed us. On 21 st Lt W. Gill was severely wounded whilst superintending operations. During the remainder of the month wire cutting was successfully carried out though at times under adverse circumstances & often under very heavy hostile fire.	
Athies	1st R.R.		Paid a battery on fatigues etc.	
Rouchecourt	8th	9 A.M.	Battery moved to Motor Lorries to Rouchecourt	
Grenglupelle	9th	10 A.M.	Reached Grenay Capelle late on 9th — W again afternoon 10th	
April	10 p 31		Settled in Arras + go up the line shoot	
"	21 st		2nd Lt. Gill wounded & sent down to the base.	

A. Morton Forkhaw 4th RFA

O.C. Y 2nd MGB

WAR DIARY or INTELLIGENCE SUMMARY

March 1917 — Army Form C. 2118.

2"/ V.M. Battery

Place	Date March	Hour	Summary of Events and Information	Remarks and references to Appendices
Albert	1st to 7th		Battery billeted at Albert. The men transferred to Fienvergs & R. & R.G. dumps remained to. Gnr. Britt & Batt. received as reinforcements on the 7th.	
Francourt	8th		Battery moved to Francourt	
	9th		Battery moved to Arras where it was attached to the 34th Div.	
Arras	11th		Work started on gun positions taken over from 34th Div. These positions were partly made.	
	11th to 16th		Work continued on gun positions.	
	16th		Gun mounted at Falkland Street G.5.d. 8½.9. Seven bombs fired. Bore stopped as could not reach mine as it was thought bed was too soft.	
	17th		Bed relaid in Falkland street.	
	18th		Twenty bombs fired but still unable to reach mine.	
	19th		Bed again relaid.	
	20th		Sixteen bombs fired but still unable to reach mine. Gr. Barker. O. joined as reinforcement.	
	21st		Reglo (?) fired at Waterloo street G.6.c.4.5½. & November avenue G.6.c.0.2.	
	22nd		Twenty bombs fired but owing to difficulty of finding an O.P. results unsatisfactory. Wire damaged.	
	23rd		Thirty bombs fired from November Avenue & Eleven from Waterloo street. Wire damaged.	
	24th		Bed in Waterloo street sunk necessitating relaying of same. Slight retaliation.	
	25th		54 bombs fired from November Avenue & Waterloo street. Guns & wire started at G.12.a.5.9.	

Army Form C. 2118.

WAR DIARY
INTELLIGENCE SUMMARY
(Erase heading not required.)

Instructions regarding War Diaries and Intelligence Summaries are contained in F. S. Regs., Part II. and the Staff Manual respectively. Title Pages will be prepared in manuscript.

Place	Date	Hour	Summary of Events and Information	Remarks and references to Appendices
Arras	26th		60 bombs fired from Iroquois Avenue & Waterloo street gun, Gap started yesterday increased to 30 yards about. Two other small gaps started.	
	27th		Guns have to be removed from Iroquois Avenue & Waterloo Street as they are main communication trenches, then is great difficulty in finding positions for the guns as the accès as all the trenches are man trenches.	
	28th		53 bombs fired from Waterloo Street gun + Gun off Iroquois Avenue. Wire damaged.	
	29th		144 bombs fired. Wire damaged.	
	30th		42 bombs fired. Wire badly damaged but no gap.	
	31st		47 bombs fired. Wire no damaged.	

Major RA
For Lt Col RA

2449 Wt. W14957/M90 750,000 1/16 J.B.C. & A. Forms/C.2118/12.

Trench Mortar Brigade
2nd Divisional Artillery.

V: X: Y: & Z. TRENCH MORTAR BATTERIES

APRIL 1917.

WAR DIARY or INTELLIGENCE SUMMARY

Army Form C. 2118.

TM 8/4/17
M Destroy
JJ 8

Place	Date	Hour	Summary of Events and Information	Remarks and references to Appendices
ARRAS. (ROLLINCOURT SECTOR)	1/4/17		Nos. 6, 7 & 9 guns in action. Day & night work on positions. Bombs carrying. Transporting of tents to Dumps. Handed over No. 6 gun position to 4/17 Batty. Heavy fogs of 1 remaining gun taken to trench 40, and thence carried to No. 6 position. 1 N.C.O. + 2 men to Hospital.	
	2/4/17		Day & night work on positions. Bomb carrying.	
	3/4/17		6's @ Nos. 9, 14 @ No. 8, and 44 between Nos. 6 & 7.) Carried (7 from 9 & 4 from 7.) in registration. Capt. ROBERTS, 2nd M.S.D. and 3 gun detachments (6 men + 1 signaller per gun) to line in the line for the preliminary bombardment. No. 8 gun in action (open fire).	
	4/4/17		"V" Day. Fired 22 rounds. 1 N.C.O. from Hospital.	
	5/4/17		"W" Day. Fired 29 rounds. 2 men to Hospital, 1 N.C.O. + 6 men from 2nd D.A.C. as Reinforcements. 4 men transferred to Brigade Batteries.	

WAR DIARY or INTELLIGENCE SUMMARY

Army Form C. 2118

Place	Date	Hour	Summary of Events and Information	Remarks and references to Appendices
ARRAS (ROEUX SECTOR)	6/4/17		"X" Day. Fired 20 rounds. Bart. carrying, 1 man from hospital	
	7/4/17		"Q" Day. Fired 29 rounds. No. 7 pit received direct hit on left hip corner of front of mantlet, rendering the collapse of the whole hind part of the pit which carries on the block of the rear revet front. Borrowed No. 6 gun & position from 1/1/17 Battery to cover gun of No. 7 gun on left hipflection. No. 6 pit working partially collapsed from concussion, so now entirely removed by night. Bart. carrying.	
	8/4/17		"Y" Day. Fired 16 rounds. All detachments except 1 man per gun to Rest Billets in ARRAS.	
	9/4/17		"Z" Day. Fired remaining 1 round from each of the 3 guns (7, 8 and 9) at 55 to 60 seconds before Zero (5.30 am) when the Attack was launched. Gun detachments relieved at 3.30 pm. Guns dismantled, covers checked and heavy parts dragged to tops	

Army Form C. 2118.

WAR DIARY
or
INTELLIGENCE SUMMARY.

(Erase heading not required.)

Instructions regarding War Diaries and Intelligence Summaries are contained in F. S. Regs., Part II. and the Staff Manual respectively. Title pages will be prepared in manuscript.

Place	Date	Hour	Summary of Events and Information	Remarks and references to Appendices
ARRAS (ROCLINCOURT SECTOR)	9/4/17		"N" Day (contd.) Patrols for remoual went out. Old German Line reconnoitred to observe effect of shooting. General effect good, much damage to dug-outs and trenches tho' having been occupied. Rounds fired = 130. Capt. ROBERTS and 2nd Lt. MEAD returned to Rest Billets in ARRAS.	
	10/4/17		Recnord repairs. Line reconnoitred for possibility of wagon roads to guns.	
	11/4/17		Recnord routine.	
	12/4/17		do. do. 1 NCO & 5 men pioneering in Line as General in Charge and above relieved. 1 gun (No. 7) brought down to Rest Billet complete in 5 half limbers.	
	13/4/17		Recnord routine. 1 NCO to hospital.	
	14/4/17		2 guns (Nos. 8 & 9) complete brought down to Rest Billet in Rtenders.	

WAR DIARY
—of—
INTELLIGENCE SUMMARY.
(Erase heading not required.)

Army Form C. 2118.

Place	Date	Hour	Summary of Events and Information	Remarks and references to Appendices
ARRAS.	15/4/17		Remaining of guns (No.6) brought down complete to Rest Billets in Hendecourt.	
	16/4/17		Removed machine.	
	17/4/17		Baths for N.C.O. & men.	
	18/4/17		"	
	19/4/17		" (including gas test and inspection of anti-gas appliances.)	
	20/4/17		29 N.C.O. & men started for BETHUNE to bring back remounts, but after waiting all day at 2nd D.M.C. dismount owing to transport having failed to turn up.	
	21/4/17		Repeated 2nd D. duty. Arr for all purposes. 29 N.C.O. & men to BETHUNE to bring back remounts. Spent night at BETHUNE VENDIN.	
	22/4/17		Remount party returned in evening.	
	23/4/17		Party of 15 engaged in bringing back horses near ANZIN. 1 man to hospital. 1 n.c.o. from hospital.	
	24/4/17		Work on trench matting on old F.L. trenches for ammunition supply to Field Batteries. All available men. 1 man to hospital.	

Army Form C. 2118.

WAR DIARY
or
INTELLIGENCE SUMMARY.
(Erase heading not required.)

Instructions regarding War Diaries and Intelligence Summaries are contained in F. S. Regs., Part II. and the Staff Manual respectively. Title pages will be prepared in manuscript.

Place	Date	Hour	Summary of Events and Information	Remarks and references to Appendices
ARRAS	25/4/17		As for 24/4/17.	
	26/4/17		Work on Light Railway. 1 M.G.O. & 1 man to Hospital.	
	27/4/17		do. do. 5 men to 3rd Veterinary Section for several days to assist in evacuation of horses.	
	28/4/17		Work on Light Railway.	
	29/4/17		Work on A.R.P. and Light Railway.	
	30/4/17		do. do.	

J. Howard Reeve.
Capt.
Commdg. 1/2 N.T.M. Bty.
2/5/17.

WAR DIARY or INTELLIGENCE SUMMARY

Army Form C. 2118

X/2 T.M. Battery

Place	Date	Hour	Summary of Events and Information	Remarks and references to Appendices
Arras	1.4.17		Continued working on positions in cord line off Victoria Trench about Sq. 6.C. 17.55 (2/20000). Positions 1 & 2 consisted of the right bay of an old 2" dugout occupied by a Stokes detachment containing 2 gun pits, one for left gun, the other (No. 2) blown in by ammunition and filled in with corrugated iron sheets &c. No. 1 pit was an excellent position - the final gun position this latter has even been ranged for this gun pit standing up & the dugout being some 30 feet below the trench & the gun pits standing up taking up an ascending passage giving a crest of about 15 feet. The passage leading to No. 2 was filled with earth. Vide plan(s). Previous to & consisted of position in the line dug in the rear of the trench covered by a screen with a camouflaged nature & ammunition. This was the plan of the positions & arrived at - Vide plan (b) & nature & ammunition.	
2.4.17			Guns brought up from Arras, timber & butts - A good deal was done on No. 1 position - Wire on the positions was continued - hindered by the carrying of ammunition & supplies -	
3.4.17			Continued with positions - Lashing through to No. 2 - got to No. 1 gun about 1 pm. Fired over 200 rounds out of Stokes gun in the afternoon at some between 90° & 6.C. 8.5 & 8.C. 8½ & 7 - The shooting was extraordinarily good & fully satisfactory. 67 rounds fired on the wire - cut several gaps - Results very satisfactory	
4.4.17			2, 3, & 4 positions up to later 4.15 finished - fired some 90 rounds from 1 all we had - Continued all possible work on position - but put in No 2	
5.4.17			Continued wire - ammunition position etc - just as available rounds with good results. The ammunition supply was extremely bad & very much time & been consumed obtaining same - Group Commander reported see Dw¼ were very satisfactory - no hitter us to continue wire cutting exclusively - Also 20 - D.7.	
6.4.17			Battery on to W.E. Wire & firing to cut wire about S.66&7 - No more rounds to cut same & pushed & fired on it but found some with a final success - all available rounds kept	
7.4.17			Same troops from trenches as ammunition supply were kept but in final battery fired about 20 rounds on new gun with fair success	
8.4.17			But tribunal japes	

WAR DIARY
or
INTELLIGENCE SUMMARY

Army Form C. 2118

Place	Date	Hour	Summary of Events and Information	Remarks and references to Appendices
St Athas	9.4.17		Arrived wound at Servoleur 2 day — Infantry Advanced @ 5.30 am. His infantry were field up by barbed wire secured who to be cut — Inspected St Athan & confident it will cut —	The battery brought forward & remains attached to supports Divisional Artillery.
	10.4.17		Withdrew from the line to Athas — (The battery were shewed that with us good protection a pill-box has been much can be done even when the ammunition supply is bad —)	
	10.4.17 to 30.4.17		Battalion at rest in Athas — during the last 15 days the battery were employed in fatigues near Roclincourt constructing dumps & assisting in Railway work —	
		10 am (Q)	positions 1 & 2 [sketch] positions 3 & 4 [sketch with 3 pit, 4 pit, Z, Y] Enemy Line	

* (a) Sleeping quarters
  (b) Ammunition dug-outs
  (c) Officers from trench
  (x) Main passage (30 ft below ground)
  (OL) Lo2 ft blown in a passage & filled in
  (e) Stairs to same " " Lo 1
  (f) " " " Lo 2
  (g) Ammn recess
  (d) Lo 1 pit — (15 ft below ground)

Lt Mylston R.F.A. X Trench Bty.

Army Form C. 2118.

1/2 Y T.M. Battery

WAR DIARY
or
INTELLIGENCE SUMMARY.
(Erase heading not required.)

Place	Date	Hour	Summary of Events and Information	Remarks and references to Appendices
ARRAS	1-4-17		The battery having been transferred from the 51st (Highland) Division and attached to the 34th Division, all guns were shifted to the front of the latter division. Worked on preparing gun positions allotted to the battery. Lieutenant Foulsham reported sick, and was evacuated.	
	1-4-17 to 6-4-17 7-4-17		Worked on emplacements. Instructions having arrived from the D.T.M.O. 34th Division to fire on enemy wire north of T3 in G6c, a new emplacement was hastily made in an assembly trench off VICTORIA STREET as the wire was out of range of the emplacements allotted to the battery. Fired on enemy wire north of T3 in G6c with good results, two large gaps being cut.	Reference maps ARRAS 1/10000 51B.N.W.
	8-4-17		Battery at rest in ARRAS.	
	9-4-17 to 30-4-17		During the last 15 days the battery was engaged in fatigues near ROCLINCOURT.	

R.P.O. Barrett
2 Lt. R.F.A.
for O.C. Y2 T.M.B.

Army Form C. 2118.

WAR DIARY Z/1. J.M.B.

INTELLIGENCE SUMMARY

(Erase heading not required.)

Instructions regarding War Diaries and Intelligence Summaries are contained in F.S. Regs., Part II. and the Staff Manual respectively. Title Pages will be prepared in manuscript.

Place	Date	Hour	Summary of Events and Information	Remarks and references to Appendices
ARRAS.	April 1st		No firing was done today on account of the luckness of the Infantry relief	
	2nd		Small lane cut in wire. 62 bombs fired.	
	3rd		18 bombs fired. Wire still further damaged.	
	4th		51 bombs fired from Pit Street junction on G.6.c.8.6. wire damaged.	
	5th		20 bombs fired from November Avenue junction. Wire at G.6.c.4.2. 3 damaged. Lottery blown in to what onto as creation observed. Gap of 15 yards + one thing 5 yards.	
	6th		Another attacked at G.6.c.4.1½. Wire much cut about. 115 bombs fired at G.6.c.2.1½. Gaps previously made greatly enlarged. Another large gap made further south of aforefront. 86 more fired on wire portion at G.6.c.4.2. + 20 rounds fired on G.6.c.8.6. Gaps cut.	
	7th		G.6.c.4.8. Wire damaged. Heavy retaliation on O.P.	
	8th		76 rounds fired in front & third line wire. Ra. 11015. Gn. Benfield became a casualty being burnt in the face by blast of the mortar which went off whilst loading.	
	9th		62 bombs fired - G.12.a.5.7. 84 + G.6.c.55.10. There is very little wire in front of G.12.a. Deputy at station on O.O.J. 20.19½. The battery couple many wire cut, of nightwind Two bombs fired at zero hour.	
	10th		Over one hundred prisoners & one officer from German dugouts	
	11th		Guns + employment brought down from the line to the billet.	
			Batteries employed in clearing up ammunition dumped in the trenches.	

Army Form C. 2118.

WAR DIARY
or
INTELLIGENCE SUMMARY

(Erase heading not required.)

Z/2 Y.M.B

Instructions regarding War Diaries and Intelligence Summaries are contained in F. S. Regs., Part II. and the Staff Manual respectively. Title Pages will be prepared in manuscript.

Place	Date	Hour	Summary of Events and Information	Remarks and references to Appendices
ARRAS	1st to 12th Dec. 1916	9.30	Battery employed in fatigues, buggying horses and making etc. Lt. Vaire R.Y.A. joined 15th Battery R.Y.A. on 29th. 2nd Lt. Naylor proceeded on one month special leave to England on 29th.	

H. Greatwood. 2nd Lt.
O.C. - Z/2 Y.M.B.

2449 Wt. W14957/M90 750,000 1/16 J.B.C. & A. Forms/C.2118/12.

TrenchMortar Brigade
2nd Divisional Artillery.

V: X: Y & Z. TRENCH MORTAR BATTERIES

M A Y 1917.

Army Form C. 2118.

V/2 T.M. Battery
Vol 9

WAR DIARY
or
INTELLIGENCE SUMMARY.
(Erase heading not required.)

Place	Date	Hour	Summary of Events and Information	Remarks and references to Appendices
ARRAS 1/5/17 (ROCKINCOURT)	2/3		Work on A.R.P. and tramway. 1 Brum from hospital.	
	4		A.R.P. for night work.	
	5		Battery moved to Bivouacs at D. 26. C. 7. 2 near ROCKINCOURT. (3 m) 29 2 r/o + 2 m posted to 11 G.S. wagons. Camp complete with 10 French stables and 1 large wagon shelter.	
Rockincourt	6/10		Work on O.R.P.	
	6		Work on old and new A.R.Ps.	
	7/8 11		2 Guns and complete stores and equipment handed over to V/51 H.T.M.B..	
	12		Work on old and new A.R.Ps. 1 2r/o on urgent special leave to England.	
	13		Work on old and new A.R.Ps. 1 2r/o on transferred to 2nd D.A.C. 5 men rejoined from 2nd A. Mobile veterinary section. 1 Brum 2r/o to Hospital	

WAR DIARY / INTELLIGENCE SUMMARY

Army Form C. 2118.

Place	Date	Hour	Summary of Events and Information	Remarks and references to Appendices
	1917 Aug			
	14		14 R.P.O. & 3 men attached to 2nd D.A.C. for escort during concentration of D.A.C. Work on A.R.P. Commenced dug-out for 38th Bde. O.P.	
	15/18		Work at D.A.C., A.R.P., and dug-out as above. Conference Day & night shifts on the dug-out work.	
	19		Work as on 15/18. Gnr. J. B. LINDSEY died of wounds at 7.30 pm., one hour after having been hit, in 13th Field Ambulance.	
	20		Work as above. 1 man to hospital. 1 man on leave. Gnr. J. B. LINDSEY buried in British Military Cemetery, Shut 51B,N.W.1, 19.24.C.3.H, Plan D, Row 15. Church parade.	
	21		Work as above. 1 man to hospital.	
	22		Work as above. Sent returning & guns and all stores and equipment to 1st Army School of Gunnery. 1 man to Beaulieu Rest Camp.	
	23		Work on A.R.P. and dug-out. Party from D.A.C. returned, 7 of whom had been inoculated. 1 Bdr. & 7 men reinoculated.	
	24		Work as above. 1 Bdr. & 7 men reinoculated.	

Army Form C. 2118.

WAR DIARY
INTELLIGENCE SUMMARY.
(Erase heading not required.)

Instructions regarding War Diaries and Intelligence Summaries are contained in F.S. Regs., Part II. and the Staff Manual respectively. Title pages will be prepared in manuscript.

Place	Date 1917 May.	Hour	Summary of Events and Information	Remarks and references to Appendices
BOULOGNE	25		6 men to BOULOGNE to bring back remounts under D.A.C.	
	26		Work as usual. 1 man to 23/24.	
	27		Work as usual. 1 man to Hospital. Church Parade. Lt. CHALMERS proceeded on leave to England.	
	28		do. 1 N.C.O. rejoined from leave.	
	29		do.	
	30		Work on D.R.P. and dug-out for 36th Bde. O.P.. 1 N.C.O. and 5 men under 2nd Lieut. SOLLAS to HERMIN to clean up village. Capt. ROBERTS on short leave to Paris. 1 N.C.O. on leave.	
	31		Work as on 30th. Remount party rejoined from Love D.A.C.	

Roberts
Capt.
Commdg. 1/2 H.T.M.B.

Army Form C. 2118

X/2 TM Battery

WAR DIARY
or
INTELLIGENCE SUMMARY
(Erase heading not required.)

Instructions regarding War Diaries and Intelligence Summaries are contained in F.S. Regs., Part II. and the Staff Manual respectively. Title Pages will be prepared in manuscript.

Place	Date	Hour	Summary of Events and Information	Remarks and references to Appendices
Arras	1.5.17		Battery at rest.	
	4.5.17		" moved to Roclincourt	
	5.5.17		Battery employed in fatigues at A.R.P. Dumps — all available men of Bn. Hqrs. employed. Sent to S.A.C. Arras.	
	17.5.17		Instructions to run a/c 36 Tm Bac re construction of dugouts for Bae up to line for O.P.	
	14.5.17		Manual plan of same. Subversion of work pure to Bruach Head X/2 Tm B. Ehino Subversion J/2 Tm B. should wire in 2 shifts of 8 hours	
			proper that battery of X/2 Tm B. should wire in each holding Repairs at Battue wire on dugouts — all men available work — a few men from each holding Repairs at	
			A.R.D. work — wire was continuous.	
	25.5.17		2 hour 10 & 15 Boulogne with O/C offices to fix revetments.	
	27.5.17		6 men inoculated.	
	14.5.17 }		Wire from 14.5.17 continued on dugout. A.R.D dumps.	
	30.5.17 }			
	31.5.17 }		11.3. Rang to 1st Army 1-M school for instruction	

1875 Wt. W593/826 1,000,000 4/15 J.B.C. & A. A.D.S.S./Forms/C. 2118.

Army Form C. 2118.

WAR DIARY 1/2 T.M.B.
or
INTELLIGENCE SUMMARY.
(Erase heading not required.)

Instructions regarding War Diaries and Intelligence Summaries are contained in F.S. Regs., Part II. and the Staff Manual respectively. Title pages will be prepared in manuscript.

Place	Date	Hour	Summary of Events and Information	Remarks and references to Appendices
Arras	1st May 1917		The Battery remained at the same billets as in the previous month & supplied parties for the A.R.P. daily.	
Roclincourt	4th	"	On the 4th the Battery personnel & equipment moved from their billets in Arras to Roclincourt, & continued sending parties to the A.R.P. On the 14th inst work was commenced on the construction of dug out M.P. for the 36th Bde under the supervision of N.C.O./Lead. the men working in shifts during the day & night until the 31st when the dugout was duly completed. On the 14th a party was also detailed consisting of 4 men & proceed to the D.C.C. for duties as regulated & to receive the	
"	22nd	"	By on 23rd at noon. On the 22nd 2/Lt R.O. Barrett left for the 1st Army Rest Camp for a fortnights rest cure.	
"	25th	"	On the 25th inst, 2 men & the Battery Groom, proceed to	
"	26th	"	Boulogne as an Officers Servants thing back remounts to the latter. On the 28th Bdr. Ferguson Wade	

Army Form C. 2118.

WAR DIARY
or
INTELLIGENCE SUMMARY.
(Erase heading not required.)

X 27 M B

Place	Date	Hour	Summary of Events and Information	Remarks and references to Appendices
Trenches	28 Mar		assisting in the construction of the dugout was accidentally hit on the head with a sledge hammer but was on his Fracture Duty on 31st with. During the month a number of men were inoculated but owing to large percentage of men being engaged on the various fatigues of no importance these were as many as were due have done.	

J. M. Jenkinson
O.C. X 27 M B

Army Form C. 2118.

2/2 T-M Battery

WAR DIARY
or
INTELLIGENCE SUMMARY
(Erase heading not required.)

2/2 T.M.B.

Place	Date	Hour	Summary of Events and Information	Remarks and references to Appendices
ARRAS.	May 1st to 3rd		Battery was billeted at Arras & was employed on fatigues on dumps etc.	
ROCLINCOURT	4th to 31st		Battery moved to Roclincourt where it remained till the end of the month. The men were employed on fatigues at A.R.P., some (4 men) were attached to the D.A.C. from 14th to 28th, & some (9 men) were employed on making a dugout for the 36th Bde. During the month as many men as possible were innoculated. On 25th 2 men were detailed to proceed to Boulogne to bring up remounts to D.A.C. Cpl. Douthwaite proceeded to the rest camp for a fortnight, the 7th for rest. On 30th, 2nd Lt. Vollar & one man were detailed to proceed to HERMIN for fatigues. On 14th Dr. HICKMAN became a casualty, having his jaw broken while acting as groom to D.T.M.O.	

H. Greenwood
2nd Lt. R.F.A.
O.C. 2/2 T.M.B.

Trench Mortar Brigade
2nd Divisional Artillery.

V: X: Y & Z. TRENCH MORTAR BATTERIES

JUNE 1917.

Army Form C. 2118.

WAR DIARY
or
INTELLIGENCE SUMMARY.
(Erase heading not required.)

V/2
HEAVY TRENCH
MORTAR BATTERY

Place	Date	Hour	Summary of Events and Information	Remarks and references to Appendices
ROCLINCOURT.	1917			
	June 6.		Went on to 5th, and examination and addition orders 2" Bomb, taking serviceable ones to A.R.P. and doing movements over on Ecurie dump.	
	7.		Went on on 5/6th. 3 R.E.O. gunners to Course under 2nd Lieut. Son Officer. 1 Man from Hospital.	
	8.		Went on on 5/6/7th. 1 Man from Hospital	
	9.		Went on A.R.P. Morope 2". (and a few Brench) T.M. Bombs selected and buried at THE LABYRINTH (formerly ECURIE) Railhead. Pte. CHALMERS rejoined from Leave.	
	10.		Went on A.R.P. Capt. ROBERTS proceeds on leave to England. 1 R.S.O. & 1 man on leave to England.	
	11.		Went on A.R.P. Sergeants, Smith and Saunders. 1 man rejoined from leave.	
	12.		Went on A.R.P. Bathing Parade, Drill etc. 1 man to Hospital.	

WAR DIARY

INTELLIGENCE SUMMARY.

Army Form C. 2118.

V/2 HEAVY TRENCH MORTAR BATTERY

Place	Date	Hour	Summary of Events and Information	Remarks and references to Appendices
ROCLINCOURT.	1917 June 13		Work on O.R.P. Battery funnels. Work for Division Ballons in the line at night. Snow from hospital. Work and Parade as on 13th.	
	14			
	15		Work as on 13/14. Guard on Race Course again, relieved by 5th Div. Lts. WATSON & Dumont Jun.	
	16		Work on O.R.P. Lts. WATSON proceeds to lint to meet Section Balloon. Officer appointed.	
	17		Work on O.R.P. Right party to work for Section Bn. in line. Party employed on chokbricking Camouflage at O.R.P. 1 Gun to 2nd D.A.C.	
	18		Work on O.R.P. and constructing Camouflage. 6 O.R. attached temporarily to 1/1 T.M.B. for work on positions in line. 4t Reinforcements from 2nd D.A.C.	
	19		Work on O.R.P. and constructing Camouflage. 1 Pay and 1 gun on loan. 2 guns to 2nd D.A.C.	

WAR DIARY
INTELLIGENCE SUMMARY

Army Form C. 2118.

V/2 HEAVY TRENCH MORTAR BATTERY.

Place	Date	Hour	Summary of Events and Information	Remarks and references to Appendices
ROCKINCOURT.	1917 June 20		Troops on on 19th. Party temporarily attached to 1/2 F.M.B. repairs. 1 Reinforcement from 2nd D.A.C.	
	21.		Troops on A.R.P. and on erection of Camouflage in the line by night.	
	22.		Troops as on 21st. Inspections and Drills.	
	23.		Troops as on 21st.	
	24.		Capt. ROBERTS rejoined from Leave. Troops on A.R.P. Church Parade. 10 Reinforcements from 2nd D.A.C.	
	25.		Troops on A.R.P. and on erection of Camouflage in the line by night. Two Inspections and Drills. 2nd Lt. WATSON returned from Sickness in Line.	
	26.		Troops as on 25th. 1 N.C.O. on Leave. Parades, Gas Kit and other Inspections. Drills.	
	27		Troops on A.R.P., Parades, Drills and Inspections. 1 Reinforcement from 2nd D.A.C.	

WAR DIARY
INTELLIGENCE SUMMARY

Army Form C. 2118.

V/2 HEAVY TRENCH MORTAR BATTERY

Place	Date	Hour	Summary of Events and Information	Remarks and references to Appendices
ROCINCOURT. 1917	June 26.		Work on B.R.P., Parapets, Gun Emplacements and Dools. 1 man rejoined from Leave.	
	29.		Work on B.R.P. Parapets and Dools. Baths.	
	30.		Work on B.R.P. Parapets and Dools. Baths. 3 men proceeded on Leave. Capt. ROBERTS proceeded to his Brevet Exchange of brigades for D.T.M.O. Course.	

Roberts.
Capt.
Comdg. V/2 H.T.M.B.

WAR DIARY
INTELLIGENCE SUMMARY

Army Form C. 2118.

Place	Date	Hour	Summary of Events and Information	Remarks and references to Appendices
ROCLINCOURT	June 1917 1		Work on R.R.P's. Billets cleaning. Party reported from HERNIN. 1 man to hospital. 1 man to R.F.C. H.Q. for Commission.	
	2		Work on R.R.P's. 1 man reported from leave, 1 O.R. HEAD to Hosp. and posted to R.I.9.M.B. & F.D.T.M.C.	
	3		Work on R.R.P's. 1 man posted to R.A.M.C. Vicinity of Camp bombed by hostile aeroplanes about 11 P.M. 20 casualties. Capt. ROBERTS rejoined from short leave to Paris.	
	4		Work on R.R.P's. Drills, Parades and inspections. 1 Pup & 5 men to Rest in Forest on Race Course near MADAGASCAR.	
	5		Work as on 4th, 1 and 15 men to dig for N.P. and H.Q. T.M. Bs. in the Line at night. Shelter formed digging in camp.	

WAR DIARY or INTELLIGENCE SUMMARY

X2 T.M.B

Army Form C. 2118

Place	Date	Hour	Summary of Events and Information	Remarks and references to Appendices
Roclincourt	June 1917		During the month of June X2 T.M.B has not been in action as a Battery. The Battery has not been stationed at Roclincourt & has been engaged in Gunnery Fatigues & has assisted Y & Z Batteries in action. Only four time has sufficient intelligence & energy been shown & were in much instances to observe on report. The officers & men continue to be quite up to battery establishment.	
	7/6/17		2/Lt Read proceeded on course of instruction at 1st Army School of Mortars 549 Bde.	
	8/6/17		2/Lt Dunning promoted Lt.	
	10/6/17		148636 Bpr Hurley promoted to Sgt. Sgt Roger now being under orders to proceed to England for commission.	
			25911 Bpr Battey promoted Cpl.	
			106106 2/c Suttrell promoted Cpl.	
			59838 Dr Blewitt	
	9–15/6/17		170156 Dr Clark } About to Battery whilst in action at	
			49355 Dr Glossop } Messines.	

Army Form 'C. 2118.

WAR DIARY
or
INTELLIGENCE SUMMARY X 2 T.M.B

(Erase heading not required.)

Instructions regarding War Diaries and Intelligence Summaries are contained in F. S. Regs., Part II. and the Staff Manual respectively. Title Pages will be prepared in manuscript.

Place	Date	Hour	Summary of Events and Information	Remarks and references to Appendices
Ractincourt	June 1917			
	15.6.17		2nd Lt Leary returned from course of instruction at 1st Army School of Mortars	
	16.6.17		25808 Sgt Roberson proceeded to England for commission.	
			298962 Gnr Blows admitted to hospital (not poisoning)	
			95388 Dr Bray } posted to X2 TMB from D.A.C.	
			811195 - Brindsale }	
	18.6.17		450576 Gnr Watt posted to D.A.C.	
	19.6.17		136606 Dr Mullington posted to X2 TMB from D.A.C	
	20.6.17		148814 Gnr Shields } posted to X2 TMB from 9th Bde.	
			2446 Dnr Bowie }	
	25.6.17		298938 Dr Blows discharged from hospital.	

WAR DIARY
or
INTELLIGENCE SUMMARY

Army Form C. 2118.

Y/2 T.M. Battery

June 1917

Place	Date	Hour	Summary of Events and Information	Remarks and references to Appendices
Between OPPY	1 & 2		During the first two days of the month the battery remained at Roclincourt working on fatigues. On the 3rd the battery moved up into action on front of O.P.Y. Wood & relieved main emplacement made by Capt. X. T.M.B. on the night of 10th. The 10 howitzers were fired every time the enemy had any kind of nature. In addition I was detailed to improve their fixed dugout before firing commenced.	
	3 to 10		Gradually work was renovated commenced and shifts were arranged & continued since the end of the month, when the howitzers moved out of the battery was drawn from the line on the night of the 29th & moved back to R.R. rolling stock. During the month Lt. A.W. Jarsham, 21st R.F.O. Barnett, Cpl. Elliott from Browne Strang proceeded on leave during the month.	

(sd) M. Sutherland
OC Y/2 T.M.B.

WAR DIARY

INTELLIGENCE SUMMARY

Army Form C. 2118.

2/2 T.M.B.

Place	Date June 1917 Hour	Summary of Events and Information	Remarks and references to Appendices
ROCLINCOURT.	1st	Battery was billeted at Roclincourt	
PLOEGSTEERT	2nd	Battery was moved to Steenwerk where it was attached to the 3rd Australian Division. Battery was billeted near Ploegsteert & attached to 4th Australian Division for duty. The billets were subjected to heavy shellfire during the evening & night so had to withdraw the men from them.	
	3rd & 4th	Could not get up the line owing to heavy shell fire. Enemy put over gas during the evening so had to withdraw men to De Romarin. Gr. Anderson & Pty wounded on the 3rd or 4th.	
	5th	Ordered to report at the "Catacomb" but could not do so as they were already shelled. Billets heavily shelled during the morning & set on fire. The whole of the Battery & men's equipment was burnt. Gr. Whitehouse was overcome by fumes while trying to salve the guns during the evening. Withdrew the men to De Romarin camp.	
	6th	Ordered to take over sector from Warneve River to River Lys & Battery to billet at De Bizet. Found no ammunition available for this sector. We lost four guns by 3rd Australian Division but no rifle mechanisms were available for same. Found that battery was unable to enter De Bizet owing to the heavy shelling, & had

WAR DIARY or INTELLIGENCE SUMMARY

Army Form C. 2118.

2/2 Y.m.D

Place	Date	Hour	Summary of Events and Information	Remarks and references to Appendices
LE ROMARIN	7th	—	Withdrawn to Nieppe.	
	8th		Returned to Le Romarin camp to take over defensive sector from 1st Divs. to River Lys from 4th Australian Div. Twenty men of 8th Div attached to Battery for duty.	
	9th		Went over front of sector with a bombadier from 4th Australian Div. This sector has a front of 2500 yards. About 100 bombs available but no component parts. Got 4 guns up the line. Ordered to take over a 300 yard sector from U.21.c.2.4, to U.21.d.4.7. (Map Ploegsteert Edition 4.B.28.S.W.4) in conjunction with Y.3 A.T.M.B.	
	10th		Went over sector with O.C. of Y.3 A.T.M.B. & chose positions for 4 guns. Y3 cannot line in bad condition & leaves little clover for positions	
	11th		Send up parts to get two positions ready, Y.3.A.T.M.B. getting the other two ready	
	12th		Took up parts to about found No.1 position hurried. Also found enemy front line occupied by our own troops. Sent up parts but 6.p.m. to get the guns out of the line.	

WAR DIARY
INTELLIGENCE SUMMARY Z/2 Y.M.B

(Erase heading not required.)

Army Form C. 2118.

Place	Date	Hour	Summary of Events and Information	Remarks and references to Appendices
Le Remarin	June 1917 13th		Took party up the line to salve ammunition from old Yser sector. The sector was very heavily shelled so could only salve a few bombs.	
	14th		Battery remained at rest.	
	15th		Battery returned to Roclincourt. From 2nd & 15th the following men were attached to the battery to bring it up to strength:— 39838 Gnr. D Low H. 170186 Gnr. Clark A. 4235.5 Dr. Yelson W. } of X₂ Y.M.B 77548 Gnr. Allan D.C. 43826 Ambrose J.A. 1143 Arthur C. } of Y₂ Y.M.B	
Roclincourt	16th-30th		Battery remained billeted at Roclincourt. They were employed in action with Y₂ Y.M.B. & also on camouflage fatigues. 2nd Lt. R. I Arnold was posted to the battery on June 2nd for 47th Battery R.G.A. — 56629 Dr. Cavan T., 75249 Dr. Willis J. joined the battery on June 2nd. 180129 Dr. Ducksthope C. & 39818 Dr. Anderson G. R. on June 20th as reinforcements from 2nd D. A. C. 30659 Gnr. Northwood R. was posted to 2nd D.A.C. from the battery on June 18th. H. Greatwood Lt O.C. Z/2 Y.M.D	

Trench Mortar Brigade.
2nd Divisional Artillery.

V: X: Y & Z Trench Mortar Batteries

JULY 1917.

WAR DIARY
INTELLIGENCE SUMMARY

Army Form C. 2118

Place	Date	Hour	Summary of Events and Information	Remarks and references to Appendices
Rocbincourt	1-7-17		2Lt GAME joined. A.R.P. promotes Inspections & drills	
	2/7		2Lt CHALMERS proceeded to BETHUNE with advance party to arrange billetting and took over from V/66. met DTMO and OC V/66 and was shown our billetment no 2,3,4,5 & 6. gun in hut 2; 5 & 6 returned to BETHUNE. Remainder of by under Mr WATSON remained at BETHUNE by lorries (2 for kits and 2½ for men)	
BETHUNE	3/7		2Lt CHALMERS met OC V/66 were shown normal OPs, dumps & took over office. 1OR reported from leave to Engineer	
	4/7		2Lt WATSON & GAME shown normal gun positions. Battery marched to billets in ANNEQUIN. 4 GS wagons took 2 Lt GAME into registered to gun positions under 2Lt. Game into positions to BHQs that we get find that place billets good but not clean guns in hut clean Reconnoitre for new posn to from TORTUE 1.9.4.5 HTH arrived 2 OR reported from leave to England	3 detachment proceeded
ANNEQUIN	5/7		Registered gun in no 2 posn. Road convoy to no 2 posn at night. 1 OR to Hospital	
	6/7		3 OR proceeded on leave to England	
	7/7		Fired 3 rds from no 2 posn	
	8/7		"	
	9/7		"	
	10/7		Registered no 5 position and no 6 position. 11 rds. 1 OR returned from Hospital	
	11/7		1 Officer and 3 OR attached from 1st Army School of Musketry 4 OR reported from leave England	
	13/7		5 OR proceeded on leave to England	
	14/7		1 OR proceeded to 1st Army School of Musketry	
	16/7		2Lt WATSON proceeded on leave to England	
	17/7		Fired 14 rds good results	
	18/7		6 P.m Railway Triangle blown up. "Minnie" Emplacement blown in & bomb store exploded	

WAR DIARY
or
INTELLIGENCE SUMMARY.
(Erase heading not required.)

Army Form C. 2118.

Instructions regarding War Diaries and Intelligence Summaries are contained in F.S. Regs., Part II. and the Staff Manual respectively. Title pages will be prepared in manuscript.

Place	Date	Hour	Summary of Events and Information	Remarks and references to Appendices
ANNEQUIN	19/July/17		Fired 7 rds. hard campaign at night	
	20		Fired 26 rds. good effect. 1 OR reported from leave to Eng Round	
	21		6 OR proceeded on Leave to Eng Round	
			2 OR reported from	
	24		Fired 21 rds with good effect - bridge on Railway Triangle destroyed	
	25		No 5 position marched on by 4 em while firing. Transportwaggons Fired 6 rds.	
	26		Fired dummy rounds	
			1 OR proceeded on Duty to Eng Round. Fired 8 rds	
			3 OR reported from Leave to Eng Round. 1 Officer + 3 OR detached	
	27		1 OR reported from Leave to Eng Round	
	28		Capt ROBERTS + 1 OR reported from 1st Army School of Musketry	
			6 OR. proceeded on Leave to Eng Round	
	29		Antiaircraft LG with ammunit'n on New position, Fired 8 rds. (IVRY TERRACE)	
	30		No 4 position knocked in by German T.M.	
			Sgt Watson reported from Crete to Eng Round 2 LT HENDERSON joined Bty	
			Gun moved from No 4 position (WILSONS WAY) to No 3 (MAISON ROUGE).	24 H rounds fired

Army Form C. 2118.

WAR DIARY
or
INTELLIGENCE SUMMARY.
(Erase heading not required.)

Instructions regarding War Diaries and Intelligence Summaries are contained in F. S. Regs., Part II. and the Staff Manual respectively. Title pages will be prepared in manuscript.

Place	Date	Hour	Summary of Events and Information	Remarks and references to Appendices
ANNEQUIN	31/7		Work done clearance of No 1 (BARTS ALLEY PIT) Construction of tunnel in No 2 pit continued (LEWIS ALLEY) Gun mounted in No 3 (MAISON ROUGE) Work continued on new (I KEY) position. Value of articles salved by the Battery during June and July 1917 £712-9-0	

O F Chalmers 2/Lt R.T.A.
for OC V/2 HTMB.

WAR DIARY
INTELLIGENCE SUMMARY

X 2 TMB.

Place	Date	Hour	Summary of Events and Information	Remarks and references to Appendices
Richebourg	1/1/17		The battery prepared to leave Richebourg for Bethune.	
Bethune	2/1/17		The battery moved to Bethune & were there billetted in outhouses of the Brie & Military Hospital for two days. Hot private baths were taken from X 66, the opportunity was taken for bathing & change of winter clothing.	
Annequin	4/1/17		The battery moved to Annequin & went into action. Fire was opened on to enemy strong points. The enemy has been continued they might has been cut out enemy strong points, light mortar in Rhum [?] emplacements. Support line, support line, Howes line & pyrene Ruff opposite Hohenzollern were heavily cut by battery fire during several raids. A retrenchment position is being constructed in the Railway — between by an overhead communication trench from D.A.C. to losa heavy construction. The trenches to Braunschweig trenches were particularly blown in by mining.	
	18/1/17			

Army Form C. 2118.

WAR DIARY
or
INTELLIGENCE SUMMARY.

X-ZTMB

(Erase heading not required.)

Instructions regarding War Diaries and Intelligence Summaries are contained in F. S. Regs., Part II. and the Staff Manual respectively. Title pages will be prepared in manuscript.

Place	Date	Hour	Summary of Events and Information	Remarks and references to Appendices
Annequin	30/7/17		Offer a successful shoot on Trench Rays. The base position was completely wrecked by enemy retaliation. Gunsmith fire on enemy support line is being carried on without	
	17/7/17		Reinforcement from [illegible] without [illegible] of enemy side arms.	
	19/7/17		Lt. Toomey & Reeves [illegible]	
	21/7/17		& 6 O.R. posted from DAC	
	22/7/17		Lt. L.C. Mcklepostel] from 216 RFA	
	28/7/17		Lt. Daly posted to X-ZTMB	
	30/7/17		Lt. L.T. Fighter] Provements to Army school of Mortars Cpl. Jamieson] Rct. Dummies [illegible] on La Bourse	

Attaching 9/// D/ff to O.C. X-ZTMB

1/2. French Mortar Bty.

Army Form C. 2118.

WAR DIARY
or
INTELLIGENCE SUMMARY
(Erase heading not required.)

Instructions regarding War Diaries and Intelligence Summaries are contained in F. S. Regs., Part II. and the Staff Manual respectively. Title pages will be prepared in manuscript.

1917

Place	Date	Hour	Summary of Events and Information	Remarks and references to Appendices
Roclincourt Bethune	1 July		On the 2nd of the month the Battery moved out of billets at Roclincourt, marched to Bethune the same day & were billeted there. The B.C. going on to ANNEQUIN to meet O.T.M.O. 66th Div. & then up the line to take over positions etc. The battery moved up on the 4th & went straight up the line into action. Recruiting was carried out during the month for suitable men, very satisfactory results, though during one of these operations a hostile T.M. struck the gun team & duly pulling it out of action, killing the two men working it. Fire was also brought to bear daily in accordance with the Infantry instructions on various parts of German trench systems. Machine gun emplacements & strong points etc. During the month a premature unfortunately destroyed a few complete M.M. was fortunately not accompanied by any casualties though the detachment were considerably shaken.	
	17		On the 17th 2/Lt R.T. Daniels was posted to the battery but transferred back to Y. F.T.M.B. 2nd Lt Hamblin proceeded on leave on 9th & Cpl Elliott. Both Grgwoer, Gnr. Cain, Andrew, Morgan, Lyle.	
ANNEQUIN	28		also during the month. Cpl Noglana Gnr Collins or 28th	

Army Form C. 2118.

1/2 Trench Mortar By

WAR DIARY
or
INTELLIGENCE SUMMARY.

(Erase heading not required.)

197

Place	Date	Hour	Summary of Events and Information	Remarks and references to Appendices
ANNEQUIN	28 July		went to 1st Army School of Mortar on a course until the 6th French Mortar Bn. Cox on the same day went on a gas course.	

A M Donaldson 4
OC 1/2 TMB

Army Form C. 2118.

WAR DIARY
or
INTELLIGENCE SUMMARY
(Erase heading not required.)

JULY Sheet I
L/2 T.M.B.

Place	Date	Hour	Summary of Events and Information	Remarks and references to Appendices
	1st July		Battery in bivouacs at ROCLINCOURT.	
	2nd July		Broke camp & moved to BETHUNE by road. Gnr Wilson J.E. admitted to hospital, sick.	
	3rd July		2/Lt Arnold took over from Z/66 at GIVENCHY. Lt Buckthorpe admitted to hospital — accidental wound in left arm.	
	4th		Battery marched to billets in dugouts on canal bank at WESTMINSTER BRIDGE & took over from Z/66 Bty — two permanent positions in "Ware Road" & "New Cut" trenches remaining three positions were exposed Temporary ones.	
	5th to 13th		Fired every day from all positions — average about 25 rounds per diem.	
	14th		Lt Greatwood returned from leave. 14th "Ware Road" position knocked out by 3 direct hits.	
	15th		2/Lt. Arnold went to 1st Army School of Instruction.	
	16th		Started making new position at "Poppy Redoubt".	
	19th		Gnr Kerridge W. posted to Bty from 71st RFA.	
	20th		2/Lt Arnold returned from course.	

WAR DIARY or INTELLIGENCE SUMMARY

JULY. Sheet II Z/2 T.M.B.

Army Form C. 2118.

Place	Date	Hour	Summary of Events and Information	Remarks and references to Appendices
GIVENCHY-LA-BASSÉE				
	20th to 24th		2/Lt R.M. Gorrie posted from X/2 T.M.B. 2/Lt Sollas returned from extended leave. Cut wire opposite C & E saps in preparation for raid. 2/Lt H.C. Leigh posted from 1st K.R.R.s, also his batman Rfn Saunders H. 2/Lt Hayter C.A. Transferred to Bty from D.A.C. to replace Gnr Conroy L.G. (Transferred to 2nd D.A.C.)	
	25th		Fired two minute barrage from seven guns (three borrowed from X/2 Bty) — for K.R.R. raid. Raid was unsuccessful but T.M's were congratulated by O.C. 6th Inf Bde on their barrage. Lt Greenwood posted to D/36 Bty R.F.A. 2/Lt Gorrie took over Bty from him	
	26th to 31st		Continued to fire average of 25 rounds per diem.	
	31st		Started mining to make new permanent position in "Upper Cut" trench	

R.M.Gorrie, 2/Lt R.F.A.
O/C Z/2 T.M.B.

Trench Mortar Brigade.
2nd Divisional Artillery.

V: X: Y & Z. TRENCH MORTAR BATTERIES

AUGUST 1917.

WAR DIARY

INTELLIGENCE SUMMARY.

(Erase heading not required.)

Army Form C. 2118.

2 D T M Bty

Place	Date	Hour	Summary of Events and Information	Remarks and references to Appendices
GIVENCHY CANAL CAMBRIN	1/8/17		Lt. WATSON proved to join R.F.C. Very wet day with bad visibility. Firing very difficult owing to flooding and caving in of pits. The weather prevented most emotional work being done, immediate repairs only being executed. 10 rounds from LEWIS ALLEY. 20 rounds from GIVENCHY – Heavy Telephonism, but the position is evidently not accurately registered by hostile guns. Infantry requested this gun to cease firing, owing to the retaliation. Bmbt. carrying.	30.
	2/8/17		Very wet day with bad visibility. Employment and thunder in very bad condition owing to continued wet weather. Bmbt. repairing done to all pits slowly to prevent them caving in and flooding. 11 rounds from MAISON ROUGE position in registration. 12 rounds from GIVENCHY. The former shoot retaliation by 4.2" and Whizzbangs. Fired 3 times again from Lewis.	23.
	3/8/17		Another bad day. All pits in bad condition, incessibility constant work mainly to keep things going. 18 rounds from MAISON ROUGE in front guarding and went over A.21.C.30.75 and A.21.A.40.60, and T.M. CHRIS. at the first named target, actual knew hidden being blown up and seen in the air; three hits must have had on CHRIS. 15 rounds fired GIVENCHY Int. front Junction 19.10.A.15.05. A.10.C. 10.85 + 15.60. Orders received from Group only to fire on request by Bn. Commander for the present. 2 men again from Lewis.	33.
	4/8/17		Again wet and dust. Breaks and emplacements in very bad condition. Took 4 LEWIS ALLEY, MAISON ROUGE, IKEY and GIVENCHY positions. Bmbt. carrying. 1 N.C.O. 3 men proceed on Leave.	
	5/8/17		A better day. Work on all positions – Bmbt. carrying.	
	6/8/17		Weather finer. Work on positions continued. The whole Battery is now engaged in making Post Hut cartridges Canister. Casualties for the present wet weather, one officer now being recovering on Sick Leave.	

Army Form C. 2118.

WAR DIARY
INTELLIGENCE SUMMARY.
(Erase heading not required.)

Instructions regarding War Diaries and Intelligence Summaries are contained in F. S. Regs., Part II. and the Staff Manual respectively. Title pages will be prepared in manuscript.

Place	Date	Hour	Summary of Events and Information	Remarks and references to Appendices
GIVENCHY CANAL CAMBRIN.	7/8/17		Generally fine, but some rain. Work on all positions continued. 2/Lt. GAME proceeded on leave. 1 N.C.O. rejoined from leave.	
	8/8/17		Fine until 6 P.M., when a heavy thunderstorm followed by hours of rain again flooded all subwork on positions continued.	
	9/8/17		Showery. Work continued at high pressure. GIVENCHY gun bed submerged under 11 inches of water, and sub-bed resting on soft mud to a considerable depth. Bed sunk 6" in front - whole structure taken up and commenced to be rebuilt. Granules fallen in very badly. Orders to fire in retaliation only. 1 N.C.O. rejoin from leave.	
	10/8/17		Work on positions continued. 1 N.C.O. & 1 man rejoin from leave.	
	11/8/17		do. 1 N.C.O. 5 men proceed on leave.	
	12/8/17		do. 11 rounds from LEWIS ALLEY on to FOSSE TRENCH (MAD POINT) A.26.J.20.22 and MADAGASCAR TRENCH A.26.C.98.18 in retaliation for enemy T.M. fire on to our trenches opposite MAD POINT. Good effective bursts, one round falling into trench.	11.
	13/8/17		Work on positions. LEWIS ALLEY tunnels meet.	
	14/8/17		do. GIVENCHY gun again ready for action.	
	15/8/17		do. R.E. finish repairs to BARTS ALLEY position. Much difficulty experienced in work at IKEY owing to having tunnelled beneath water level in one part, and excavated front stove in loose slag in another. 10 rounds from GIVENCHY in registration on to SAXON WAY trench. Good bursts, timber and material being thrown up. Shooting rather erratic, probably owing to the settlement of the new bed. 5 rounds from MAISON ROUGE on T.M. A.26.A.65.50 in retaliation for enemy T.M., at request of Bgr. Commdr. 14 rounds from LEWIS ALLEY at T.M. emplacements A.26.B.18.30 (CHRIS)	29.

K.3. A.8534 W.W.4973/M687 759,000 8/16 D.D.&L.Ltd. Forms/C.2118/13

WAR DIARY
INTELLIGENCE SUMMARY
Army Form C. 2118.

Place	Date	Hour	Summary of Events and Information	Remarks and references to Appendices
GIVENCHY CANAL CAMBRIN	16/8/17	6 P.M. 6.30 P.M.	and A.26.a.50.20. Three direct hits on CHRIS, exhib. amn. attained. and A.26.a.90.45. 11 rounds on large sandbag mound at A.9.2.90.45 from GIVENCHY in conjunction with M.T.M. and 8" how. Excellent results. Of the 11 rounds fired, 5 burst a few yards behind the work, 3 burst a good 10 yds in front, 1 off the line, 1 dud, 1 air burst. All the 8 bursting close to the work seemed to do great quantities of sandbag any further, and the mound itself was greatly damaged. 7 Germans were observed to climb out of one of our craters front made in front of the work, and to run for the trench. They showing chests & legs, and to make attempts hit been blown in. 1 man appeared to England to join Cadet School. Cpl. LAZENBY promoted Sergeant to replace him. Bomb carrying. 1 Pte. & 1 man rejoin from hum. Troops on positions continued.	11.
	17/8/17 18/8/17		do. 20 rounds fired from GIVENCHY at T.M. Trench was emplacement. One round fell actually in the trench, doing considerable damage to a large quantity of trench boards and revetting. Another round blew 75 up in the air. Numerous mining parties and a long target of telephone wire observed. 2 N.C.O. & 2 men rejoin from leave. A.10.C.c.8.92. Good effective bursts were obtained, doing considerable damage to	20.
	19/8/17		Troops on positions. Bomb carrying. 9 rounds fired from MAISON ROUGE at T.M. A.9.2.b.9.6.4. in retaliation for enemy T.M. fire. Direct hits on trench near T.M. observed and considerable damage done. T.M. silenced.	9.

WAR DIARY or INTELLIGENCE SUMMARY

Army Form C. 2118.

Place	Date	Hour	Summary of Events and Information	Remarks and references to Appendices
GIVENCHY CANAL CAMBRIN	20/8/17		Shoots on hostile emplacement. 13 rounds fired from LEWIS ALLEY on to C.T. A.18. C.96.92 and T.M. A.28. B.1.3. In retaliation and registration. Enemy severely damaged – good registration. 4th GAME GAME reports from scene.	13.
	21/8/17	6.30 pm 6.30 pm	Guns in position. Special shoot carried out with Medium T.M. and Arty. 13 rounds from LEWIS ALLEY on to trench junction A.28.C.98.92 and T.M. at A.26.A.70.30. 11 rounds from MAISON ROUGE on to RYAN'S KEEP and T.M. at A.22.C.50.45. 12 rounds from CHINCHY on to T.M. at A.22.A.65.60 and Post on Ridge at A.16.C.30.30. General effect except good. Bosch crumping.	36.
	22/8/17		Guns in position. 2 rounds fired from GIVENCHY at T.M. A.9.D.95.81. In support by retaliation of British T.M. Enemy fire reduced. Bosch crumping.	2.
	23/8/17		Guns in position. Shoot on IKEY greatly hindered by continual heavy fire of the Boer Sting forming the railway embankment on which our Vickers gun being sent. Bosch crumping, 1 man to 2nd D.9.C. 1 Pig + 5 men. Region from heavy.	
	24/8/17 25/8/17		Guns in position. 2 rounds from MAISON ROUGE on to an actual shot on enemy trenches. A.23.C.29.55. These two rounds were the first of a pre-arranged shoot for 1 hour with Arty, support, the shoot was then stopped by the receipt of an order that no further firing was to take place by F.7.R or 8 th Bde artillery orders.	2.

WAR DIARY
INTELLIGENCE SUMMARY
(Erase heading not required.)

Army Form C. 2118.

Place	Date	Hour	Summary of Events and Information	Remarks and references to Appendices
GIVENCHY CANAL CAMBRIN	26/6/17		Work on positions. 1 N.C.O. 3 men journeyed on leave. 1 man to hospital. Work continuing.	
	27/6/17		Handed over BART'S ALLEY and LEWIS ALLEY positions, with 2 guns and stores complete to W/6 T.M.B. Much work on West positions has been done during our occupation of them. BART'S ALLEY. Repaired with R.E. assistance. Sand-bell laid. Gun taken to VERSAILLES, and everything left in readiness for getting in action at short notice. Railway from VERSAILLES to position refomed. LEWIS ALLEY. A shaft from the C.T. has been connected with the dug-out thus making the latter habitable. The work was very difficult owing to the run-in so that in the shaft and dug-out caused the tunnels not to be run as but in the shaft and dug-out caused the trouble not known there. Constant pumping alone made it were possible. Now, however, the air is quite fresh, the dug-out forms an excellent living place with good cover. Trenches round the position are out and rebuilt, pit and ponengre repaired and strengthened, and everything kept in readiness for immediate action.	
	28/6/17		2nd Lt CHALMERS and 14 O.R. of A Sub-section attached to W/6 H.T.M.B. This party moved complete to SNIFFY LABOURSE (w/o Rest Billets.) Work on MAISON ROUGE, IKEY and GIVENCHY positions. The GAME and second forward on course at rest Army S. of M.	
	29/6/17		Work as on 28th.	
	30/6/17		Handed over MAISON ROUGE position and gun complete to W/6 H.T.M.B. Much work had been done on this position whilst its appropriate benches. The position at present over was considerably advanced land cleared. GIVENCHY gun mount. Shelter kept in the field.	

WAR DIARY

INTELLIGENCE SUMMARY.

Army Form C. 2118

Place	Date	Hour	Summary of Events and Information	Remarks and references to Appendices
GIVENCHY CANAL CAMBRIN.	31/8/17		Work on position continued. Dug-out and turnout at IKEY hut. MAISON ROUGE and LEWIS ALLEY guns under Fd. CHALMERS fired 28 rounds in conjunction with our Brigade Battery. 1 N.C.O. 5 men return from leave.	
			Value of articles ashed by the Battery during the month £25.	

Jocelyn Roberts
Capt;
2/c H.T.M.B..

Army Form C. 2118.

WAR DIARY
or
INTELLIGENCE SUMMARY.
(Erase heading not required.)

X2 TMB

Instructions regarding War Diaries and Intelligence Summaries are contained in F. S. Regs., Part II. and the Staff Manual respectively. Title pages will be prepared in manuscript.

Place	Date	Hour	Summary of Events and Information	Remarks and references to Appendices
Annequin	August 17		During this month X2 TMB has been in action & has fired out enemy strong points, emplacements, supports line & trench mortar batteries. He also taken part in two organised shoots (21.8.17 & 31.8.17). S.O.S. fire has been continuous on the various positions & a line position in (A.S.) Brainwork position on partially wrecked by 9" minenwerfer on 15.9.17 but retaliation & other have been returned. All positions of TMB has been advanced to bound for instruction since 23rd. Front & have maintained their position & also wire firing.	
	4.9.17		Lt Stevens & Cpl Sullivan \} returned from Sch Army School, Montana	
	7.9.17		Br Dunning returned from the Course	
	10.9.17		2/Lt Ray temporarily attached to X2 TMB	
			39118 Gr Edwards attached from DAC rejoined his attachment from DAC returned to unit	

Army Form C. 2118.

WAR DIARY
or
INTELLIGENCE SUMMARY.
(Erase heading not required.)

Instructions regarding War Diaries and Intelligence Summaries are contained in F. S. Regs., Part II. and the Staff Manual respectively. Title pages will be prepared in manuscript.

Place	Date	Hour	Summary of Events and Information	Remarks and references to Appendices
Annyeur	August		X=TMB	
	15.8.17		201/19 Gr Bradwell } Proceeded to 1st Army Review of Mortars 11154 Gr Blog }
	16.8.17		Headquarters of X=TMB removed from 118 Uneyeur to 231 Bussy
	18.8.17		2/Lt Rooy returned from I=TMB
			Lyr Bradwell } returned from 1st Army Review of Mortars Gr Blog }
	21.8.17		133/194 Gr Morrison Wounded accidentally
			6066. Gpl Wight to hospital returned to duty
	27.8.17		105511 Gr Gora Coser from D.A.C. Lt Walker } Lt Oates } Proceeded to 1st Army Sch of Mortars Pte Power }

Army Form C. 2118.

WAR DIARY
or
INTELLIGENCE SUMMARY

(Erase heading not required.)

Instructions regarding War Diaries and Intelligence Summaries are contained in F. S. Regs., Part II. and the Staff Manual respectively. Title Pages will be prepared in manuscript.

Place	Date	Hour	Summary of Events and Information	Remarks and references to Appendices
ANNEQUIN	1-8-17		During the first three weeks the battery continued in action, covering the 99th Brigade front. Wire-cutting was not carried out to any great extent, most of the shooting being on hostile Trench Mortars, Trench systems, dug-outs & Machine Guns, much material damage being done. In one instance whilst firing on a hostile Minnie, a large explosion occurred after the 4th round. During the month, work was continually carried out improving emplacements, bomb-stores, etc.	
BEUVRY	16-8-17		On the 18th, Billets were moved back to BEUVRY on account of billets increased hostile shelling in close vicinity of billets. On the 26th, on account of 99th Bde, Y.2 T.M.B. was moved further North, taking over part of X.2 battery front, namely from the LA BASSEE ROAD to RUSSELL'S KEEP. The following day 2 guns were handed over to Y.5, making them into a 6 Gun Battery.	
	31-8-17		On August 31st, a combined Strafe was organised between X's, Y.2 T.M.B.'s & a Section of Portuguese. One Gun & 3 men from the C.E.P. were attached to the Battery during the latter part of the month, for practical instruction & to help when needed. They proved themselves very useful, & did excellent shooting during the Strafe on 31st August.	

R.P.O. Barrett
2/Lt. R.F.A.
f/o C. Y.2 T. M. B.

WAR DIARY
INTELLIGENCE SUMMARY

Army Form C. 2118.

Z/2 T.M.B. Sheet I
AUGUST 1917.

Place	Date	Hour	Summary of Events and Information	Remarks and references to Appendices
GIVENCHY LA BASSEE	1st Aug.		Four guns in action in the sector. Visited O.C. 41st Bde R.F.A. to ask for more support from our artillery during T.M. shoots. 2/Lt R.G. Arnold R.F.A. posted to 4/11th Bty R.F.A. 2/Lt G.D. Peacock R.F.A. posted to this battery from D.A.C. to replace him.	
	2nd		Fired 12 rounds from "Church" gun – good effect on Agd T.7 new Boch workings. Gnr Goldstein received 14 days F.P. No II for being drunk when he had been warned to act as guide to a carrying party. Cpl. Eatough rejoined after seaside rest camp.	
	3rd to 4th		All the temporary pits flooded owing to heavy rains – firing impossible.	
	4th		#Lieut R.M. Gorrie went on leave, & the same day 2/Lt H.G. Leigh K.R.R's went into hospital with "trench fever" — 2/Lt Peacock left in charge of battery.	
	7th		2/Lt F. Keay attacked from X/2 T.M.B.	
	7th to 14th		Very little firing owing to objections of O.C. 1st Kings.	
	10th		2/Lt H.E. McKenna posted to us from D.A.C. – also his batman Gnr Ashdown. 2/Lt G.D. Peacock sent to 38 I.B.D owing to some error in his posting.	
	14th		A premature occurred in New Cut pit during a shoot in retaliation of 2 guns. Bdr Haynes was wounded & badly burned, while Gnr G.P. Anderson was badly shaken; he went in search of help & subsequently returned to the gunpit to put out the fire, which had been caused by the explosion. For this act Gnr Anderson was awarded the Military Medal on 30/8/17.	

Army Form C. 2118.

WAR DIARY
or
INTELLIGENCE SUMMARY

2/1 T.M.B. Sheet II.
AUGUST 1917.

(Erase heading not required.)

Place	Date	Hour	Summary of Events and Information	Remarks and references to Appendices
GIVENCHY LES LA BASSÉE	14th cont.		Cpl Gatough & Gnr Rix went on 5 days course of instruction on new 6" mortar.	
	16th		Lieut. Gorrie returned from leave. 2/Lt Keay returned to X/1 T.M.By. Three gun shoot of 7 rounds on to Spoil Dump A9a95.45. in conjunction with H.T.M. & 8" howitzers.	
	17th		Did 20 rounds "Sniping" at Bosch mineshaft.	
	18th		30 round shoot on E Bosch sap behind new crater Ducks Bill - Warlingham Crat. 6/1 Bdr Sutton promoted full Bdr from 14/8/17 in place of Bdr Haynes, who has been evacuated to England.	
	20th		Continuing construction of new permanent position in Upper Cub trench. Bosch retaliating more quickly against our shoots.	
	22nd		Bad luck in combined strafe with artillery on New Crater sap - only got away 3 rounds when Bosch retaliated on Strathcona Terrace gun pit with Minnie hit on pit which wounded Gnr Gott very badly in both thighs & Gnr Rix slightly in back. We had an extremely difficult task in getting Gott removed from the position under heavy fire. Gnr Rix was recommended for the Military Medal for this work.	
	23rd		Gnr Gott died of wounds at 33 C.C.S. & was buried on the 24th in Bethune Cemetery	
	24th 25th		Mr Valroe & 2 Soldiers of the 4th Portuguese T.M.B. attached to us for instruction. 2/Lt H.F. Mc Kenna detailed for Court Martial	

Army Form C. 2118.

WAR DIARY
or
INTELLIGENCE SUMMARY

(Erase heading not required.)

Z/1-T.M.B. Sheet III.
AUGUST 1917.

Instructions regarding War Diaries and Intelligence Summaries are contained in F. S. Regs., Part II. and the Staff Manual respectively. Title Pages will be prepared in manuscript.

Place	Date	Hour	Summary of Events and Information	Remarks and references to Appendices
GIVENCHY	Aug 26th		Order received re no shooting except in retaliation during until further orders.	
	27th		2/Lt C.F.H. Hamilton posted from Y/1 T.M.B. 2/Lt H.G. Leigh returned from hospital to duty. Pte John W. posted from D.A.C. Gnrs Britt + Gascon sent to 5 days course on new 6" mortar.	
	30th		Work continues on Upper Cut position + also on several new temporary positions. 2/Lt J.G. Renner posted from 17th Middlesex.	

R.M.G.
Lieut R.F.A.
O/C Z/1 T.M.B.

Trench Mortar Brigade
2nd Divisional Artillery.

V: X: Y & Z. TRENCH MORTAR BATTERIES

SEPTEMBER 1917.

WAR DIARY or INTELLIGENCE SUMMARY

Army Form C. 2118.

JUNE 1918 — 41st L.T.M.By

(Erase heading not required.)

Place	Date	Hour	Summary of Events and Information	Remarks and references to Appendices
Stoney Castle Camp Pirbright	28/6/18	8.0 pm	41st L.T.M.By. taken over from Lieut Smith R.F.A. Stores and Equipment incomplete but all weather placed under sentry	
	29/6/18		8 Stokes' 3" Trench Mortars drawn from D.A.D.O.S. at Aldershot. Inspected by this Command.	
	30/6/18		Promotions: 96026 SERGT PORTER G.G. 18th Y+L to be acting Battery Sergeant Major from this date (unpaid) 37370 CPL. POOK A. 2/9th D.L.I. to be acting SERGT from this date (unpaid) Battery ready for France as regards stores and Equipment. Lieut FLECK J.D. returned Battery from leave (about 17.30 hrs)	Appx I Condition 7 T.M. By.s

W.B. Barrington Lieut
for OC
41 L.T.M.By.

CONFIDENTIAL.

WAR DIARY

- of -

41st LIGHT TRENCH MORTAR BATTERY.

From: 1st July, 1918.
To: 31st July, 1918.

VOLUME II.

WAR DIARY
or
INTELLIGENCE SUMMARY.

(Erase heading not required.)

JULY 1918   41st T.M.Bty

Army Form C. 2118.

Place	Date	Hour	Summary of Events and Information	Remarks and references to Appendices
Stony Castle Camp, Brookwood	1/7/18	3.20 a.m.	Stores complete. Sent to Frimley Guard. N.C.O. Queen	
	2/7/18	8.30 p.m.	Battery marched to Brookwood Station and entrained for FOLKESTONE	
Folkestone	3/7/18	3.0 a.m.	Arrived Folkestone	
		7.30 a.m.	Marched down to Quay, embarked boat. Arrived Boulogne. Marched to OSTROVE CAMP	
Ostrove Camp Boulogne		12.0 midnight	Orders received from B.O.A. H.Q. Boulogne to entrain at Boulogne for RETT and the next day	
	4/7/18	6.30 a.m.	LIEUT FLECK T.D. proceeded with billeting party to area at MARQUISE	
		8.30 a.m.	Battery marched to Boulogne Station and proceeded to MARQUISE. Marched from MARQUISE to LOQUINHEN 7miles E of MARQUISE	
			Lorry convoy arrived and at this place	
Loquinhen	7/7/18	11.30 a.m.	LIEUT FLECK T.D. admitted into hospital	
		12.0 noon	2/LIEUT ATKINS R.V. reported for duty	
		9.0 p.m.	Battery proceeded by motor lorry to 39 N.Z.T.M. School at MARONHILLE	

Army Form C. 2118.

WAR DIARY
or
INTELLIGENCE SUMMARY.
(Erase heading not required.)

Instructions regarding War Diaries and Intelligence
Summaries are contained in F.S. Regs. Part II.
and the Staff Manual respectively. Title pages
will be prepared in manuscript.

Place	Date	Hour	Summary of Events and Information	Remarks and references to Appendices
LAPONVILLE	8/7/18		2 miles S. of NORDAUSQUES (HAZEBROUCK 5A)	
	8/7/18		2/Lieut A.S.KIN. reported for duty	
	8/7/18 to 14/7/18		Battery training at T.M School, meanwhile Bde moved to EPERLECQUES area	
LECOSTHOL	14/7/18	6.0 pm	Battery proceeded by motor lorries to LECOSTHOL, MOULLE area. Billets good.	
			Inspection by Army Commander at MOULLE.	
	16/7/18		1 N.C.O, 5 men attended medical board by medical Inspector of Drafts	
	18/7/18		1 N.C.O. 2 men sent to Labour Corps Base Depot Boulogne	
	19/7/18 to 31/7/18		Steady training	

CONFIDENTIAL.

WAR DIARY

- of -

41st TRENCH MORTAR BATTERY.

From: 1st August, 1918.
To: 31st August, 1918.

VOLUME III.

Army Form C. 2118.

WAR DIARY
INTELLIGENCE SUMMARY.

AUG. 1918.
41st L.T.M.B.

(Erase heading not required.)

Instructions regarding War Diaries and Intelligence Summaries are contained in F. S. Regs., Part II. and the Staff Manual respectively. Title pages will be prepared in manuscript.

Place	Date	Hour	Summary of Events and Information	Remarks and references to Appendices
LECOSTHOL	18/8/18	-	T.M. Demonstration by the Battery.	
	11/8/18	-	Capt. FLECK. J.D. rejoined Battery and took command from this date.	
ST. JAN-TER-BIEZEN	19/8/18	-	Battery moved from MOULLE area to ROAD CAMP. ST. JAN-TER-BIEZEN. 4 miles W. of POPERINGHE. Entraining at ST. OMER on 19.8.18 and detraining at PROVEN 19.8.18.	
BRAKE CAMP.	27/8/18	-	Battery moved to BRAKE CAMP (Sheet 28. A.30.c.8.5.) by light railway, arriving at 10.30 p.m and took over Defence Scheme from 102nd L.T.M.B.	
	28/8/18	-	Battery relieved 103RD L.T.M.B. in YPRES SECTOR taking over guns from 103rd L.T.M.B.	See Appx. II by O.C. 41st L.T.M.B.

A.W. Scott
for O.C.

Appendix I.
    Condition of Battery before leaving
    England 2.7.18

The personnel of the Battery was recruited from 12 different Battalions. They had all had courses of Trench Mortars in England and had fired dummy ammunition. It was found that only 6 N.C.Os and men had fired live ammunition. 2 of these were N.C.Os. No one had fired in the line including all N.C.Os.

    General discipline was bad especially amongst the N.C.Os.

A.H.Booth Lt.
for O.C.
451st T.M.B.

War Diary

Appx II

This Battery relieved the 103 LTMB on Aug 28 in the Ypres Sector.
The Ammunition was found to be practically useless & the Ranges laid down on SOS lines could not have been reached. New Ammunition was brought up & before this unit left the lines on 5. 6th Sept: all old ammunition had been replaced & Ranges correctly laid on. The work of salving the old ammunition was carried on by the 242nd LTMB. The work of preparing new Emplacements was also carried out by this Battery.

NS Heck Capt
O/C 41 TMB

CONFIDENTIAL.

WAR DIARY

- of -

41st TRENCH MORTAR BATTERY (LIGHT).

From: 1st September, 1918.
To: 30th September, 1918.

VOLUME IV.

WAR DIARY
INTELLIGENCE SUMMARY

(Erase heading not required.)

Army Form C. 2118.

2 D T M Bty
V.2. L.H.Bakery
Vol 13

Place	Date	Hour	Summary of Events and Information	Remarks and references to Appendices
GIVENCHY CANAL CAMBRIN	1/9/17		Work on positions continued.	
	2/9/17		do.	
	3/9/17		do.	
	4/9/17		do.	
			11 rounds from CUINCHY at T.M. A.16.C.6.5. Shooting good as to line, but no b range. Pity I burst really close to target. 1 round fell short. Several rounds thrown up tender from other enemy trenches.	21.
			10 rounds from GIVENCHY in organised shoot on SPOIL DUMP A.9.D.95.45. Shooting good. 1 direct hit, doing great damage to target. 1 man wounded.	
	5/9/17		Work on positions continued.	
			15 rounds from CUINCHY on to Bridge on Railway at A.16.C.85.35. Excellent results. 4 direct hits. Rails not demolished but considerably undermined. Limber blown up by nearly every shot.	20.
			5 rounds from GIVENCHY at T.M. A.9.D.95.85. Effect good.	
	6/9/17		Work on positions continued.	
			5 rounds from GIVENCHY on to HANS T.M. A.10.C.08.92. Good effect.	
			15 rounds from CUINCHY on to 'N' Brickstack A.16.C.75.02 and Dumb at A.16.C.78.04 (Movement observed here frequently by observer). Very good results. 1 direct hit on Brickstack. Some bombs were observed to go up where firing on Dumb. A lot can be seen in the Centre of the Brickstacks where it turns Whit.	20.
			1 Pnr to 2nd D.A.C.	
	7/9/17		Work on positions continued.	
			9 rounds from CUINCHY on to A.22. A.6.5. and 'N' Brickstack and where spent in neighborhood. Excellent results. CUINCHY gun recently shelled with 5.9".	
			2/Lt. HENDERSON proceeds to join 38th Division. 1 Reinforcement from 2nd D.A.C.	9.

WAR DIARY or INTELLIGENCE SUMMARY.

Army Form C. 2118.

(Erase heading not required.)

Instructions regarding War Diaries and Intelligence Summaries are contained in F. S. Regs., Part II. and the Staff Manual respectively. Title pages will be prepared in manuscript.

Place	Date	Hour	Summary of Events and Information	Remarks and references to Appendices
GIVENCHY CANAL CAMBRIN	8/9/17	10 am	Work on positions continued. 10 rounds from GIVENCHY on to trenches in vicinity of A.10.C.1.9. Observation difficult owing to heavy ground mist, but last round observed to fall right into trench. Shrapnel effects good. Faintly registering immediate T.M. Retaliation. Strong and accurate shelling of position about 5 pm. Pit discharged. 1 man evacuated. Bomb carrying to GIVENCHY. 1 n/o 3 men rejoin from leave. Pte: CHALMERS on leave.	
	9/9/17		Work on positions continued. Re firing. GIVENCHY gun dismounted and stored in Bomb store in LAMBETH ROAD. Pte. A.G. SMITH attached from 174th Battery.	10.
	10/9/17		Work on positions continued. 1 man rejoins from hospital. Pte. GAME & 10.12. rejoin from 1st Army School of Bombing.	
	11/9/17		13 rounds from GIVENCHY on to BRICKBAT ALLEY from A.22.A.6.5 to A.22.A.8.7 in conjunction with shoot by Brigade. Effects very good. 1 n/o 9 men attacked from 2nd D.A.C.	
	12/9/17		Work on positions.	13.
	13/9/17		1 n/o 9 men attacked to H/Q T.M.B. 1 man rejoins from leave.	
	14/9/17		do. 2 n/o, 2 men rejoin from leave.	
	15/9/17		18 rounds from GIVENCHY on to suspected tunnel under CANAL BED A.16.c.5.6. Good results. 4 direct hits observed. 1 in entrance of tunnel. Many rounds fell on Rly. embankment, doing considerable damage.	16.

WAR DIARY
INTELLIGENCE SUMMARY

Army Form C. 2118.

Places	Date	Hour	Summary of Events and Information	Remarks and references to Appendices
CUINCHY CANAL. CAMBRIN.(Contd)	15/9/17		2 fell in THE TORTOISE. Commenced laying tramway track from A.15.c.5.7 to new IKEY position (completed 6-day). Carried point of gun to IKEY.	
	16/9/17		Continued rail-laying. Carried remainder of gun to IKEY and bombs to CUINCHY. 1 Sic. 2 men on Plive.	
	17/9/17		Rail-laying. IKEY in action. Bomb-carrying to IKEY.	
	18/9/17		do. Bomb transport to A.15.c.5.7 for IKEY.	
	19/9/17		do. Bomb carrying to IKEY. Laying of permanent telephone system.	
	20/9/17		5 rounds from new IKEY gun in registration on to N. Britakour. 1 direct hit, 3 other good bursts close to target. 1 shind. Rather heavy retaliation by 5.9o on to THE ORCHARD and CUINCHY gun, the entrance to the latter being blown in. Took over BART'S ALLEY, LEWIS ALLEY and MAISON ROUGE guns from 1/4b H.T.M.B. Removed F.H.Q. & MAISON ROUGE ALLEY. 2/Lt A.D.CHALMERS promoted to Lieutenant with effect from 1.7.17	5.
	21/9/17		5 rounds from IKEY on to A.22.B.30.55 in registration. Good registration secured. 5 rounds from CUINCHY on to Tramway on N. Bank of Canal. 2 hits on objective, 2 on Rly. embankment, 1 air burst. Extent of damage could not be observed from O.P. Bomb-carrying to IKEY. Rail-laying. Repairs to CUINCHY Pit.	10.

WAR DIARY

INTELLIGENCE SUMMARY.

(Erase heading not required.)

Army Form C. 2118.

Place	Date	Hour	Summary of Events and Information	Remarks and references to Appendices
GIVENCHY CANAL CAMBRIN	22/8/17		3 rnds from MAISON ROUGE at LES BRIQUES TRENCH A28 a 90 65 in retaliation by request of Battalion Commander. Unobserved. Rail-laying at night to IREY R.R. INCO very slightly wounded	
	23/8/17		Work on positions and road laying. 2O.Rs. proceed on Leave to United Kingdom	
	24/8/17		Work on positions and road laying	
	25/8/17		do do do do Capt Roberts proceeds on leave to U.K.	
	26/8/17		do do	
	27/8/17		do do	
	28/8/17		do do Lt Chalmers returns from leave to U.K.	
	29/8/17		do do	
	30/8/17		do do 3 O.R. proceeded on leave to U.K	
			Value of salvage during the month £8-6-0	

A.K. Chalmers Lt. R.F.A.
for Capt Comdg. V/2HTMB

WAR DIARY
or
INTELLIGENCE SUMMARY.

Army Form C. 2118.

X.2. T.M. Battery

Place	Date	Hour	Summary of Events and Information	Remarks and references to Appendices
La Bassé	1-9-17 to 1-10-17		Battery in action all the month 20 rounds were fired the Battery participating in several joint shoots with R.F.A. and 6" Considerable damage was done in three shoots to Brickstack Alley, Thanks Keep, and other Trench Work. 93 casualties were sustained Except one N.C.O. slightly. Concealment a great deal of constructive work was done during the month and the Battery was fortunate in obtaining some outside assistance. A large deep pit was dug of a dugout made by the Battery 16/L underground which should prove very useful. Work was also commenced on pits new positions with a view to further 6" Stokes in them. A new type of outpost bed was built of a number of 4" by 3" bolted together by D bolts and 9 by 3 by 2 planks. Two beds have the advantage of being portable — the beds are withdrawn and when put together place to be very solid. They proved very satisfactory indeed when fired with its two zeros at 0⁰. wooden sub bed. The two way bed with a bed of codgr it would apply about 30 dgr apart enable the gun to fire over a 60 dgr arc of codgr. It would apply about — that beds of this type might be generally which to a great	

(A7692). Wt. W12859/M1293. 750-850. 1/17. D. D. & L., Ltd. Forms/C.2118/14.

Army Form C. 2118.

WAR DIARY
or
INTELLIGENCE SUMMARY.
(Erase heading not required.)

Place	Date	Hour	Summary of Events and Information	Remarks and references to Appendices
			advantage, the shooting during the month shows that J.J. Range the 2" even at extreme range is extraordinary accurate. Having regards to the bombs, J/J an example at 500 yds. out of 13 9dr. Burst - his were obtained on a Richstack Several of the men were well given courses of instruction at the school of Musketry - the ordinary routine firing on a considerably quiet ected day about - the month work	

Raymond Davies
2/Lt 7.2 2nd B+A
Comdg s/o trench By 2nd Battery

Army Form C. 2118.

WAR DIARY
or
INTELLIGENCE SUMMARY.

(Erase heading not required.)

Y.2 D/Battery

Instructions regarding War Diaries and Intelligence Summaries are contained in F.S. Regs., Part II. and the Staff Manual respectively. Title pages will be prepared in manuscript.

Places	Date	Hour	Summary of Events and Information	Remarks and references to Appendices
BEUVRY	1/9/17 to 10/9/17		During this period the battery carried out retaliatory shoots, constructed emplacements, and made preparations for the "strafe" of the 11th.	
	11/9/17		An organised shoot, with artillery outpost, was carried out from 12.30 p.m. till 1 p.m. on the Brickstacks and Brick fat Alley, with good effect.	
	16/9/17		From 7.30 a.m. till 7.45 a.m. an organised shoot was carried out on selected targets, from 5 p.m. till 5.30 p.m. a destructive shoot was carried out on an enemy post and sniper's plate on A.2.d.90.50. Five direct hits were obtained.	
	20/9/17 to 23/9/17		The battery changed fronts, covering the sector occupied by the 99th Infantry Brigade, and fired in retaliation.	
	24/9/17		Wire cutting took place for a raid on A.28.a.00.10 to A.27.b.95.35. The Battalion which carried out the raid reported that the wire was completely cut, and presented no obstacle.	
	25/9/17		An organised shoot took place from 3.3 p.m. till 3.23 p.m. on Ryan's Keep, Train Alley and Mine Trench. 96 rounds were fired and much damage done to the enemy trenches at these points.	
	26/9/17 to 3/9/17		The battery moved its Trench H.Q. to Swab Trench. Retaliation was carried out effectively.	

R.P.O. Barrett
2 Lt. R.F.A.
Y.2. D/M.B.

Army Form C. 2118.

WAR DIARY
or
INTELLIGENCE SUMMARY

(Erase heading not required.)

SEPT. 1917.
2/1 T.M.B.

D48

Instructions regarding War Diaries and Intelligence Summaries are contained in F.S. Regs., Part II. and the Staff Manual respectively. Title Pages will be prepared in manuscript.

Place	Date Sep.	Hour	Summary of Events and Information	Remarks and references to Appendices
GIVENCHY lez LA BASSÉE	1st		Battery in action with 4 guns in and around GIVENCHY village. Order in force for no firing except in retaliation to combined shoots.	
	2nd + 3rd		Preparing six new temporary emplacements for a six gun shoot carried out registration of the guns which caused considerable retaliation by Boche Minnies & artillery.	
	4th	6.30pm	Fired 150 rounds from six guns on mine dumps — Special "Pump" at 47.d.95.45. also one west Prussian Way A6.d.7.7.9. Portugese attached to us fired two of the guns & worked guide well under supervision. Shooting rather erratic owing to beds giving way in soft ground.	
	5th + 6th		Fired 75 rounds "sniping" working parties which are repairing damage. 8 yesterdays shoot.	
	7th + 8th + 9th		Very little enemy Minnie activity so only fired a few rounds in retaliation to his desultory fire.	
	10th		Made reconnaissance of Cover Trench + game CANADIAN ORCHARD with the intention of doing eight-gun shoot. Commenced by driving piles to put beds on, as the ground is extremely marshy there.	
	11th		R.E.s progressing very slowly with construction work on Utopia Cut permanent position. O.C. Battle (Col Hunt) prohibited all firing, including retaliation.	
	12/3		R.E.'s projected gas during night fired in expiration with that. Rule established that we are to retaliate at once with at least three to one for every Boche Minnie larger than "Pineapples"	

WAR DIARY
INTELLIGENCE SUMMARY

Army Form C. 2118.

SEPT. 1917.

Z/2 T.M.B.

D 4 1

Place	Date Sept	Hour	Summary of Events and Information	Remarks and references to Appendices
GIVENCHY LEZ LA BASSEE	14/15		No offensive firing allowed owing to GOC 6th Bde's wishes as the trenches are full of Portuguese under instruction.	
	15th-17th		Enemy Minnies fairly active so had occasion to retaliate daily — generally successful in closing him & Stop.	
	18th & 20th		Enemy Mortar's very quiet, but his artillery who were very active registering on various points in the sector, & his infantry (busy on trench work at night), REs again shot over 900 which caused considerable retaliation.	
	21st & 26th		Hostile T.M.s again more active — fired 78 rounds in retaliation during three days.	
	26/27th		Carried eight guns + 1120 bombs during night to Cover Trench S.27 b + 28 a. (Three gun borrowed from Portuguese battery, one from Z/2 + one from Y/2) This was an extremely heavy nights work getting the guns in action in time for Shoot at 5:30 am. The shoot was quite successful and we had no casualties in spite of heavy retaliation on + behind the breastworks. The targets were enemy wire, support trench + STORM LOOP between S.27 & S.28 a 6.2 + S.28 a.8.7. + we fired 1056 rounds during the minute. Dummy flashes were put up from a flank which drew away part of the retaliation. The guns were withdrawn early the morning + taken back to GIVENCHY the same night.	
	28th & 30th		Slight T.M. activity. Blew up store of Very lights + other inflammables during a registration shoot on "Spoil Dump."	

H.B.Co sounded fired during the month. Lieut Gorrie + three men attacked Gorrie's Instruction on G Trench, Mortar at Clarques. 2/Lt H.G. Leigh attached to Z-29 gun RFs from 30th.

R W Gorrie / R F A
Lieut Z/2 T M B
O/C Z/2 T.M.B.

Trench Mortar Brigade
2nd Divisional Artillery

V: X: Y: & Z. TRENCH MORTAR BATTERIES

OCTOBER 1917.

WAR DIARY or INTELLIGENCE SUMMARY.

Army Form C. 2118.

2D T M By
V2 M Roberts
Vol 14

Place	Date	Hour	Summary of Events and Information	Remarks and references to Appendices
CANAL, GUENCHY, CAMBRIN.	1/10/17		Rain-laying.	
	2/10/17		Rain-laying. Reconnaissance of sites for position for new Long H.T.M. behind CUINCHY. 1 Pdr. from Yr H.T.M.B.	
	3/10/17		do. do. in LE PLANTIN.	
	4/10/17		New Long H.T.M. Mark III arrived on 3 motor lorries. Received orders to prepare to hand over. 7 rounds from 46th Div.	
	5/10/17		General preparation of positions etc for handing over. IKEY on to SPOTTED DOG.	7.
	6/10/17		10 rounds from BARTS ALLEY — night firing in conjunction with 46th Div. (Raid), motored, on to CORONS DE MAROC. 2 Bm from Kerne.	10.
	7/10/17		Off. W/25 H.T.M.B. shewn round gun positions, H.Qs, O.Ps, etc. Capt. ROBERTS returns from leave. Personnel of W/25 H.T.M.B. arrive.	
	8/10/17		W/25 take over. Rounds fired by Yr shewing occupation of station = 500. 3 men proceed on leave.	
AMES.	9/10/17		Battery move to AMES in 2 motor lorries making 2 journeys each. 1 Pdr of Yr H.T.M.B. proceeds to 36th Div. rejoins his unit. 1 man cold from 36th Bde. rejoins his	

Army Form C. 2118.

WAR DIARY
INTELLIGENCE SUMMARY.

(Erase heading not required.)

Instructions regarding War Diaries and Intelligence Summaries are contained in F. S. Regs., Part II. and the Staff Manual respectively. Title pages will be prepared in manuscript.

Place	Date	Hour	Summary of Events and Information	Remarks and references to Appendices
AMES.	12/10/17		Capt. ROBERTS & Lt. CHALMERS attend Instructional Demonstration on new Long 9.45" H.T.M. Trench M at HERSIN. 1 man attd. Town Major AMETTES for Police duty.	
	13/10/17		Mr. SMITH and servant posted to 17th Bty. R.F.A.. 1 man from hospital. 2 men from Leave.	
	15/10/17		Lt. CHALMERS and servant to Instruction Course at 1st Army School of Gunnery.	
	16/10/17		2 men on Leave.	
	10/10/17 – 16/10/17		Refitting, Inspections, Parades, Drills, Signalling Class and Route Marching.	
STNBQE.	17/10/17		Move to STEENBECQUE. Three cars in convoy at VENDIN. Move completed in 4 motor lorries tightly packed without guns. Billeted for night in STEENBECQUE.	
GDSVLDE.	18/10/17		Move in same lorries to GODEWAERSVELDE. Billeted there for night. 1 man to hospital.	
SIEGE CAMP	19/10/17		Battery (less 2 R.S.O. & 22 men attached A.R.P.) moved in lorries to SIEGE CAMP between VLAMERTINGHE and ELVERDINGHE. Billeted in hessian huts.	
	20/10/17		Routine.	
	21/10/17		Lt. Hon. SHIPLEY joins from D.G.C.	

Army Form C. 2118.

WAR DIARY
INTELLIGENCE SUMMARY.
(Erase heading not required.)

Instructions regarding War Diaries and Intelligence Summaries are contained in F. S. Regs., Part II. and the Staff Manual respectively. Title pages will be prepared in manuscript.

Place	Date	Hour	Summary of Events and Information	Remarks and references to Appendices
SIEGE Camp.	23/10/17		3 men rejoin from Leave. 1 N.C.O. & 2 men attd. 41/st Bde. R.F.A. 4 men attd. D.A.C. 9/Bdr. THOMAS promoted Corporal vice LAZENBY struck off list from 19/9/17.	
	25/10/17		4 men on Leave. 1 man rejoined from D.A.C. 1 3mm attd. D.A.C.	
	26/10/17		Hr: SHIPLEY and Servant attd. 2/36 Bty, R.F.A.	
	26-29/10/17		1 man wounded by aeroplane bomb (to hospital). Routine.	
	30/10/17		Lt. CHALMERS and Servant attd. 47th Bty, R.F.A. 3 men on Leave. 1 man killed by aeroplane bomb.	
	31/10/17		Routine. Value of stores sold during month = £5:3:6.	

Rowland
Capt.
Comm'g. 1/2 H.T.M.B.

WAR DIARY or INTELLIGENCE SUMMARY

Army Form C. 2118.

Place	Date	Hour	Summary of Events and Information	Remarks and references to Appendices
La Boisselle	1/10/17 to 5/10/17		In action. Battery fired some 60 rounds in retaliation work. Enemy firing was not heavy. Local gas shells fell fairly close to O. Trench. H.Q. but fortunately the wind was very unfavourable to enemy. Infantry were attacked on 2nd inst: number of battery were attacked but after R.E. & N.C.B. overhead work the beginning work well returned to duty. Thirteen O.R.'s were attached returned to unit.	
	6/10/17 7/10/17		Lt. B.T. Stephen granted leave to U.K. & Lieut R. Bailey Blount returned. Lt. Wilson attached to School of Gunnery Shoeburyness. Lt. Gage returned from leave. Brig. Bung F. Seddon returned from Lt. Keay. Lieut. Brown to Shoeburyness. Lt.-Col. Beck slightly wounded returned from hospital.	
	8/10/17			
Amiens			Left Beaune for Amiens	
	9/10/17			
"	11/10/17		Bdr. Robinson promoted Battery Seft. Continues back in Cpl. Corporal. Although intended for the was not L. Corporal. Although intended for it was not inspected by possible owing Came before.	
"	13/10/17		Gnr. Black Baillie T. Neeson returned from School of this day the Battery into a Concentration camp. Short ros. a great success.	
"	14/10/17		Cpl. Burchell returned off leave. Lt. Keay granted Leave to U.K. Cpl. Bishop returned from hospital. Gnr. Clark A. Cpl. Buckley L.B.R. officer	
"	15/10/17		To L.O.R. Tucker. Lt. Emory attached School of Gunnery.	
"	16/10/17		Gnr. Baillie granted leave to England.	

Army Form C. 2118.

WAR DIARY
or
INTELLIGENCE SUMMARY.
(Erase heading not required.)

Instructions regarding War Diaries and Intelligence Summaries are contained in F.S. Regs., Part II. and the Staff Manual respectively. Title pages will be prepared in manuscript.

Place	Date	Hour	Summary of Events and Information	Remarks and references to Appendices
Aura.	6/10/17.		During the period at Aures were held every day. The route marches F. daily for recreation. & a football match was played.	
	17/10/17. 18/10/17.		Left Aures for Steenbecque.	
Steenbecque.			Left Steenbecque for Godewaersvelde, & there for Reige Camp.	
Reige Camp. 19/10/17. Steenvoorde			Eight men attached to 2nd D.A.C. Lt. F.J. Stephen returned from leave.	
"	23/10/17.		One S.L.O.T. three men attached to 2nd D.A.C. One C.S.M. & C.S.L.S. damages received from 5th Division. Maj. 68490 Dr. Coble L. looked for 1/2 Feb. 17. B. No. 111436 Dr. Gray admitted to hospital.	
"	26/10/17.			
"	28/10/17.		Lt. King returned from leave. Col. Bewley, Lt. Clark, Lt. St. Anstether, Lt. Sent Wakefield L.C. or Uddington. The Pomeroy returned from leave &	
"	29/10/17.		2nd Bailie returned from leave. Y. to Lt. Trotter granted leave to U.K.	
"	30/10/17			

A.K. Stephen Lt. O.C. N2. Y.M. D.V.
R.E.

WAR DIARY
or INTELLIGENCE SUMMARY

Army Form C. 2118.

½ TM Batt.

Place	Date	Hour	Summary of Events and Information	Remarks and references to Appendices
CAMBRIN	1/10/17		10 DAC men + 25 men + 1 Sgt of 2nd R. Berks Regt attd for work on new DUNDEE WALK 6" howitzer emplacement.	
"	2/10/17		Heavy retaliatory fire from own Quarry Boat alley & Munster Tunnel guns	
"	3/10/17		Registering on wire in front of Little Willie trench for proposed raid by 3rd KRRC	
"	4/10/17		Bores retaliation from Munster Tunnel & Quarry guns Received orders to prepare to hand over to incoming division	
"	5/10/17		Attached DAC ~ R Berks R. men returned to units. Work on Dundee Walk "Emplt ceased. 30th Retaliation fire from Mason Rouge Alley & Quarry guns Retaliation Bomb's from Mason Rouge Alley & Quarry guns	
"	6/10/17		41st Bde fired in conjunction with 46th Div raid, onto French junction & hostile "morine"	
"	7/10/17		Gnr Craig, Dotson, Morgan returned from 1st Army School of Mortars O.C. Z/25 showing round positions preparatory to taking (over) 2/Lt Daniel, Gnrs Taylor, Holden, Adams, Cain & Pte Cox proceed on 6" course at 1st Army School of Mortars 2nd Lieut R.P.C. Barrett proceeds on leave to U.K. Lieut H.M. Fordham returns from leave	
BEUVRY	8/10/17		Z.25 takes over from ½	
AMES	9/10/17 10		Moved to AMES in Motor Lorries Billet here for one day	
"	11/10/17		Parade inspection, kit fitting, etc. Then men on course of telephony with RE.	
"	13/10/17		Lieut R.P.Daniell + 5 men return from Army School of Mortars	

Army Form C. 2118.

WAR DIARY
or
INTELLIGENCE SUMMARY

Y/2 T.M Bat'y

(Erase heading not required.)

Instructions regarding War Diaries and Intelligence Summaries are contained in F. S. Regs., Part II. and the Staff Manual respectively. Title pages will be prepared in manuscript.

Place	Date	Hour	Summary of Events and Information	Remarks and references to Appendices
STEINBECQUE	17/10/17		Move to Steinbecque. Motor Lorries Billet for night.	
GODEWAERSVELDE	18/10/17		Move to Godewaersvelde via same lorries. Billet in barn for night.	
GOD/DE & SIEGE CAMP	19/10/17		Moved in same lorries to Siege Camp between Sherdinghe and Planrintinghe. Billetted in Nissen huts. 1 Sgt & 8 men attached to 2 DAC for duty at A.R.P. St Jean Station	
SIEGE CAMP	22/10/17		Gnr Taylor att'd to HQ 5th DAC	
"	23/10/17		BQMS Coton Stoneman & Wilson att'd 2nd DAC	
"	"		Lieut H.M. Jonesham & servant att'd to 15th Batty R.F.A.	
"			6" Howitzer motion stores taken over from 9th Army T.M.S	
"	24/10/17		Gnr Adams proceeds leave to U.K.	
"	25/10/17		2nd Lieut W Graham recommended for immediate award in connection therewith	
"	27/10/17		Lieut R.B. Barrett returns from leave. also posted to 7/1st Batt R.F.A.	
"	29/10/17		Lieut S. Luylew rejoins from leave. also Gnrs Bentley & Jeune from 6" Course at 1st Army School of Mortars	
"	30/10/17		2 Lieut Olding posted from 2nd DAC & granted leave to U.K. Gnr Dotson granted leave to U.K.	

Raymond Daniels 2/Lt
/OC Y/2 T.M Battery

A5834 Wt.W4973 M687 750,000 8/16 D. D. & L. Ltd. Forms/C.2118/13.

WAR DIARY or INTELLIGENCE SUMMARY

Army Form C. 2118.

OCTOBER 1917

Z/2 T.M.B.

D42.

Place	Date	Hour	Summary of Events and Information	Remarks and references to Appendices
GIVENCHY LEZ LA BASSEE.	Oct 1st		Battery in action in GIVENCHY Sector, firing daily in retaliation to enemy M.mr. useful fire. Fired 25 rounds this morning at 7.30 a.m. & succeeded in stopping a heavy trench mortar strafe, also 10 rounds at 4 p.m. in response to enemy evening fire.	
	2nd		Fired 16 rounds at 12.15 a.m. in co-operation in barrage for raid by 1st/5th King's, also 12 rounds at 4.45 p.m. on to "SPOIL DUMP" in A9d9545.	
	3rd		12 O.Rs attached to this battery from 2nd A.C.D. to assist in the construction of a 6" gunpit near BIRDCAGE WALK. 5 rounds fired in registration on a mining crater at A9d 58.72. blown by enemy this morning — apparently no attempt made by him to consolidate it.	
	4th		10 rounds fired from 2 guns at 11.38 p.m. in cooperation in projected retaliation shoot by R.F.A.(Group) & garrison a large scale fired 7 rounds at 6.15 p.m. in combined retaliation. DTM.O. 725th Bde made tour of this sector in preparation for taking over.	
	5th		Line exceedingly quiet all day owing to the relief of the 6th Bde by the 7th Bde.	
	6th		Y/2 T.M.B.Y took over from this battery in this sector, taking over our guns & kit in 7R.H./o/5.	
	7th		Completed relief. Men attached from D.A.C. were returned to duty.	
	~~8th~~ 9th		Battery moved with the remainder of 2nd Div. T.M.s transported in mo. lorries to AMES, where we found billets for the men in a barn.	
AMES.	10th		Commenced training during the period in rest — with daily parades for gun cleaning, gun drill, gun drill and rifle drill, + football. 2/Lt. H.C. Leigh, R.F.A. returned from leave.	
	11th		Church parade for divisional artillery — service conducted by the Bishop of Khartoum. 2/Lt C.T.Hamilton & 3 O.Rs returned from 6" Centre at 1st Army School of Mortars.	

WAR DIARY or INTELLIGENCE SUMMARY

Army Form C. 2118.

OCT. 1917.   Z/2 T.M.B.

D43

Place	Date Oct	Hour	Summary of Events and Information	Remarks and references to Appendices
AMES	15th		Lieut R.M. Gorrie attached for a few days training to 71st Bty R.F.A. Lieut F.G. Bower Middlesex Regt & 4 O.R.s went to 2nd course at 1st Army School of Mortars. Battery moved with remainder of Div. T.M.s to STEENBECQUE where Battrie. were billeted in a farm.	
STEENBECQUE	17th			
GODWAERSVELDE	19th		Battery moved to GODWAERSVELDE via HAZEBROUCK & STEENVOORDE.	
VLAMERTINGHE	19th		Further move to SIEGE CAMP nr VLAMERTINGHE, via POPERINGHE. Billeted in Nissen huts. 10 O.R.s sent to D.A.C., attached for work on ammunition dumps & fatigues.	
	20th		2/Lt. H.G. Leigh & 2 KRRC's posted to 483 (East Anglian) Field Coy. R.E. Remainder of battery (excepting Sergeant, naick orderly & officers servants) attached to D.A.C.	
	24th		2/Lt Ct. Hamilton granted leave to U.K.	
	30th		Lieut R.M. Gorrie temporarily attached to 71st Bty R.F.A.	
	31st		Lieut F.G. Bower granted leave to U.K.	

R.M. Gorrie
Lieut R.F.A.
O/C Z/2 T.M.B.

Trench Mortar Brigade
2nd Divisional Artillery.

"V" Battery disBanded 19.11.17.

V: X: Y & Z. TRENCH MORTAR BATTERIES.

NOVEMBER 1917.

Army Form C. 2118.

WAR DIARY
~~INTELLIGENCE~~ SUMMARY.
(Erase heading not required.)

Instructions regarding War Diaries and Intelligence Summaries are contained in F. S. Regs., Part II. and the Staff Manual respectively. Title pages will be prepared in manuscript.

Place	Date	Hour	Summary of Events and Information	Remarks and references to Appendices
SIEGE CAMP	1/6/17		Work for D.A.C. and on A.R.P. 1 man killed by aeroplane bomb. 1 man to hospital.	
	2/6/17		1 man wounded.	
	3-5/6/17		do.	
	6/6/17		do. 14 N.C.O. & men attached D.A.C.	
	7/6/17		do.	
	8/6/17		do.	
	9/6/17		do. 1 N.C.O. & 8 men from 36 & 41st Bde. arrived.	
	10/6/17		do. 2 men from kennel.	
	11/6/17		do.	
	12/6/17		do. 1 N.C.O. & 1 man posted from D.A.C. to D.A.C.	
	13/6/17		do. " 1 " " "	
	14/6/17		do. 1 man from kennel.	
	15/6/17		do. 1 man from kennel.	
	16/6/17		do.	
	17/6/17		do.	
	18/6/17		BATTERY DISBANDED. Capt. ROBERTS, M.C., attached X/ T.M.B. Lieut. CHALMERS posted to D.A.C, Lieut. SHIRLEY posted to D/36 Bde, R.F.A. 2/Lt: GAME posted to X/ T.M.B. 42 O.R. to D.A.C., 5 O.R. to X/, 9 to Y/, 9 to Y/, 9 to Z/, 1 to D/36 Bde, R.F.A. *Forward Roberts* Capt: 9/c Y/ H.T.M.B.	

Army Form C. 2118.

2D TM Bgy
5/1/5

WAR DIARY
or
INTELLIGENCE SUMMARY.
(Erase heading not required.)

Instructions regarding War Diaries and Intelligence Summaries are contained in F. S. Regs., Part II. and the Staff Manual respectively. Title pages will be prepared in manuscript.

Place	Date	Hour	Summary of Events and Information	Remarks and references to Appendices
Siege Camp	1/11/4 to 18/11/4		Work for D.C., C and A.N.Q.	
Siege Camp	19/11/4		Farewell from Siege Camp to Lt Lawrence	
Lawrence	20/11/4 to 22/11/4		Lt Lawrence.	
Lawrence	23/11/4		Left Lt Lawrence. Marched to Hephebourg advanced for Bapaume.	
Hephebourg	24/11/4		Arrived Hephebourg.	
Hephebourg	25/11/4		Left Hephebourg for Hg advanced.	
Bapaume	26/11/4		Left Bayard and for Herms the resting a AKP Heren	
Herms	27/11/4 to 30/11/4		[illegible]	

WAR DIARY or INTELLIGENCE SUMMARY

Army Form C. 2118.

Place	Date	Hour	Summary of Events and Information	Remarks and references to Appendices
Mamalonghe	Nov 1st 1917		The personnel of the battery continued working on S. Jew. Dump & D.A.C. fatigues as during the latter part of previous month. Lt. I. McDonoghan still attached to 15th Bty R.G.A. reported on 18th. All men return to Bty on 19th.	
St Lawrence	20		Battery moved to St Lawrence with S.A.A. section	
Goguelberque	24		Battery moved to Goguelberque by road & entrained by rail leaving there at early next morning & detraining at Bapaume & proceeded to Stapleworth	
Stapleworth X.				
Royaulcourt	27.		The Bty moved to Royaulcourt by road on the 27th	
Hermies	29		The Bty moved to Hermies by road on 29th 2nd Lt. Daniels proceeded on leave during the month.	

J.M. Donohue Lt. RFA
O/C 72th Bty

Army Form C. 2118.

D 44

WAR DIARY
or
INTELLIGENCE SUMMARY

Z/2 T.M.B.
NOVEMBER 1917

(Erase heading not required.)

Instructions regarding War Diaries and Intelligence Summaries are contained in F. S. Regs., Part II. and the Staff Manual respectively. Title Pages will be prepared in manuscript.

Place	Date	Hour	Summary of Events and Information	Remarks and references to Appendices
VLAMERTINGHE	1/11/17 to 18/11/17		All available men working for 2nd D.A.C. at St JEAN STATION Ammunition Dump, & wagon lines at BRIELEN in very bad conditions with mud & poor billets.	
	19/11/17		Lieut. Comie attached to 71st Battery R.F.A. in action at St JULIEN from 1/11/17 to 3/11/17 and then as Bde. Sig. Officer of 36th Bde R.F.A. from 9/11/17 to 12/11/17.	
			All men returned to duty from D.A.C. 1 N.C.O. and 9 men posted to D.A.C. and replaced by 1 N.C.O. and 9 men posted from V/2 T.M.B. which was disbanded.	
ST LAURENT	20/11/17		Battery moved with divisional T.M.'s to ST LAURENT.	
ESQUEL-BECQ	24/11/17		Battery moved by road to ESQUELBECQUES.	
BAPAUME	25/11/17		Battery entrained at 2 a.m. Turned by rail to BAPAUME and thence by road to HAPLINCOURT.	
HAPLINCOURT	26/11/17		Battery moved by road to ROYAUCOURT.	
	27/11/17		Battery moved to HERMIES — all available men attached to D.A.C. for work on APPLE DUMP &c.	

R. M. Gorrie
Lieut. R.F.A.
D.C. Z/2 T.M.B.

Trench Mortar Brigade.
2nd Divisional Artillery.

X: Y: Z. TRENCH MORTAR BATTERIES

DECEMBER 1917.

2D TM By
J/a/16

WAR DIARY
or
INTELLIGENCE SUMMARY.

Army Form C. 2118.

(Erase heading not required.)

Place	Date	Hour	Summary of Events and Information	Remarks and references to Appendices
Henin	1/15 4.12.17		Battery engaged in APP work at this place.	
Rogincourt	6.12.17 to 7.12.17		Battery move to Rogincourt at 15.40 [?] were attached to the APP artillery escort.	
	7.12.17		Gun withdrawn from APP work & allotted to Z² Zone to have a 6" replacement in the line.	
	12.12.17 to 15.12.17		Battery withdrawn from work at Z² position & schedule to have a 6" replacement for their own battery. - Orders to move on to position.	
	15 R 17		Orders not to fire owing to consolidation infantry work, generally for our heavy in consolidation were received.	
Eng. posn	15.16.17.12/17		Were in position continued -	
	17.12.17		Battery moves to billets @ Dug Heap near camel move in position continued - gun to bed feet in position.	
	17 to 25.12.17		worked on improving position	
	25.12.17 to 28.12.17		Enemy shelled our position. Trenches caved in cups & recesses of loose 7 - communication were severed. Dugouts & neighbourhood mostly escaped damage.	
	28 to 31.12.17		Enemy shelling continued — work on our Z² position & new Campbell gun during the period 24 to 31/12/17 one cartridge was dropped to another emplacement position were also begun — about 12 trenching parties [?] put in.	

1st Lieutenant
O/c 2 [?]

4/1/18

WAR DIARY or INTELLIGENCE SUMMARY

Army Form C. 2118.

½ T M B

Place	Date	Hour	Summary of Events and Information	Remarks and references to Appendices
Romeo	January 1918. 1		Battery when billeted in Hermies. 8 men & NCO attached to A.R.P. Respirator Inspection duty (two shifts of 4 men per day)	
Ryaulcourt	4	11	Battery moved to Ryaulcourt men continued on A.R.P. duties on 6" T.M. will remainder of Battery detailed on A.R.P.	
	12		Battery moved up into action men having been withdrawn from A.R.P. & commenced in digging positions. Conducted one permanent position & one temporary one. But were not able to fire as no orders were received by others.	
			Had no firing to be done until ordered. Lieut. Singleton & four men attached to A Army Schools Mortars for instruction.	
	17		Battery continued working up the types of making positions until end of month.	

G. M. Southern Lt.
O.C. ½ T.M.B.

WAR DIARY or INTELLIGENCE SUMMARY

Army Form C. 2118.

7/2 T.M.B.

DEC 1917.

Place	Date DEC	Hour	Summary of Events and Information	Remarks and references to Appendices
HERMIES.	1st		Battery billetted in dugouts in Rue de Haucourt, HERMIES; men working on 8-hour shifts on WINDY CORNER Ammunition Dump.	
	2nd		Lieut. Gorrie returned from leave.	
RUYAULCOURT.	3rd 4th		Battery moved into hessian huts in RUYAULCOURT.	
	5th		All available men commenced work on A.R.P. under Capt Weston of 2nd D.A.C. D.T.M.O. & battery commander reconnoitred ground of left of CANAL DU NORD near LOCK 7 for 6" positions in preparation for defence of new line which was being taken up by our infantry after the retreat from BOURLON WOOD.	
	7th		Battery went into action & commenced digging a position in old German M.G. position at K 9 a 7.2.10.4. (Trench Map 57 C NE 1/10000)	
CANAL du NORD	8th to 11th		Work continued steadily on position in spite of considerable shelling.	
	11th		Received orders from D.T.M.O. to stop work, as this position was too far forward. Men withdrawn to rest billets at RUYAUL COURT.	
	12th		Reconnoitred the front of div. on right (K10 & K16) for 6" emplacements — no prospect of action there until enemy line is pushed forward in front of GRAINCOURT.	
	17th		Battery's rest billets moved to unfinished cupola shelters on Canal bank at K35 c 6.7.	

Army Form C. 2118.

WAR DIARY
or
INTELLIGENCE SUMMARY

Z/2 T.M.B.

DEC. 1917

(Erase heading not required.)

Place	Date	Hour	Summary of Events and Information	Remarks and references to Appendices
CANAL du NORD (HERMIES)	18th		Reconnoitred positions in reserve line in K20 (Trench map 57C NE 1/10000)	
	20th		Battery commenced work on reserve emplacement at SLAGHEAP (K20 b.1.1.)	
	21st to 31st		Work continued steadily on this position, with the exception of Xmas Day which was observed as a holiday.	

R.W.Gourie
Lieut R.F.A.
OC Z/2 T.M.B.

2ND DIVISION
DIVL. ARTILLERY

'X', 'Y' & 'Z'
   TRENCH MORTAR BATTERIES,
      JAN - DEC 1918.

2nd Divisional Artillery.

X: Y: & Z: TRENCH MORTAR BATTERIES

JANUARY 1918.

Army Form C. 2118.

WAR DIARY
or
INTELLIGENCE SUMMARY

N.Z. F.A. 4 B. Aug/15

Vol 17

(Erase heading not required.)

Instructions regarding War Diaries and Intelligence Summaries are contained in F. S. Regs., Part II. and the Staff Manual respectively. Title Pages will be prepared in manuscript.

Place	Date	Hour	Summary of Events and Information	Remarks and references to Appendices
Unauthorised	1 to 4		The Battery continued working on emplacements in front of Browles Wood.	
Elephant	5	19	On the 5th the Battery was relieved by 4th the Battery and ordered to Taylor's end. Seven Guts and one 4.5" was carried out on harbours of stats from front.	
"	23		The Battery moved by tram to help in cutting & also in Taylor carried out to 6 Gun Battery in the sea.	
Faith	30		Battery took on left group of guns from 4 " B.A.	

[illegible signature annotations]

WAR DIARY or INTELLIGENCE SUMMARY

½ T.M.B.

JAN 1918.

Army Form C. 2118.

(Erase heading not required.)

Place	Date	Hour	Summary of Events and Information	Remarks and references to Appendices
Royaulcourt	Jan 1 to 4		The Battery continued working on emplacements in the line in front of Boulon Wood.	
Hyplincourt	5 to 19.		On the 5th of the month the battery were relieved by Y.17. the battery moved to Hyplincourt into Nissen Huts. Work was carried out on prolickon against tanks.	
"	20		Lt. Bugden reconnoitied 63rd divnional front on Welsh Ridge prior to taking over from the	
"	21		Advance party went into the line & took over position	
Metz en Couture	23		Remainder of battery moved from Hyplincourt to Metz in Metz.	
"	24	31.	Registration shoots checked & retaliation & obstructive shoots carried out. 86 rounds being fired during the month except Lt Daniel & 1 O.R. attended 3rd Army School of Mortars	

2nd Lieut Foulsham
O.C. ½ T.M.B

WAR DIARY or INTELLIGENCE SUMMARY

Army Form C. 2118.

Z/2 T.M.B.
JAN. 1918.

Place	Date JAN	Hour	Summary of Events and Information	Remarks and references to Appendices
CANAL DU NORD (HERMIES)	1st		Battery working on construction of 6" positions in reserve line of defence near Canal Bank at K20.b.1.1. Rear billets also near Canal Bank at K35.c.7.1 (Ref/100000, 57C)	
HAPLINCOURT	4th		Relieved in the line by the 17th Div. T.M.Bs, and moved to rest billets in huzen huts at HAPLINCOURT.	
	5th to 19th		Work carried out in improvement & protection of huts from bombing, and daily parades for rifle drill & gas drill.	
	20th		2/Lt Gorrie reconnoitred 63rd Div. T.M. positions on WELSH RIDGE in front of VILLERS PLOUICH.	
	21st		Advance party went into line.	
	22nd		2nd Howitzer took over in line from Z/63 T.M.B. Three guns in action in open gunpits.	
METZ en COUTURE	23rd		Remainder of battery moved from HAPLINCOURT to new rear billets in METZ.	
	24th to 31st		Gun daily in registration on trench junctions, crossroads, around LA VACQUERIE. Put fourth gun in position in Quarry in FARM RAVINE, but only allowed to use it for S.O.S. lines or direct tank attack owing to dry line + in retaliation, & occasionally on slight enemy activity.	
	23rd to 31st		Kept 2/Lt Binder attached Q.M.S. T.M. Course, + five other ranks, its 6" Course at 3rd Army School.	

R.M. Gorrie
Lieut. R.F.A.
O.C. Z/2 T.M.B.

2nd Divisional Artillery.

X & Y TRENCH MORTAR BATTERIES ::: FEBRUARY 1918.

Army Form C. 2118.

2 A. T. M. Bty
FEB 18

WAR DIARY
or
INTELLIGENCE SUMMARY.
(Erase heading not required.)

Instructions regarding War Diaries and Intelligence Summaries are contained in F. S. Regs., Part II. and the Staff Manual respectively. Title pages will be prepared in manuscript.

Place	Date FEB '18	Hour	Summary of Events and Information	Remarks and references to Appendices
METZ	1		Work on improving positions on left section continued. 2nd Lt K.T. Stofen M.C. returns from leave to U.K.	Rate fixed
	2		Improving positions continued. 2 O.R. proceed on leave to U.K.	
	3		do. Sui Officers of American Army attached for instruction.	15.
	4		Work continued 1 O.R. proceeds on leave. 2nd Lt. J.P. Genne returns from M Salire	
	5		Took over other positions on right of Divisional front and over left positions to Y Battery. 4 guns in action	
	6		Work on improving positions, Levels, stores, trenches and dug out commenced. 1 O.R. proceeds on leave to U.K.	
	7		"	
	8		Work on positions etc continued 1 O.R.	
	9		New dug position for " started with a vertical shaft Entrance. Work on other positions continued	
	10		Work continued	10 rds
	11		" 1 O.R. to Hospital American Officers return to their HQ	
	12		" 2nd Lt Sch. Nebe proceeds on leave to UK	25 rds
	13		"	
	14		" 1 O.R. proceeds on leave to U.K.	
	15		" Bty A.D. Charlwood attached x Bty by arrangement with D.T.M.O.	
	16		" New position on extreme right commenced 1 O.R. on leave to U.K. 1 O.R. (Bdr.) wounded	65 rds

Army Form C. 2118.

WAR DIARY
or
INTELLIGENCE SUMMARY.
(Erase heading not required.)

Instructions regarding War Diaries and Intelligence Summaries are contained in F. S. Regs., Part II. and the Staff Manual respectively. Title pages will be prepared in manuscript.

Place	Date 1918 Feb.	Hour	Summary of Events and Information	Remarks and references to Appendices
METZ	17		Work on new and old positions continued	
	18		" "	
	19		Ditto	2 O.R. return from leave to UK	10 rds
	20		do	1 O.R. proceeds on leave to UK	50 rds
	22		"	1 O.R. proceeds to I.O.R. returns from UK wounded at nose wheel	
	24		"	1 O.R. proceeds to & 1 O.R. return from UK	5 rds
	25		"		
	26		do	One gun in position on Epr - of section Kaban over from Y Battery	17 rds
	27			1 O.R. on leave. 1 O.R. surrendered. A shoot was carried out with aeroplane rotation. An attempt was made to register 3 guns simultaneously. Trouble was experienced with guns breaking at No 1 gun and with the bed at No 5 gun. Able registration for No 2 gun was successful.	48 rds
	28			A second aeroplane shoot was attempted. Single gun registration. Results were not satisfactory. S.D.S.C. Sweep natives from Reserve	40 rds

H.S.Thompson
Capt xxxxx

WAR DIARY
or
INTELLIGENCE SUMMARY.

Army Form C. 2118.

½ 7 M B

(Erase heading not required.)

Place	Date	Hour	Summary of Events and Information	Remarks and references to Appendices
Ritz	Jan 1918	1.	The Battery continued working on defensive positions in Ritz.	
		2.	I.O.R. proceeded on leave. Work on defences continued.	
	"	3.	Lt E Sugden proceeded to M.K. Four American Officers joined. Reach Motor for practical instruction in the Lewis Gun. 2/Lt Daniels & 5 O.Rs returned from III Army School of Artillery. Work continued on defensive positions. 1 O.R. proceeded on leave.	
		4.	1 O.R. proceeded on leave. Work continued on defensive positions.	
		5.	Maj. M.C. Salley rode the Battery. Proceeded up line to Y°f Pte K. Ptg who had relieved the Battery on the takeover from to. One American Officer went up the line. 30 h. nit. One American Officer went up to relieve Practical instruction. 10 rounds fired in relation improved on line. Motor defensive positions continued	10.
	"	6.		
	"	7.	2 O.Rs proceeded on leave. Lewis Master & positions in the line improved. 4 American officers left. 1 O.R. proceeded on leave. Capt Taylor returned from Artillery Base Depot. Work continued on defensive	20.
	"	8.		

WAR DIARY
or
INTELLIGENCE SUMMARY. ½ T.M.B.

(Erase heading not required.)

Army Form C. 2118.

Place	Date	Hour	Summary of Events and Information	Remarks and references to Appendices
Holy	8		Positions	
"	9.		Work on defensive positions continued. Second half Bty near Capt Jordan proceeded up the line. 8 rounds fired.	8.
"	10		Proceeded on leave. Work on positions in line. 20 rounds fired during day & 17 rounds on recept. One Coll.	20
			Bumps at 11.35 p.m. American officer reports 10 men into	17
"	11.		Work on defensive positions continued. Lt Daniels reports No 3 defensive position with fired shell. 20 rounds	28
"	12.		fired in retaliation. Work in line continued. 1st & 3rd Coldn. Leave. Work on positions continued.	
			ARIAL	
"	13		Work on defensive positions continued.	
"	14.		1 OR proceeded on leave. 25 rounds fired.	25.
"	15.		Lt Daniels proceeded on leave. One line well relaid.	
"	16.		Work on positions in line continued. 10 rounds fired. 1 OR proceeded on leave. Work continued on defence.	10

WAR DIARY or INTELLIGENCE SUMMARY.

Army Form C. 2118.

Place	Date	Hour	Summary of Events and Information	Remarks and references to Appendices
H.Q.	Feb 1918		Positions	
	16.			
"	17.		MG continued on defence of positions in front system.	27.
"	18.		1 Offr proceeded on leave. 27 rounds fired on retaliation.	
"	19.		MG positions continued. 1 Sgt & 2 other ranks to 34th Div School. 2 O.R's from 34 Div Mgr Coy.	
"	20.		Mortars. 18 rounds fired on enemy communications. Enemy struck gun team. 1 O.R. for 24 hrs.	18.
"	21.			15.
"	22.		MG continued on all positions. Party 6:30 from halftroops came in enemy fire. 1 O.R. left 24 hrs. on leave during "crash" by enemy M.G. gun. 34 Bomb fired in reply. Half on bombardment.	34.
"	23.		2 Again took & left by turn.	
"	24.		1 O.R. to England on leave. Defensive positions taken over by 4th Division. 38 rounds fired on retaliation.	38.

WAR DIARY or INTELLIGENCE SUMMARY.

Army Form C. 2118.

½ TMB

(Erase heading not required.)

Place	Date	Hour	Summary of Events and Information	Remarks and references to Appendices
TMB	24		Work on new O.P. commenced in front system on new front.	
"	25		Cpl Loveny returns from hospital on light duty.	
"	26		1 O.R. sent on leave. 74 rounds fired in retaliation for hostile minnies.	74
"	27		New O.P. ready for action except for runaway trench. In firing number fired 18 rounds.	18
"	28		O.R. B.T.R. fired during L.O.L. on left B.de front. Both guns out of action after firing 18 rounds. M.G. on account of Lewy heating. Total number of rounds fired. To casualties in Lachen rd. Prematures nil.	18 35 - #4

[signature] Cap RFA
O.C. ½ TMB

2nd Divisional Artillery.

"X"/2nd DIVISIONAL TRENCH MORTARS.

MARCH 1918

Army Form C. 2118.

WAR DIARY
or
INTELLIGENCE SUMMARY.
(Erase heading not required.)

X/2 T.M. Battery

March 1918

Place	Date	Hour	Summary of Events and Information	Remarks and references to Appendices
	Mar 1st		Capt H.W. Roberts M.C. posted as 2.T.M.O. & H.Q. X.T.A. - 1 o.r. proceeded to U.K. for duty. 1 o.r. returned off leave. Rounds fired. 18. Casualties Nil.	
	2		2 Beds & 1 Gas Ejector handed over to X/XXI T.M.B. 1 o.r. proceeded on leave to U.K. 3.3.18 to 17.3.18 Rounds fired. Nil. Casualties Nil.	
	3		1 o.r. Evacuated to 3rd C.C.S. Suffering P.U.O. Rounds fired. 12.	
	4		2 o.r. proceeded on leave to U.K. 5.3.18 to 19.3.18. Rounds fired 10 on ridge left of Lakagourne. Casualties Nil.	
	5		Rounds Fired 7 Casualties nil.	
	6		1 o.r. proceeded on leave to U.K. 7.3.18 to 21.3.18. 1 o.r. admitted Hospital sprained Ankle. 1 o.r. returned off leave. Rounds fired 26 Registered No.1 Gun on tank. 6 Mining Frames fired in pit. Casualties Nil.	
	7		1 o.r. returned off leave. 1 o.r. admitted Hospital Injury to Knee. Rounds fired Nil. 2 reserve positions chosen. Carried on with work at pit. 2 Guns brought from line	
	8		1 o.r. proceeded on leave to U.K. 9.3.18 to 23.3.18 Work contn on b.p. position. New reserve pit started near Dead Mans Corner. Rounds fired Nil. Casualties Nil.	
	9		Work contd on position at Shaftesbury Alley & Dead Mans Corner. Sergt & 2 men rets from School of Mortars Rounds fired Nil. Casualties Nil. 1 o.r. returned off leave.	
	10		Work Contd at Dead Mans Corner. Sub Bed laid at No.1 Pit. 1 o.r. proceeded on leave to U.K. 11.3.18 to 25.3.18 Rounds fired 40 Casualties nil.	
	11		1 o.r. returned off leave. 1 o.r. Evacuated 29th C.C.S. Injury to Knee. Gun 8 Bed fixed No.2 position 10 Rounds fired in retaliation. 9 o.r. gassed night of 11th admitted No.105 F.A.	
	12		1 o.r. Evacuated No.6 F.A. Complaint N.Y.D. 3 o.r. from D.A.C. as reinforcements. 1 o.r. ret.d off leave. Work Contd on Dead Mans Corner position. Rounds fired Nil. Casualties nil.	
	13		1 o.r. ret.d off leave. Work contd on Dead Mans Corner position. Rounds fired Nil. Casualties nil. Rounds fired 70.	
	14		1 o.r. proceeded on leave to U.K. 15.3.18 to 29.3.18. Mostyn reserve position started. Rounds fired Sick. Lieut. J.P. Grehme adm.d to Hospital Sick.	

WAR DIARY
or
INTELLIGENCE SUMMARY.

(Erase heading not required.)

Army Form C. 2118.

March 1918.

Instructions regarding War Diaries and Intelligence Summaries are contained in F.S. Regs., Part II. and the Staff Manual respectively. Title pages will be prepared in manuscript.

Place	Date	Hour	Summary of Events and Information	Remarks and references to Appendices
	Mar 15		Lieut A.D. Chalmers posted X/2 T.M.B. Work Cont⁰ on New Turn position. Rounds fired 35. Casualties nil.	
	16		1 or. ret⁰ from Hospital. 1 or. proceeded on leave to UK. M.318 t. 21.3.18. Rounds fired 35. Casualties nil. Work Cont⁰ on New Turn position. 2 Guns & Beds taken up.	
	17		1 or. proceeded on leave to UK 18/3/18 t. 1/4/18. Work cont⁰ on New Turn position. Rounds fired 15. 1 or. ret⁰ off leave. 1 or. admitted Hospital - Gas	
	18		Work cont⁰ on New Turn position. 1 or. admitted Hospital Gas. 2/Lt V.R. Waugh posted X/2 T.M.B. Rounds fired 25.	
	19		1 or. proceeded on leave to UK 20/3/18 t. 3/4/18. 1 or. ret⁰ off leave. Work Cont⁰ to New Turn position. Rounds fired 30 on Night of 18th/19th in raid. Rounds fired 19th 10. Casualties nil	
	20		1 or. ret⁰ off leave. Work Cont⁰ New Turn position. Rounds fired nil. Casualties nil	
	21		1 or. ret⁰ off leave. do. do.	
	22		Left Metz for Manancourt. Left Manancourt for Bus after destroying & burning Stores, Books, papers, maps &c	
	23		Arrived Bus - Left Bus Arrived Sailly Saillisel	
	24		Left Sailly Saillisel - Arrived Combles	
	25		Left Combles - Arrived Bazentin le petit. & reached Albert.	
	26		Left Albert - Arrived Millincourt	
	27		Arrived Hennincourt & marched to Vauchelles	
	28		Left Vauchelles - Arrived Acheux.	
	29		Arrived Varennes	
	30		Lieut A.D. Chalmers attached Y/2 T.M.B.	
	31		AT Varennes	

K.T. Stephen
Capt. X/2 S.A.

2nd Divisional Artillery.

X/2 TRENCH MORTAR BATTERY

APRIL 1918.

(7)

H.Q. 2. T. M. B. 13

Army Form C. 2118.

April 1-30

WAR DIARY
or
INTELLIGENCE SUMMARY.
(Erase heading not required.)

2 D.T.M.Bty

VK 20

Instructions regarding War Diaries and Intelligence Summaries are contained in F. S. Regs., Part II. and the Staff Manual respectively. Title pages will be prepared in manuscript.

Place	Date	Hour	Summary of Events and Information	Remarks and references to Appendices
Tavernes	1 to 3		2.6 O.K. attached D.A.C.	
do	5		Left Tavernes and marched for Bout des Joues	
Bout de Joue	6		4 O.K. rtd from leave. Left Bout des Joues and marched to Berlancourt. 1 O.K. "	
Berlancourt	7		28 O.R. returned from 2 D.A.C. to rejoin Battery	
"	8		Received from Ordnance 6 Guns 2" Beds, 6 Char Baston 6 Ebour Handed to Hq TMB 3 " 3 " 3 " 2/Lt W.J. Halletts (S.R.) 2 D.A.C. posted to H2 TMB Left Berlancourt and marched to Capelle Hamert. Lt Hallwell reported for duty 2nd Batty R.F.A.	
"	9			
Capelle Hamert	11		Left Capelle Hamert. Marched to Origny Ste Benoîte. 2/Lt W.J. Waugh accidentally injured & admitted to Hospital Left Capt B. G. Hooper 2 D.A.C. attached Hq 2 TMB	
Origny S.B.	12		Capt R. S. Stephen R.A. proceeded to bm to choose position A B & 6 Sections proceeded to br until L Coln de Bois	
do	14			

WAR DIARY
or
INTELLIGENCE SUMMARY.

Army Form C. 2118.

Place	Date	Hour	Summary of Events and Information	Remarks and references to Appendices
Asjn. L. Arbre	15		Bde Reopendro inspected at Gas Depot. D.E.&F had section practise through Gas Chamber.	
"	16		A & B Sub sections returned from divi C Section remained with Capt H.J. Elphick O. No. 1 Gun fired a Red Flare in	
			2 " " "	
			3 " " "	
"	18		D & E Sub section relieved on line under Lt. Searle "off" Bocks. 20 Rounds fired on Registration of Guns. No. 1 & 3 in H.28 A.52.93. No. 2 in H.28 C.65.65. Heavy hostile shelling of our Gun Position.	
"	19		Firing Report. 15 Rounds on H.28 C. 65.65. with excellent results. Hostile shelling of our position continued.	
"	20		Firing Report. 35 Rounds. 15 on H.28 a.53.90. 20 on H.28 C.65.65. Lewis direct hit was obtained on enemy Shelter, in trench reports by L/S. It is very strongly held. No. 1 Gun Position was damaged by a direct hit. Gr O. N/S slightly wounded.	

Army Form C. 2118.

WAR DIARY
or
INTELLIGENCE SUMMARY.
(Erase heading not required.)

Place	Date	Hour	Summary of Events and Information	Remarks and references to Appendices
Asgn St Aubyn	21		Work in improvement of position. Bent carrying etc.	
	22		Capt. R.J. Hughes R.C. asst. Shells Truff detachment proceeded to relieve the line	
			Infy Report 28 Hours at or S.28.a.55.95 got bombs in support of the	
			raid on S.28.a.55.95 and S.28.c.65.65"	
	23		Capt. H.J. Hughes R.C. wounded whilst observing Dpts of wounds late in day.	
			Lt. Daniels Y2 TMB proceeded to line to [illeg] take charge of detached guns covert.	
			left Clube. No. 2 position destroyed by hostile shelling.	
	24, 25, 26		Work in trench connecting to 3 position and Dug Out	
			New position started.	
	27, 28, 29, 30		Y2 TMB lest one forward position + K2 TMB the alternate position	
			Work in improvement of defence position.	

[signature]

"2nd Divisional Artillery.

"Y"/2nd DIVISIONAL TRENCH MORTARS

MARCH 1918

Army Form C. 2118.

WAR DIARY
or
INTELLIGENCE SUMMARY

(Erase heading not required.)

Instructions regarding War Diaries and Intelligence Summaries are contained in F. S. Regs., Part II. and the Staff Manual respectively. Title pages will be prepared in manuscript.

Place	Date	Hour	Summary of Events and Information	Remarks and references to Appendices
Metz-en-Couture	1.3.18		Lieut. A. Bowles R.I.O.R. (11th Middlesex Regt.) Posted to V/V Heavy T.M. Bty.	
"	2.		2/Lt. R.T. Daniels (S. Staffs) x 1 Gr. On leave to U.K. 14 Days.	
"	5.		Capt. Elliott W. x Coxon T. Posted to V/V Heavy T.M. Bty.	
"	"		Bdr. Naylor R x Bdr. Turton H. Promoted Corporals. vice Elliott & Coxon to V/V H.T.M. Bty.	
"	6.		1 Gr. on leave to U.K. (14 Days)	
"	8.		5 O.Rs from 3rd Army School of Mortars.	
"	9.		1 N.C.O. " " " " "	
"	10.		1 O.R. Admitted to Hospital. (Sick) 2 Gunners posted from 2nd D.A.C.	
"	12.		1 O.R. " " " " 1 " on leave to U.K. (14 Days)	
"	13.		1 O.R. Posted to V/V Heavy T.M. Bty. 1 " " " " "	
"	14.		2 " Admitted to Hospital. (Sick) 1 " " " " "	
"	16.		1 " on leave to U.K. (14 Days)	
"	17.		Captn. H.M. Foulsham. Admitted to Hospital (Sick) 1 O.R. on leave to U.K. 14 Days.	
"	19.		2/Lt. R.T. Daniels. (S. Staffs) from leave to U.K.	
"	20.			
"	21.		Opening of German offensive. 50 Rounds fired from Guns on Welsh Ridge. Rear Billet shelled heavily during morning 2 N.C.Os + 1 Gr. wounded. 1 N.C.O. sniped in the forward Area. 2 Guns on Welsh retire to Highland Ridge.	
"	22.		Trescault Line manned in morning. 2 Guns on Highland Ridge brought back to here, Rear Billets retire to Eriscourt. In the evening all Battery Stores, Ropes, Kits burned. Personnel retire on Bus v Albert. About mid-night 5 Guns in Trescault man-handled to Neuville R.H. Geos v Guys in Trescault Line destroyed & Dug outs blown up.	
"	23.		(Gun from Rear H.Q. Handed over to 5. S.A.R. Sect. 4th D.A.C. at Combles Ridge at 10.0.a.m. 5 Guns at Neuville put out of action v buried Personnel retire to Bus arriving 5.0.p.m. Joined 4th Dvn. T.M.B. Through Mesnil to wards Sailly - Saillesel. 2 O.Rs from Hosp. 4th Dvn T.M.B. Through Mesnil to wards Sailly - Saillesel lined ridge in front of Sailly-Saillesel. Roll Called v find only 25 O.Rs present. At 5.0 p.m. retire with 10 O.Rs Retired to Combles 10.0 p.m. Retired from Combles. through Guillemont, Longueval to 2nd D.A.C. H.Q. at Bazentin le Petit.	
"	24.		Leave Bazentin le Petit and retire to Albert. 2 Officers join composite Battalion on road. anchor men in Trenches all night Remainder reach Albert which is heavily bombed. Boring night by enemy aircraft.	
"	25.		Men assist in digging out civilians from ruined houses. Roll Call. 38 present 1 unaccounted for. Leave 11-0 am join No.1 Sect. D.A.C. at Hennencourt. 1 O.R. to Hospital. (Sick).	
"	26.		Leave Millencourt v join 2nd D.A.C. H.Q. at Henencourt Roll Call. 41 O.Rs present. 4 unaccounted for. March to Vauchelle. 2/Lt. G.F.H. Hamilton Wounded by Aeroplane Bomb.	
"	27.		March from Vauchelle to bivouac outside Acheux. 2 O.Rs rejoin from S.A.R. Sect. D.A.C. It appears from information gathered That 1 N.C.O. is captured & 1 Gunner wounded.	
Verennes	28.		Move to billets in Verennes.	
"	29.		1 N.C.O. v 6 Grs. Posted from D.A.C.	
"	30.		Lieut. A.O. Chalmers from X/2 T.M.B. to Y/2 T.M.B.	

A. Chalmers Capt. Y/2 T.M.B.
O.C. Y/2 T.M.B.

2nd Divisional Artillery.

Y/2 TRENCH MORTAR BATTERY

APRIL 1918.

Army Form C. 2118.

WAR DIARY or INTELLIGENCE SUMMARY

for APRIL 1918
½ T M Bty

(Erase heading not required.)

Place	Date	Hour	Summary of Events and Information	Remarks and references to Appendices
VARENNES	1/4/18		Parade & organise remainder of Bty (34 men attached to Zedu Bty) Col Jones & Dr Hayter return from leave U.K. Lt Johnstone & Dr Back.	
"	3/4/18		Parade etc.	
VARENNES - GROUCHES	5/4/18		Move from VARENNES to GROUCHES via march. 1 G.S. waggon for stores via Billets to-night.	
GROUCHES - BERLENCOURT	6/4/18		Move from GROUCHES to BERLENCOURT " " . Billets in huts	
"	7/4/18		Parade features etc.	
"	8/4/18		Bt Brunnell & Gr Dale return from leave U.K. 3 N.C.O.s & 17 O.R. report from D.A.C. 3 men 6" Newton T.M.G. 16 head arrive from Ordnance. Sawing parades etc.	
BERLENCOURT	9/4/18		Moves from BERLENCOURT to CAPELLE-FERMONT in 3 Motor Lorries remainder by new march	
CAPELLE-FERMONT	10/4/18		Lieut A.D. CHALMERS had formation (? was taken ill) mark of Capt while comdg ½ T M Bty Capt to hospital (sick) with account	
CAPELLE-FERMONT - ANZIN	11/4/18		Moved in same 3 Motor Lorries to ANZIN remainder from march.	
ANZIN	12/4/18		Lieut N. BENTON posted from 2nd D.A.C. Lieut S.V. UPHAM actg from 2nd D.A.C. Training - gun drill etc.	
"	13/4/18		2nd Lt Johnstone to hospital (sick) Gun Bata Barlow return from leave U.K. receiving warning notice to take over front E. of ARRAS	
"	14/4/18		1 officer & 20 men from 20 Mun Masses of 2nd D A at ACQ D T M O & O/C & NCO's reconnoître 3 different T M positions astride R. SCARPE	

WAR DIARY
or
INTELLIGENCE SUMMARY for APRIL 1918

Army Form C. 2118.

Place	Date	Hour	Summary of Events and Information	Remarks and references to Appendices
ANZIN	15/4/18		D,E & F Sub sections with 2/Lt DANIELS & 2/Lt UPHAM go into action constructing these defensive positions (covering Right Brigade 1st CANADIAN DIV) at H20a 58 03 H13d 6.2 and H13 t99 30. B & C sub sections provide working party on same	
"	16/4/18		5 sub sections continue work on positions	
"	17/4/18		3 positions completed & guns ready for action. C.R.A. 2nd Div inspect positions Complete telephone communications established to forward OPs	
"	18/4/18		Dumps of bombs for defensive guns arrive	
"	19/4/18		A, B & C sub-sections relieve D, E, & F	
"	20/4/18		Capt A D Chalmers adjutant report from Hospital	
"	23/4/18		D" " returns from hospital. D E & F sub sections relieve A,B, & C	
"	25/4/18		Sgt Winston " " Bn Bdes admitted to Hospital (sick)	
"	26/4/18		Bdr Harborn Kingan & Uttridge promoted Corporals. L/Bdr Collier promoted Bdr. Gnr Dix Nicholls Scott & Attwell promoted Bdrs. Gnr Attwell & Dale promoted L/Bdrs	
"	27/4/18		Started work on new position N of R. SCARPE in H16. t 45 30.	
"	28/4/18		working party 1 NCO & 5 men proceed to line to work on Nos 1 & 2 Guns	
"	29/4/18		3 No "6" NEWTON T.M & 6 beds arrive from Ordnance	
"	30/4/18		Oct Relief carried out. Working party 1 N.C.O & 5 men proceed to line to work on Nos 1 & 2 Guns	

Raymond Daniels 2/Lt
for Capt Conroy O/C T.M. Bty.

2nd Divisional Artillery.

X & Y TRENCH MORTAR BATTERIES ::: M A Y 1918.

Army Form C. 2118.

WAR DIARY for MAY 1918. (page 1)
INTELLIGENCE SUMMARY.   X/2 T.M.B.

Ref. MAP of FRANCE, sheet 51B N.W.

(Erase heading not required.)

Place	Date MAY	Hour	Summary of Events and Information	Remarks and references to Appendices
ANZIN — ST AUBIN.	1st		Work was carried out in improvement of three defensive positions in ARRAS — LENS Railway Embankment astride the RIVER SCARPE.	
	2nd		2/Lt. A. BOSWORTH attached X/2 T.M.B. from 2nd D.A.C. Handed over the three defensive positions in this sector to Y/2 T.M.B. Our detachments thus relieved returned to rear billets at CHATEAU DE LILACS, ANZIN.	
	3rd		2/Lt. TUCKER + 2/Lt. CHALKER + HESTER proceeded to line to take over GAVRELLE Sector from Y/1 Cdn.Sdn. T.M.B. Our Right Section took over active guns at ① H11a7.4 ② H10b9.9. ③B28d5.6 @B29C.06.15. while Centre Section took over defensive guns at ① H70d77 ② H8a.5.5 ③ B26b0.5. A direct hit by a 4.2 shell destroyed the gunpit and ammo recess of No 1 gun, damaging several bombs. Repairs were carried out + the No 1 gun was again put in action. No 4 gun was dismantled + the piece was brought from in front of our front line to our dugout in K TRENCH, as no supply of bombs was available.	
	4th		Six guns complete were handed over to 1st Can. T.M.B.'s at rear billet in exchange for those taken over by us in the line. 2/Lt CHALKER carried out a shoot of 36 rounds from No 2 gun in which much damage was caused to enemy trenches HOARY and HAGGARD in H6C, also 5 rounds from No 1 gun on to HYDERABAD TRENCH in H12C. Work was done in construction of ammo. recess at the 2nd Defensive gun.	
	5th		10 rounds were fired in registration of No 3 gun on enemy front line at B29d8.4. 2/Lt BOSWORTH and men of Right Section relieved the defensive detachments, + 2/Lt CHALKER + Right Section returned to Rear billets from forward positions.	
	7th		No 1 + 2 forward guns at H11a.7.4 + H10b9.9 handed over to Y/2 T.M.B.	

WAR DIARY

INTELLIGENCE SUMMARY for MAY 1918. (page 2.)

X/2 T.M.B.

Army Form C. 2118.

Place	Date MAY	Hour	Summary of Events and Information	Remarks and references to Appendices
ANZIN—ST.AUBIN	7th (cont.)		2/Lt R.M. GORRIE posted as A/CAPTAIN to X/2 T.M.B. from 71.Sg.By. R.F.A. vice CAPT. K.T. STEPHEN (died of wounds 23.4.18). CAPT. GORRIE assumed duties as O.C. 2/R.P.C.J. HAMILTON, R.F.A. attached to X/2 T.M.B. which 1/c of 2nd D.A.C. wagons allotted to 2nd Div. T.M's.	
	8th		Capt. GORRIE relieved Lt. TUCKER at forward H.Q. Work was continued on N.OH. gun position at B29.c.05.15 in getting gun into action; an O.P. was constructed in K TRENCH at B28.c.4.2.	
	9th		Forward guns in B29.c. + B28.d + one defensive gun in Railway Cutting at H2.6.b.0.5, handed over Y/15 T.M.B. Centre Section this relieved returned to Rear billets. Three guns complete were received from 15th D. iss. T.M's at Rear billets in exchange for these handed over in the line.	
	10th		2/Lt BOSWORTH + Left Section took over two active guns at (1) H11.a.7.4 (2) in SUNKEN ROAD + (2) H.10.6.99 from Y/2 T.M.B. 8 rounds fired in registration of N°1 gun; Zero-line found to be 77° True Bearing. 8 rounds fired in registration of N°2 gun on trench junction at H6.c.3.2; Zero line 78° True Bearing. Work continued on N°1 defensive gun in H7d in resetting gunpit + completing runaway traverse.	
	11th		Destructive shoot carried out at dugouts at B.C.13 9/ ROYAL SCOTS; 48 rounds fired from 2 gun with excellent effect. The newly formed loopholes in HAZARD TRENCH at H11.b.7.3. were completely destroyed. A satisfactory arrangement of Carrying parties of 50 strong every night was provided by H.6th Inf. Bde. The bed of N°2 gun was taken up + relaid more satisfactorily to work on both defensive positions was continued.	
	12th		10R was admitted to hospital with sprained ankle.	
	13th		2/Lt CHALKER proceeded to defensive positions while 2/Lt. PARTNER took over from 2/Lt. BOSWORTH of forward guns to carry out a shoot of 34 rounds in which many direct hits were obtained on a new trench dug from H12a.1.7 to H11.b.9.5. to form enemys new front-line system. Transport of bombs was arranged by Decauville tramway, but this was found unreliable, so a dump was formed	

Army Form C. 2118.

WAR DIARY for MAY 1918 (page 3)
or
INTELLIGENCE SUMMARY. X/2 T.M.B.

(Erase heading not required.)

Instructions regarding War Diaries and Intelligence Summaries are contained in F.S. Regs., Part II. and the Staff Manual respectively. Title pages will be prepared in manuscript.

Places	Date MAY	Hour	Summary of Events and Information	Remarks and references to Appendices
ANZIN — ST. AUBIN	14th (cont'd)		formed on ARRAS — GAVRELLE Road at H 3 d 8.4. 8 rounds were fired in retaliation for intermittent Minnie fire during day, and 6 rounds in registration of targets detailed for raid barrage.	
	15th		71 rounds were fired by us in support of a raid by 13th ROYAL SCOTS on H.6.c. at 3.45 a.m. Three prisoners were secured, many casualties caused to the enemy by our fire & by blowing up of dugouts by raiders. The enemy S.O.S. barrage was very poor indeed.	
	16th		Work was commenced in the construction of a twin gun position in CAM VALLEY for defence of CAROLINE — EFFIE SWITCH LINE. Increased precautions for S.O.S. arrangements were made in expectation of enemy attack on this front.	
	17th		20 rounds were fired on to new work observed in H 11 b. Lt. TUCKER relieved Capt. GORRIE at forward H.Q.	
	18th		2/Lt CHALKER & the Right Section took over at the forward guns. A shoot of 30 rounds was carried out on enemy support line in H.6.c. with fine effect, much material & sandbags being thrown up. Retaliation opened from a Minnie which was observed firing from HYDERABAD TRENCH, which was immediately engaged by us & silenced, 2 hits being obtained on its emplacement.	
	19th		10 rounds were fired at the same Minnie emplacement at H.12.a.00.01 & several hits were made.	
	20th		A destructive shoot by No 2 gun was started on HARRY TRENCH but heavy retaliation came & the pit was set on fire by a H.2 burst, the camouflage & revetting frames burning fiercely. Cpl WHITEHOUSE & his detachment climbed up on top & shovelled earth on the fire & succeeded in getting it under, after several minutes work, under Machine gun fire & the continued shell fire. It was only by the men's strenuous efforts that the fire was kept from setting the ammunition	

WAR DIARY for MAY 1918. (page 4)
INTELLIGENCE SUMMARY. X/2 T.M.B.

Army Form C.2118.

Place	Date MAY	Hour	Summary of Events and Information	Remarks and references to Appendices
ANZIN — STAUBIN	20th (contd)		ammunition alight. Talks putting the fire out the men volunteered to go on with the shoot. 46 rounds were fired and a hostile Minnie observed firing from H.6.c.70.24 was engaged, one hit on the emplacement causing a fire amongst ammunition which burned fiercely for 5 minutes. Large quantities of material were thrown up by our hits on HARRY TRENCH in H.6.c. Work on defence position in CAM VALLEY proceeding satisfactorily.	
	21st		Capt. GORRIE relieved 2/Lt TUCKER at Forward H.Q. A destructive shoot of 36 rounds was made on suspected TM E's in HYDERABAD TRENCH at H.11.b.95.05 & H.12.a.02.35 — much damage was done & large quantities of sandbags were thrown up. Two hostile T.M.s were observed while firing in retaliation & they were both engaged & silenced by a further 28 rounds. 2/Lt HESTER & Gun/Lt Section relieved the forward gun detachments, which returned to Rest billets. In a shoot of 36 rounds on a hostile T.M. observed at H.12.a.45.18 excellent shooting was made one hit on the emplacement causing a fire which shot up dense clouds of smoke for some time — presumably Minnie ammunition. There was some retaliation by a T.M. battery which shot up Sunken Road in H.11a.but which wounded Major WYE (B.M,R.A) while inspecting our gun emplacement.	
	23rd		17 rounds fired on activity observed in CHILI TRENCH - several hits raised wood &	

Army Form C.2118.

WAR DIARY for MAY 1918. (page 5)
or
INTELLIGENCE SUMMARY. X/2 T.M.B.
(Erase heading not required.)

Place	Date MAY	Hour	Summary of Events and Information	Remarks and references to Appendices
ANZIN	23rd (contd)		and revetting material. I.O.R. returned from hospital.	
ST.AUBIN	24th		A shoot was carried out at dawn in which 579 rounds were fired. 12 hits were made on a new trench dug at H6.c.90.05 & several around an M.G. Emplacement observed yesterday at H12.a.1.1. 10 rounds in addition were fired at CHILI TRENCH, of which 6 hits damaged trench. Considerable retaliation by H2 shelling of Sunken Road near 7.0.1 gun in H11a	
	25th		The following promotions were made dating from 22.5.18 :— 68661 Bdr. EDGE.T. to be Corporal; 32996 4/Bdr CATER.W.W. and 25911 4/Bdr BENTLEY.W. to be Bombardiers. 24684 a/Bdr HOWARTH.J. 170136 Gnr CLARK.A. and 96849 Gnr. TODD.H. to be 4/Bdrs. A shoot at the request of O.C. 6th BLACK WATCH was made on wire in front of HAZARD TRENCH & on M.G. emplacement at H11.b.67.27. 41 rounds were fired & the wire was effectually cut & scattered. Infantry patrols reported later that HAZARD TRENCH had been practically obliterated by our 6" Newton fire. Continued enemy shelling round 7.0.1 gun & LEMON TR.	
	26th		A shoot of 579 rounds was made in conjunction with heavy how's on HARRY TRENCH which had been recently improved — great execution was done 15 enemy new "island traverse" at H6.c.0.2. by our fire. Enemy shelled Sunken Road at 7.0.1 gun & LEMON TRENCH very heavily all day. No phone communication & ration carrying very difficult. All infantry carrying	

WAR DIARY for MAY 1918. (page 6)
INTELLIGENCE SUMMARY. X/2 T.M.B.

Army Form C. 2118.

Place	Date MAY	Hour	Summary of Events and Information	Remarks and references to Appendices
ANZIN – ST AUBIN	26th	(contd)	Carrying parties for T.M's stopped by order of G.O.C. 15th Div.	
			10 rounds fired in retaliation for Minnie fire during "Stand To" at dusk in midst of heavy H.E. shelling of Sunken Road around Gun. Detachments stood to all night in expectation of enemy attacks. Considerable mustard gas shelling of rear areas & Battery positions during night. until	
	27th	6 a.m.	657913 Corp. WHITEHOUSE A.V. awarded Military Medal for his work on 20th inst.	
	27th		Handed over both forward guns + one defensive gun at H8 a 5.5 to Y/5 Canadian T.M.B., & remaining defensive gun at H7d.77 to V/2 T.M.B. Detachments from line returned to ANZIN.	
	28th		Batting parades for gundrill in gasmasks & instruction in musketry. Details of sections re-organised. Night working party provided to work for Y/2 T.M.B. on their position in CABLE TRENCH (FAMPOUX SECTOR) 7308 Gr MAYLEN, G. wounded in leg & arm while in charge of this party. I.O.R. also admitted to hospital with synovitis. I.O.R. posted from 5th A.F.A. Bde.	
	29th 31st		Instructional parades & physical training carried out daily, and working & Carrying parties for day & night provided to assist Y/2 T.M.B. in work at CAM VALLEY & on forward positions in FAMPOUX SECTOR	

R.M. Gorrie.
Capt. R.F.A.
O.C. X/2 T.M.B.

WAR DIARY for Month of MAY 1918.

INTELLIGENCE SUMMARY ½ T.M. Battery.

No. 71

Army Form C. 2118.

Place	Date	Hour	Summary of Events and Information	Remarks and references to Appendices
ANZIN St AUBIN.	1/5/18		1 NCO & 6 men relieve sect at new poster N of R. Scarpe at H16 b 45.30 (CABLE TR.) Fired 19 rounds in registration etc from No 2 Gun (BATTERY VALLEY) on to ICELAND TR & IONIAN TR at H28a 40.50 & H28a 55.40	
"	2/5/18		Centre Sect relieves section of "X" 2 Bty. in Defensive positions & Left Sect takes over forward positions in BATTERY VALLEY. Fire 18 rounds in registration etc of No 1 Gun (BATTERY VALLEY) on to ICELAND & IONIAN TRS. at H28a 40.50 & H28a 55.40. Battery Hq moves forward into RAILWAY TRIANGLE at H19 a 20.30	
"	3/5/18		40 rounds fired on ICELAND & IONIAN TRS. with No 1 & No 2 Gun several direct hits were observed from O.P. at H20 C 90.85.	
"	4/5/18		40 Rds fired from No 1 & 3 Guns so on previous day. Receive orders to evacuate 2 positions in BATTERY VALLEY owing readjustment of Divl boundaries. All Guns Ammunition etc removed to Bty H.Q.	
"	5/5/R. 6/5/18		Mens billets & Rear HQ moved to C150 Road to ANZIN. Intersection relief carried out. 60 rounds of Ammo taken to CAM VALLEY Dump.	
"	7/5/18		Centre Section take over 2 Guns N of R. Scarpe from X & Bty. Coordinates of guns {H 10 b 88.90 1 Officer 2 NCO & 15 men 28 min 3 horses & G.S. Wagon attached from 2 Dac. {H19 a 65.35.
1 hangin't Limber
B^t NICHOLLS J awarded MM for devotion to duty on 22.4.18.	

Army Form C. 2118.

WAR DIARY for MAY 1918.
or INTELLIGENCE SUMMARY
(Erase heading not required.)

Place	Date	Hour	Summary of Events and Information	Remarks and references to Appendices
ANZIN St AUBIN.	10/5/18		X2 Bty takes over 2 forward guns again at H10 b 88 90 & H11 a 65 35. Inter sec relief carried out. 1 O.R. to hospital (sick) Right Sect. Continue work in continuous shifts on CABLE TR position dugout.	
"	11/5/18		Reconnoitre Spares H22 a + b for positions for 3 guns for special gas shoot	
"	13/5/18		610 Railway Cutting in H23 a + b Commence work on temporary positions for special shoots Aug/5/18 at H22 b 50 35. 3 Guns complete 160 rounds one standard at CAM VALLEY for these above positions	
"	14/5/18		Inter green relief carried out. Log kept at forward positions in DINGWALL TR. 35 Inter gunners camo Buss + motored from CAM VALLEY to DINGWALL TR for Special Shoot. 66 Waggoners Camp 60 rounds of ammunition from CAM VALLEY & DINGWALL TR round guns + final preparations for shoot by 3 guns on night of 17th	
"	15/5/18			
"	16/5/18		1 O.R reports to OC Central Workshops St Pol	
"	17/5/18	2 am to 4 am	3 Special Guns at H22 b 55 90 & H22 b 45 35 (DINGWALL TR) Shoot on RAILWAY Cutting No 1 Spec firs 20 rds on H23 c 5 9. No 2 Spec firs 17 rds on H23 b 65 35. No 3 Spec firs 20 rds on H23 c 7 8. First 5 rounds from each fused with instantaneous remainder with delay fuses. Infantry observers report good bursts in the cutting and causing very heavy to be put up by the enemy. Spanning mortars opened in relation of nearer were undoubtedly obtained	

2449 Wt. W14957/Mg0 750,000 1/16 J.B.C. & A. Forms/C.2118/12.

WAR DIARY for Month of MAY, 1918.

INTELLIGENCE SUMMARY

Place	Date	Hour	Summary of Events and Information	Remarks and references to Appendices
ANZIN St	17/5/18		Contd. Immediately behind the guns. A good deal of annoyance was, it is certain, caused to the enemy.	
AUBIN	18/5/18		In action relief carried out. I.O.R on leave to UK (special) 19/5/18 to 2/6/18	
"	20/5/18		New position at H17a 90.90 CAMEL TRENCH Commenced	
"	21/5/18		I.O.R on special leave to UK 22/5/18 to 5/6/18	
"	22/5/18		Inter Sec Relief Carried out. Subsec 3 taken to CAMEL TR position	
"	24/5/18		Dr Chapple & Sgt Davis promoted Bomdr.	
"	26/5/18		1 Gun at Defensive position H17d 68.69 taken over from "X2" Bty "B" Bty now mans 4 Defensive gun positions. Subsec relief carried out	Total No of Rds fired during Month: 2044.
"	27/5/18		2 New Defensive positions in CAM VALLEY Commenced Amn sent up to the 2 New Def Positions in CAM VALLEY. 1 Lt Hcd + 2 beds	
"	28/5/16		12 men of X2 Bty Car 8 boxes from CASTLE DUMP to CAMEL TR position 5 men of X2 Bty work on CAM VALLEY positions No 1 Def Guns at H20 a 48.05 dismantled	
"	29/5/18		VALLEY Defensive positions X2Bty providing ammunition handover to CPH. Hand over Def Guns at H17d 68.69. Handed over 3 Y/s CTMB, on reallotment of front over Def Gun. No 1 Def Gun 3 CAMVALLEY Continues	
"	30/5/18		Work of transferring ammunition from 4/5CTMB to replace one taken over in line Durin/ Gun. Complete from 4/5CTMB to replace one taken over on CABLE TR position 2 Gets have been in action above while one is resting at ANZIN	
"	31/5/18		During month Canteens work has proved a great success	

Raymond Daniels 2/Lt
W.O.C 1/5 T.M Bty

2nd Divisional Artillery.

X & Y TRENCH MORTAR BATTERIES ::: JUNE 1918.

Army Form C. 2118.

WAR DIARY of X/2 T.M.B.

INTELLIGENCE SUMMARY for JUNE, 1918.

(Erase heading not required.)

Ref: Map:- FRANCE 1/20,000
Sheet 51b NW.

Vol 22

Place	Date JUNE	Hour	Summary of Events and Information	Remarks and references to Appendices
ANZIN — ST AUBIN	1st/7th		The battery personnel was employed in providing working & carrying parties for Y/2 T.M.B. Day & night shifts worked on the construction of a dugout position in CABLE TRENCH positions under construction at CAMEL TRENCH & in SCARPE VALLEY & defence positions in CAM VALLEY.	
	8th		The battery relieved Y/2 T.M.B. in the FAMPOUX sector. Taking over the following positions. Active guns at H.22.a.13.70 ("A2") & H.16.b.95.95 ("A4"), position under construction at H.16.b.48.30 (A3), & defence guns at H.16.b.60.45 ("B1" & "B2"), H.13.d.55.20 ("C1") & H.13.b.95.20 ("C2") with battery H.Q. at Railway Embankment at H.13.b.85.20. 2/Lts BOSWORTH & PARTNER with D, E & F Subs took over the forward guns while 2/Lt Chalkin with A, B & C Subs took the defensive guns. Registration of A2 gun was made with 8 rounds on the Railway Cutting at H.22.d.30.20 for S.O.S. & also for raid covering fire. Observation was done from PERU TRENCH. 2/Lt J.P.GAME returned to duty from hospital.	
	9th		50 rounds were fired from A2 gun at 1.30 a.m. as covering fire for raid by 6th Camerons on posts in Junction south of FEUCHY COPSE — no identifications were obtained. The enemy carried out a raid on THE SNOUT at 2.30 a.m. & shelled back areas with gas — being both Green Cross & Yellow Cross. Corporal EDGE was slightly gassed.	

Army Form C. 2118.

WAR DIARY

of X/2 T.M.B.

INTELLIGENCE SUMMARY. for JUNE, 1918.

(Erase heading not required.)

Place	Date	Hour	Summary of Events and Information	Remarks and references to Appendices
ANZIN – ST AUBIN	9th (contd)		Work was commenced on "A1" position at H 22 a 10.72, the site being in the floor of a line hut whose roof was protected by a layer of chalk rubble.	
	10th		8 rounds fired in registration on junction of INDIAN TRENCH & the Railway Cutting – shoot curtailed owing to enemy balloons going up. Dr DONNACHIE admitted to hospital with injury to knee caused by falling chalk in mining work.	
	11th		24 rounds fired from A2 at dawn – 14 direct hits observed on Railway Cutting where much movement is reported. A second shoot was carried out at stand-to of 21 rounds of which 10 fell in the Cutting & 5 on INVERNESS TRENCH. Corporal Gates & men proceeded to 1st Army School of Mortars for a Course. Carrying parties were provided nightly by Y/2 Bty. to assist in removing chalk spoil from the "A3" dugout workings. 2/Lt. C.T. HAMILTON (attached as i/c DAC personnel attached to TMs) was transferred to 2nd Div. ARP	
	12th		A shoot was carried out from A4 gun during the heavy morning mist – 26 rounds were fired – 16 rounds were cutting on new enemy wire in front of his CAMEL SAP & 20 rounds on the QUARRY at H 18 a 20.40 of which effect could not be observed. Another shoot of 20 rounds was made at 3.15 p.m. from A2 gun during the barrage for a daylight raid carried	

WAR DIARY

INTELLIGENCE SUMMARY of X/2 T.M.B. for JUNE 1918.

(Erase heading not required.)

Army Form C. 2118.

Place	Date JUNE	Hour	Summary of Events and Information	Remarks and references to Appendices
ANZIN-	13th (cont.)		out by us South of FEUCHY. Excellent shooting was obtained on various points in the Cutting	
ST AUBIN	13th		13 rounds were fired in retaliation on active T.M at H.23.C.9090 which was silenced by our fire. The dug out at A3 position was finished & the subbed was laid. Our supply of bombs was cut down to 20 per diem owing to a shortage in the supply.	
	14th		The subsections were interchanged A B & C Subs going to forward positions & D & F coming back to the defence guns. The following changes were made amongst our Officers:- Lieut S.C. TUCKER posted to 1/1 T.M.B. 2/Lt J.F. GAME & 1/F PARTNER transferred from the Bty & 1/1 T.M.B. Lieut F. SUGDEN posted from 1/2 to this bty as second in command. 2/Lt B.G. HESTER posted to this bty from 1- attached	
	15th		To provide a supply of ammunition 50 rds from each of the defence guns were transferred to the active guns, leaving 150 rds per gun at the defence positions. Wirecutting at request of the infantry was carried out. 15 rds were fired on wire on PAMPOUX- GAVRELLE road in H17.b while 11 rds were fired in trenches in rear to "camouflage" the wirecutting. The effect on the wire was uncertain owing to the long grass but the battalion commander would not allow enough shooting to ensure an early accurate destruction of the wire in case it should arouse the enemy's suspicions. A destructive shoot of 23 rds was fired from A2 gun	

WAR DIARY
INTELLIGENCE SUMMARY.

of X/2 T.M.B. for JUNE, 1918.

Army Form C. 2118.

Place	Date	Hour	Summary of Events and Information	Remarks and references to Appendices
ANZIN-	JUNE			
	15th (contd)		from the usual targets south of the SCARPE — one round caused a fire of ammunition or camouflage in the cutting – the flames rose along a stretch of 60 yards & burned fiercely for several minutes.	
SEAUSIN	16th		A shoot was begun from A4 gun but on the first round retaliation by M.G.'s on & around the pit started, so the shoot was discontinued until the afternoon. The G.O.C. 4th inf Bde. asked for further wirecutting to be done "surreptitiously." 23 rds were fired of which 12 fell in & around enemy wire in front of CAMEL SAP & remainder did considerable damage to wire & ZION TRENCH. The O.P. for this shoot was established in STOKES SUPPORT TRENCH. 41 rounds were fired from A4 as covering fire for raid by 8th Seaforths in evening just in CAMEL TRENCH. The raiders were held up by wire hidden in the long grass, but the 4th/5th Black Watch obtained identifications on the left.	
	17th		The A3 gun was registered with 11 rounds on a house in FAMPOUX. O.P. for this gun being selected near FAMPOUX CHURCH. 13 rds fired from A2 as retaliation on hostile T.M. fire at 11 pm – Our fire silenced the enemy. Lieut SUGDEN relieved CAPT. GARRIE at the Bty. Forward H.Q. 2 O.R's posted from 2nd D.A.C.	
	18th		Wirecutting in H.17.b was carried out with 22 rds from A3 gun, result was uncertain owing to the long grass. 2/Lts CHALKER & HESTER returned from leave to ANZIN-	

Army Form C. 2118.

WAR DIARY
or
INTELLIGENCE SUMMARY.
(Erase heading not required.)

of X/7th T.M.B. for JUNE, 1918.

Instructions regarding War Diaries and Intelligence Summaries are contained in F. S. Regs., Part II. and the Staff Manual respectively. Title pages will be prepared in manuscript.

Place	Date	Hour	Summary of Events and Information	Remarks and references to Appendices
ANZIN - ST AUBIN	19th		Retaliation of 12 rds fired from A2 against enemy T.M. active + wirecutting observed + continued from A2 during afternoon. 10 rds fired from A2 on M.G. spotted firing from the bank of cutting - one rd fell in the M.G. emplacement + caused considerable fire.	
	20th		The battery was relieved by X/115 T.M.B., all the guns in the forward H.Q. being handed over. The relief was completed by 8 pm.	
	21st		2 men evacuated to Base as sick from 6th Army School of Mortars.	
ST AMAND	22nd		Inspection parades, refitting of clothing + equipment + fatigues of cleaning up billets. The battery moved from ANZIN to ST AMAND. The A.D.C. wagons left at 9 am. + remainder of bty moved in motor lorries (provided by VI Corps) through DAINVILLE + 6A C.A.V.C. H/E. The men were billeted in barns.	
	23/24th		Epidemic of "P.U.O." influenza started - 4 men admitted to hospital. The D.T.M.O. fell sick leaving Col. CURRIE to act as D.T.M.O. in his place.	
	25th		Battery commanders went forward to reconnoitre the positions held by 31st Div T.M.B's preparatory to taking over :- V Bty on the right from BLAHNZEVILLE SANETTE. X Bty from AVETTE to MOYENNEVILLE on the front held by 2nd Div. infantry.	
BERLES - AU BOIS	26th		Bty moved from ST AMAND to near billets for the line at BERLES-AU-BOIS to relieve	

WAR DIARY
of X/7 T.M.B.

INTELLIGENCE SUMMARY. JUNE 1918.

(Erase heading not required.)

Army Form C.2118.

Instructions regarding War Diaries and Intelligence Summaries are contained in F. S. Regs., Part II. and the Staff Manual respectively. Title pages will be prepared in manuscript.

Place	Date	Hour	Summary of Events and Information	Remarks and references to Appendices
BERLES AU BOIS	26th (cont)		X/31 T.M.B. at L gun position in COIEUL VALLEY at F5.a.95.80 (ref map FRANCE Edition 5 7d N.E.) & 2 defence guns in open at F8.a.60.10. covering the PURPLE LINE. Bty H.Q. in MONCHY-AU-BOIS. The ammunition was in a disgraceful state & much damp.	
	27th		Work on the unfinished dugout was started at the forward position. Moving forward ammunition were taken up at night — (some men getting up to the actual position.) 5 men went feet to Y/7 Bty. Same third defensive guns - Y Bty. having only 13 men fit for duty owing to the P.U.O. epidemic.	
	28th		3 men went to hospital. 3 men returned from 1st Army Cal Mary School	
	29th		2 Hendes fired in registration & S.O.S. lines from Infantry post — Great difficulty was experienced with the old Pattern fuzes (leading + snapping off. Capt. GORRIE accompanied the front to the left as far as BOIRY ST MARTIN for new positions. 2/Lt HESTER admitted to hospital with P.U.O. — 14 men now in hospital.	
	30th		Bdr. Head attached to 36- Bde R.F.A. for discipline whilst in the line. Gr. BROWN remanded for F.G.C.M. by Col Goschen 258	

R.W. Gorrie
Capt. R.F.A.
O.C. X/7 T.M.B.

A6945. Wt. W14422/M1160. 35,000 12/16. D. D. & L. Forms/C./2118/14.

WAR DIARY or INTELLIGENCE SUMMARY

Army Form C. 2118.

for MONTH of JUNE 1918

Y/2 1 M.Bde

2nd Divisional Artillery

Place	Date	Hour	Summary of Events and Information	Remarks and references to Appendices
ANZIN ST AUBIN	1/6/18		New Gun position at H32a 10.70 reconnoitred & taken to this position on the Riverside. Defensive Action continue work on Reserve position in CAM VALLEY. 1 sub sec, bed & mortar	
	2/6/18		Work on new RIVERSIDE position commenced by converting old 9.2" How gun pit. Work on CAM VALLEY Gun positions continued. 1.O.R to hospital	
	3/6/18		Left Section relieves Right Section at Defensive positions WORK on CAM VALLEY Right " " " Centre " " " forward	
			RIVERSIDE positions continued	
	5/6/18	11ᵃᵐ to 6ᵃⁿ 8ᵃᵐ	21 Rounds fired from No 2 (CAMEL TR) Position. This shoot was in registration of a new Gun. Co-operation was arranged with 4.5" How forward section who fired a few rounds on each of the targets engaged. Fire the RED HOUSE at H33a 4.3.4 was registered, several hits being obtained was then brought to bear into QUARRY at H33a 3.4. Enemy retaliated briskly with M guns only on Roof Line and PORT TRENCH. ½ OR returns from half an hour! Defensive officers HQ moved to CAROLINE TR dugout OR returns from leave U.K.	
	6/6/18	10 pm to 8.30 pm	He Rounds fired from new position at H33a 10.70 (RIVER) onto RAILWAY CUTTING in H33C and INDIAN TR at H33C 35.60. 22 direct hits on the cutting were observed from OPs for PERU TR and CAM AVENUE. A Minnie at H33C 40.60 was silenced after	

Army Form C. 2118.

[Stamp: 2nd Divisional Artillery]

WAR DIARY
or
INTELLIGENCE SUMMARY

(Erase heading not required.)

for JUNE 1918.   1/2 T.M.B.

Place	Date	Hour	Summary of Events and Information	Remarks and references to Appendices
ANZIN ST AUBIN	1/6/18		O.P.'s allotted during for Guns ("B") in CAM VALLEY O.P. in EFFIE TR. & CAM AV. Forward Liaison Officer moved HQ to CAROLINE TR Dugout. 1 O.R. returns from leave to U.K.	
"	11/6/18 10pm to 11:30pm		One O.R. wounded from RIVERSIDE GUN into RAILWAY CUTTING in H32 & H23C. This shell was carried out to shaping & was very successful 20 rounds were observed 6 fell exiting & hostile Minnies commenced retaliation from H23C but were silenced after firing 4 rounds each. The forward HQ is connected by phone an & buried cable to Battery HQ & also to Guns (reserve) in CAM VALLEY. Whole battery return to Billets	
	3/6/18		X/2 T.M.BK. relieve forward reserve sections A 1/2 BK & 1M Co. + 2 men remaining behind at gun at H32 & 10.70 to H22 in & rd by 6th CAMERON H 15 NCO's & men. Go forward for 8 hours work in line for X/2 Bk. Back O.5 N.COs & men work at X Bk positions supplying sandbags at CABLE TR position.	
	5/6/18 6/6/18		Box Respirators worn by all ranks for hour for test purposes. 1.N.Co to hospital – O.R. Captn. A.D.CHALMERS proceeds to ORDNANCE COLLEGE WOOLWICH.	
	11/6/18		16 N.CO's & men working party for X Bk. on the line. N.Co + 4 men proceed to ARMY School of M.G.R. thru CLARQVES.	
	14/6/18 15/6/18		17 N.CO's & men working party for X Bk with line. Lieut S.C.TUCKER (24/RF) posted to 28 N.CO's & men working for X B4 on line on 8 hours. Lieut E. SUGDEN posted to 6 x B4. Command 1/2 B4 with much of actual Captain. Lieut J.F.PARTNER RFA add'd to Y B4. posted from X B4 to Y B4. 2 LIEUT F. PARTNER RFA add'd Y B4. 2LIEUT J.P.GAME RFM	

Army Form C. 2118.

WAR DIARY for MONTH JUNE 1918.
or
INTELLIGENCE SUMMARY
(Erase heading not required.)

Y/2 T.M.B.

Stamp: 2nd Divisional Artillery

Instructions regarding War Diaries and Intelligence Summaries are contained in F. S. Regs., Part II. and the Staff Manual respectively. Title Pages will be prepared in manuscript.

Place	Date	Hour	Summary of Events and Information	Remarks and references to Appendices
ANZIN S? AUBIN	15/6/18		27 N.C.O's men working parties for X Bty in line	
	16/6/18		12 M.C.O's	
	17/6/18		Gns. BECK & NEWMAN report as reinforcements from 2nd D.A.C. L/Bdr. CAIN wounded to hospital. 13 NCO's men work for X Bty in the line	
	18/6/18		13 NCO's men work for Y Bty attached for discipline to 4/d R.F.A. while out of the line to 2nd D.A.C. Powers of Bty. Commander delegated powers to O.C. Y. Bty.	
	19/6/18		13 NCO's men work for X Bty in line	
	20/6/18		1 O.R. to hospital sick	
	21/6/18		20 as 15th army L/M admitted hospital sick	
	20/6/18		2nd Div T.M.B. relieved by 15th Div T.M.B. Y Bty being out of action not affected. From ANZIN to ST AMAND in 17 Motor Lorries + 4 G.S. wagons for the personnel	
ANZIN — AUBIN — ST.AMAND	22/6/18		from ANZIN to ST.AMAND Moved c/o of 2/4 Bty's	
ST AMAND.	23/6/18		1 O.R. hospital sick	
	24/6/18		2 LIEUT. J.P. GAME admitted hospital sick. 9 O.R. admitted hospital sick CAPT. S.C. TUCKER admitted hospital injured. 6 O.R's to hospital sick. Receive warning order to move & take over from 31st Div T.M.B.- Reconnoitre line AYETTE - ABLAINZEVILLE.	
	25/6/18		in 6 G.S. wagons	
ST.AMAND — BERLES-AU-BOIS and MONCHY-AU-BOIS.	26/6/18		Move to BERLES-AU-BOIS & MONCHY-AU-BOIS. in 6 G.S. wagons Y/31 Bty relieved Y/31 in line taking over 4 Howard guns & forward HQ at F.10.b.30.00. and 2 Reserve guns at ESSARTS at F.13.c.00.60 & also Bty HQ at MONCHY-AU-BOIS Take over WAGON LINES at BERLES-AU-BOIS. 2 Defensive Guns manned temporarily by a detachment of X Bty owing to shortage of personnel in Y Bty Take over 6 MORTARS 13 hels & 5 Adhesa from Y/31 T.M.B. 474 Rounds fired by 4 mortars in 2 efforts of barrage + patrol at 2.a.m. 5 O.R. to hospital sick. 2 O.R. from hospital	

WAR DIARY or INTELLIGENCE SUMMARY

Army Form C. 2118.

for MONTH of JUNE 1918.

Stamp: 2nd Divisional Artillery

Y/2 TMB

(4)

Place	Date	Hour	Summary of Events and Information	Remarks and references to Appendices
MONCHY-AU-BOIS	27/6/18		Telephone Communication established between Bde HQ & Forward HQ via D/36th Bde R7A. 2/Lieut J.C. GAME returns from hospital. 3 O.R. for School of Musketry. 3 O.R. admitted hospital sick.	
"	28/6/18		Wire O.P. at ANT LANE. 40 rounds of ammunition fired by No. 1 & 2 Guns at F16 b 4 8	
	29/6/18		Fire 40 rounds - with No.1 Gun at F16 b 40 70 + No.4 Gun at F11 c 60.90. To various ark posts & sunken road at F9a 53 in shaping line 3 good hits were obtained. 8 Rounds with No.1 & 7 Rds with No.4 registering new S.O.S. targets at F17 d 1.4 & F17 c 95.95. 8 Rds with No.1 Gun put were at F17 c 60.11 & F23 a 48.34. Both guns bde became out of action and were cutting shoot had to be abandoned for the day. 3 Beds & 2 outhers in sunken road at F10 b 50.10 were pulled out. Sea-rampage & brushes used for the 18 lost guns. 6 O.R. return from hospital.	
	30/6/18		Fire 54 Rounds from No.1 & No.4 guns Both Sets burning new places re-regulation. Carried out with 8 round heygen on Sunken point at F17 c 85.35. S.O.S. line at F17 d 1.5 & F17 c 95.95 (SUNKEN ROAD)	

Con.to

[Stamp: 2nd Divisional Artillery]
Y/2 TMB

WAR DIARY
INTELLIGENCE SUMMARY
for Month of JUNE 1918

Army Form C. 2118.

(Erase heading not required.)

Place	Date	Hour	Summary of Events and Information	Remarks and references to Appendices
MONCHY- AU-BOIS	30/6/18		Was then checked until it reached the Gun. 60 rounds were then fired and were at F17c 6.4 & F23a 5.5 also into HOSTILE CAMP in F17 & F23. These targets were allotted by the 1st R. Berks who wished one gun of the Coy to assist. The wire was much damaged by our fire. Very good effect was observed on the Camp and a very violent explosion caused in one of the huts. 4 of the enemy ran across the open from one hut to another just towards the Camp. Our outposts which had two been damaged were known to be out to the Infantry concerned. 40 rounds sent to forward guns. 19 R. returns from hospital. Total Number of Rounds fired in month = 231. No. of days in action = 12. Average firing per day = 19.25.	

Raymond D. Webb
Lt 100 Y/2 TM By
2/7/18

2nd Divisional Artillery.

X & Y TRENCH MORTAR BATTERIES ::: JULY 1918.

WAR DIARY
of X/2 T.M.B.
INTELLIGENCE SUMMARY
(Erase heading not required)

Army Form C. 2118.

JULY, 1918.

Ref. Maps: FRANCE 1:20,000
57C SE
57d NE
57b SW
57C NW

Place	Date	Hour	Summary of Events and Information	Remarks and references to Appendices
BERLES-au-BOIS	JULY 1st		Battery in action on AVETTE—MOYENNEVILLE front. A Section relief was carried out in daylight.	
	2nd		A shoot of 50 rounds was carried out on the AVETTE-MOYENNEVILLE road in A.1.b. — three "outly hole" shelters were knocked in + that timber thrown up. 2 O.R's admitted to hospital with "Spanish Flue".	
	3rd		A new forward position on the Left Bde front at 57.26.C.15.20 in a bank near BOIRY ST. MARTIN aerodrome, also a new defence position (covering the PURPLE LINE) at X.27.b.30.40 were selected. Two mortars were taken from the main position to the new defence position in F.S.B 15 the newly selected position, the two defence mortars were taken from the present position at F8.a.50.10 (near LITTLE FARM) to the new position at ADINFER BANK (X.27.b).	
	4th		2/Lt. J.W. SCHALKER admitted to hospital. 3 O.R's returned to duty from hospital. 2/Lt. B.G. Heald was evacuated to Base.	
	5th		The new guns on Left Bde front ("AX 3" and "AX 4") were registered on various points of AERODROME TRENCH in A.8.a and A.2.d. — The O.P. selected was in DART LANE at A.2.a 35.70.	
	6th		The C.R.A. 2nd Div. visited the various gun positions & witnessed a short shoot from the O.P. A section relief was carried out. 2/Lt. R.A. BOSWORTH went to forward guns & Lt. SUGDEN relieved Capt. GORRIE at H.Q. 102 rounds were expended in night firing at request of 2nd S. STAFFS on troublesome M.G's, + in destructive shoots on AERODROME TR. and M.G. Emplacement at A.7.b.90.95. — Several O.K's on their targets.	

Army Form C. 2118.

WAR DIARY
of X/2 T.M.B.
INTELLIGENCE SUMMARY. JULY, 1918.

(Erase heading not required.)

Place	Date	Hour	Summary of Events and Information	Remarks and references to Appendices
BERLES au BOIS	JULY 7th		A shoot of 229 rounds was carried out on the junction of enemy front line & the road in A3a. There was retaliation by 4.2's on the gunposition but the shoot was continued, when its gun was overheated with firing gunpit. The charge of one bomb caught alight & blazed up while still in the loaders hands, burning him severely. The grass on the bank in front of the gun also caught fire & caused considerable smoke. The detachment behaved very coolly & promptly in extinguishing it.	
	8th		The Battery HQ. was moved from MONCHY to its dugout evacuated by the 48th Siege RFA in ROTTEN RAVINE. A report was forwarded on the faulty shooting experienced when using the present supply of 5th Charge Cordite bags. An effective shoot of 64 rounds was carried out, obtaining many good hits on AERODROME TR in A8a & also a small trench at F12a6.8.	
	9th		Gnr BROWN M was awarded 28 days F.P. No 2 by F.G.C.M. 2 O.R's returned from hospital.	
	10th		A temporary position was constructed in a disused trench in AYETTE village at F11b05.85. 2 reinforcements joined from 2nd D.A.C.	
	11th		A section relief was carried out. Capt. GORRIE relieved Lt. SUGDEN at H.Q.	
			A shoot of 140 rounds was made from the new AYETTE gun, cutting wire in front of enemy outpost line at A12b65.65. His concertina wire was effectually scattered. The O.P. for this zone was in AYETTE hedge at F5d65.65. 1/2 Bty carried out an experimental shoot	

Army Form C. 2118.

WAR DIARY
of X/2 T.M.B.
INTELLIGENCE SUMMARY. JULY, 1918. (3)

(Erase heading not required.)

Instructions regarding War Diaries and Intelligence Summaries are contained in F. S. Regs. Part II, and the Staff Manual respectively. Title pages will be prepared in manuscript.

Place	Date	Hour	Summary of Events and Information	Remarks and references to Appendices
BERLES	JULY			
au-BOIS	11th		with the "spade" pattern of improvised mobile bed.	
	12th		A shoot of 60 rounds was carried out on New work in AERODROME TR in A3a + A2d - several good hits on the desired points of suspected dugout building - also on registration of the new shell hole trench at A2c 90.50 + the derelict R.F.A. limber at A2b 20.10.	
			2/Lt SUGDEN went on Special leave.	
	13th		A shoot of 30 rounds was made on the T.M. emplacement in the COURCELLES-ADETTE road at F/12c 96.35.	
			a fire was caused which smoked for about 10 minutes + several O.Ks were registered.	
	14th		39 rounds were fired on A17d as covering fire for a raid by 1st K.Rings on posts in F17c + 9 prisoners were caught with very light casualties to the raiders.	
			The ammunition was cleared from the disused defence position at LITTLE FARM + removed to the ADINFER position where the guns have been put ready for action.	
	15th		30 rounds were fired on a M.G. Emplacement at A18.1.6 + on wire at F6c. The 24th R.F's objected to our guns firing on their front. The ammunition allotment was reduced to 400 rounds per Division per week.	
	16th		A shoot of HA rounds was carried out on the newly constructed loopholes in the parapet of AERODROME TR at A8a 95.95. A Boch carrying a blue flag was chased from the parapet	

A6945 Wt. W14422/M1160 35,000 12/16 D. D. & L. Forms/C/2118/14.

WAR DIARY

of X/2.T.M.B. JULY 1918. (4)

INTELLIGENCE SUMMARY.

(Erase heading not required.)

Army Form C. 2118.

Place	Date	Hour	Summary of Events and Information	Remarks and references to Appendices
POMMIER	JULY 16th		one loophole was destroyed & the contour of the parapet changed in several places	
	17th		The Trench Mortar Wagon was moved from ISERLES-au-BOIS to POMMIER. 61 rounds were expended in retaliation at night on the enemy using a 3" Stokes mortar, & in destructive shooting. Sandbags were thrown up from the trench in A3a. A Bosch was seen clearing from A8a 95.95 - 10 direct hits were made on this point. 1 hive was thrown up from the junction of the C.T. with AFRODROME TR at A8a 90.75. A section relief was carried out, 2 signallers were located from 2nd A on Centre Bolefont	
	18th		highfiring was carried out on 2 M.G.s which had been troubling out wiring parties - this was effected in silencing them entirely. The enemy carried out a gas bombardment of RIVETTE TDo UCHY at dawn. Ammunition allotment received 8. 1200 per Division for week.	
	19th		2/Lt RARTNER relieved 2/Lt BOSWORTH in the line. 38 rounds were fired in retaliation at night at request of 2nd H.L.I, ten new work spotted in AERODROME TR.	
	20th		Nightfiring was carried out on troublesome MGs on the left of Bolefont.	
	21st		69 rounds were expended in a destructive shoot. A Bosch was bolted from A7 b 00.95. + infantry observers reported 3 stretcher cases being taken from this point immediately. stopped firing. Considerable damage was done to AERODROME TR. in sweeping 16	

Army Form C. 2118.

WAR DIARY
of X/2 T.M.B.
INTELLIGENCE SUMMARY. JULY 1918.
(Erase heading not required.)

Instructions regarding War Diaries and Intelligence Summaries are contained in F. S. Regs., Part II. and the Staff Manual respectively. Title pages will be prepared in manuscript.

Place	Date	Hour	Summary of Events and Information	Remarks and references to Appendices
	JULY			
POMMIER	21st		Whole length throughout, A8a, A8b, A2b + A3a - direct hits on it at many points.	
	22nd		Section relief was carried out. 92 rounds were shot on the usual targets on the T.M. emplacement at F12c9.5.5. Good shooting was obtained.	
	23rd		Retaliation was asked for by Left Batt. for enemy area strafe on our front line.	
	24th		A M.G. was spotted firing at our planes from A2d 30.20. A direct hit was obtained by our first round + a Boche body was thrown up amongst the debris. 67 rounds were fired on this + the favourable targets.	
	25th		106 rounds were fired - partly in night firing on front, some MGs at request of 17th R.F.'s - this was effective in silencing them - + partly in a destructive shoot on A2a where the trench was knocked about by our bombs.	
	26th		55 rounds were fired on different points in AERODROM F.T.R. where trouble was troublesome by our bursts. The enemy raided the front line near our AX 3rd position at night but he obtained no identification + the Boche officer was killed.	
			A complimentary report on the work of the two 6" Newton batteries was received from the G.O.C. 2nd Div. praising out good work + keenness.	
	27th		Section relief. Lt. BOSWORTH relieved Lt. RAETNER forward. 31 rds were fired on A3a.	

Army Form C. 2118.

WAR DIARY
of X/2 T.M.B.
INTELLIGENCE SUMMARY. JULY 1, 1913. (6)
(Erase heading not required.)

Place	Date	Hour	Summary of Events and Information	Remarks and references to Appendices
POMMIER	JULY 28th		All rounds were fired in registration for a forthcoming shoot on new work (a suspected O.P.) in AERODROME TR. Several good O.K's were registered in a destructive shoot.	
	29th		A shoot of 40 rounds at dawn was carried out. The first round scattered a dozen Boches who were looking over the parapet & heavy timber + duck boards were thrown up from the junction of the C.T. + AERODROME TR. at A8 & 70 75".	
	29th/30th		116 rounds were fired from 3 guns on MOYENNEVILLE ROAD in F6 c + A1 d in support of the raid by 15th Kings on enemy pk. in F1 b a. O.C. Kings reported that there was no M.G. fire at all during the raid + that this was chiefly due to the 6" Howitzer fire. 5 prisoners were obtained.	
			At dawn a 40 round shoot was carried out. The Boches stayed standing - 10 were killed by our first round + the shape of the parapet was changed in 5 places by our bombs.	
	31st		10 m.e. from D.A.C. were attached for working under R.E's in construction of a new battery H.Q. dugout behind DOUCHY at F 3 a 60.40.	
			Night firing was carried out on M.G's in F1 b c + A 7 b. Total rounds fired by the battery during JULY = 1481 rounds.	

R.W. Gozzard
Capt. R.F.A.
O.C. X/2 T.M.B.

2nd Divisional Artillery

WAR DIARY For July 1918.
or
INTELLIGENCE SUMMARY

Y/2 T.M. B'tty Sheet I Vol 2

Army Form C. 2118.

Place	Date	Hour	Summary of Events and Information	Remarks and references to Appendices
MONCHY-au-BOIS	1-7-18		Fire 40 Rds with Nos 1, 2 & 3 Guns in to Sunken Road & Huts in F.17.c. Material thrown into the air also on to dug-outs & suspected T.M.E in F.18.a. obtaining good registration. 4 O.Rs from Hospital.	
"	2.7.18		Hostile T.M. observed to be firing from approx. F.23.a.8.7. 22 Rds fired by No 1 Gun, Hostile T.M. only fired 4 rds. after our shoot commenced. 14 rds fired in registration & checking S.O.S. lines. Ceased work on ESSARTS Def. Position 1 O.R. from Hospital.	
"	3.7.18		Salvage 2 Beds from Old Def. Position at QUESNOY FARM. 54 rds fired in retaliation for hostile T.M. fire. on to F.23.a.8.7. and were successful in silencing the 2. or 3 hostile T.M's.	
"	4.7.18		Relief of 14 men forward. 2 O.Rs from Hospital	
"	5.7.18		Fire 32 rds on Work in F.18.a. 14 rds fired in retaliation on to F.23.a.8.7.	
"	6.7.18		Fire 24 rds on Huts. F.17.d. & F.23.B. excellent results being obtained 3 Huts were demolished and much debris thrown up. 61 rds. were fired with Nos 2, 3, & 4 Guns on enemy work and suspected Empl. in F.18.d. Two Def. Positions at ESSARTS dismantled and timber taken from dug-out to New Position at F.Z.c. 90.50. G.R.S.M. Inspects all Positions etc. of Battery in Line. Dvr. EDWARDS severely wounded by E.S.F.	
"	7.7.18		15 rds fired in retaliation on F.18.d. 80. 80. with No 2 Gun.	

Army Form C. 2118.

Sheet II

WAR DIARY for July 1918
INTELLIGENCE SUMMARY
(Erase heading not required.)

Place	Date	Hour	Summary of Events and Information	Remarks and references to Appendices
ROTTEN RAVINE F.2.d.08.25.	8-7-18		Battery H.Q. moves to F.2.d.08.25. from Monchy-au-Bois. 2 new Def. Positions started at F.2.c.90.20 & F.2.c.99.20. on T. Bearings of 136° & 75° respectively. Fire 20 rds. with No. 5 Gun. in registration on TREE at F.12.d.20.15. and on enemy work and wire at F.12.c.4.8. with very good results. Also fire 50 rds from No. 2 & 3 Guns on new work reported at F.17.d.80.40. & 90.30. No retaliation for either of these shoots. 2/Lieut. S.V. Upham granted leave to U.K. from 8th to 22nd.	
"	9-7-18 10-7-18		Fire 20 rds. in retaliation on New work at F.18.d. Fire 79 rds on new enemy trench at F.17.d.7.5. & F.17.c.7.8. with No. 4 Gun. Many direct hits were obtained and camouflage and timber thrown up. Infantry Officers since report several very large craters more than 6 feet deep. in this work. Fire 8 rds in retaliation on F.17.c.50.10. 2 O.R.'s posted from 2nd D.T.C.	
"	11-7-18		Test of Special Mobile Bed. witnessed by C.R.A., A.D.T.M.O. and several O.T.M. O's. Fired 1/2 rds. onto F.17.d. & 23.B. (Huts). Special proved fairly satisfactory but soil too hard for spades to sink in properly. Fire 34 rds with No. 1 Gun in retaliation on to suspected E.T.M. in F.23.d. Effective and rapid silencing of same ensued. 46 rds. fired from No. 2 & 3 Guns with good effect on work in F.18.d. S/A request of Infantry. 18 rds were fired with No. 4 Gun on M.G. Nest at F.17. Central. Several hits being obtained on supposed Empl's. All 4 Guns fire 2 rds each at 10-10 pm on Test S.O.S. First rounds from each Gun being fired before rocket reached ground.	

Army Form C. 2118.

Sheet (1)

WAR DIARY or INTELLIGENCE SUMMARY
July 1918

(Erase heading not required.)

Place	Date	Hour	Summary of Events and Information	Remarks and references to Appendices
ROTTEN ROW	12/7/18	01.45	Forward relieved at Guns. Fired 10 rds. in retaliation from N°1 Gun & 29 rds. from N°5	
F.I.d.			4,3 & 4 Guns. Fired 23 rds. on trench & M.G. Post at F.17.a.9.5. to F.17.a.3.5.	
			This shoot was in co-operation with 18 Pdrs. N°2 Def. Position completed.	
			Build new Ammunition recess at N°3 Gun.	
- do -	13/7/18		Fire 25 rds. in registration for raid by 1st Kings for the night of 14th, 15th on	
			the following targets. N°1 Gun. M.G. nest at X roads F.17.c.95.95. N°2 F.17.a.20.60.	
			N°3. F.17.b.50.50. N°4. F.17.b.0.7. Registration of about 15.4.25 in the	
			vicinity of N°2 1,2 & 3 Guns. 1 O.R. to Hospital "Sick"	
- do -	14/7/18		2 Def. Positions Completed and 80 rds. of Ammunition brought up. No firing	
			until Zero Hour. (11-30 p/m) N°1 Gun fires 44 rds., N°2, 27, N°3 - 54,	
			N°4, 31. All Instantaneous fuzes on Barrage Lines. F.17.b.45.10. to F.17.b.55.65.	
			and F.17.c.95.95. Firing was from Zero to Zero + 20. Nine prisoners	
			were captured in this raid on enemy outpost Line at F.11.d.4.2 to 5.4.	
- do -	15/7/18		Fire 22 rds. in support of daylight raid by 15t Royal Berk's Regt. on	(F.17.d.7h.10, F.17.c.8.8.)
			F.17.a.90.80. to F.17.d.10.60. The raiding party reached their objective	
			unmolested which they still hold. No further Artillery or T.M. support was	
			required. S.O.S. Lines for N°1 & N°4 Guns are adjusted to meet altered	
			requirements to F.17.c.8.5. to F.17.d.4.5.) 1 O.R. to Hospital "Sick"	

Army Form C. 2118.
Sheet IV

WAR DIARY for July 1918
INTELLIGENCE SUMMARY

(Erase heading not required.)

Instructions regarding War Diaries and Intelligence Summaries are contained in F. S. Regs., Part II. and the Staff Manual respectively. Title Pages will be prepared in manuscript.

Place	Date	Hour	Summary of Events and Information	Remarks and references to Appendices
ROTTEN ROWINE F.Z.d.08.25.	16/7/18		Fired 30 rds on Bank in F.18.d. and 10 rds on Huts F.23.d. Two huts being destroyed.	
" -	17/7/18		Wagon Lines moves from BERLES-au-BOIS to PONNIER. Men at Def. Guns relieved. 12 rds were fired during night at request of 1st K.R.R's. at 3.55 a/m. 24 rds were fired on X Roads at F.17.C.90.90. At request of 1st K.R.R's at 3.55 a/m. 24 rds were fired from Nos 2, 3 & 4 Guns on BANK and Sunken Road. F.17.C. 30.50. 47 rds fired from Nos 2, 3 & 4 Guns on BANK F.18.d. 05.35. to F.18.d. 20.30. Good effect was observed. 3 white Very Lights were fired from BANK after Third round. L.O.R's posted from Lr. D.H.G. by the enemy	
" -	18/7/18		30 rds on repeated T.M.E. at F.12.d.90.55. from No 5 Gun. Good hits were observed.	
" -	19/7/18		30 rds fired with 2, 3 & 4 Guns on BANK in F.18.d. in registration	
" -	20/7/18		34 rds fired at M.G.E. F.11.d.30.15. with good results Gun being silenced	
" -	21/7/18		10 " registration on F.17.C. 80.40. Forward Section relieved at Guns. 27rds fired at T.M.E. F.12.C.90.55. and O.P. and work in F.7.C. 30.70. Another 8 rds fired on trench F.11.d. 53.35. Several direct hits being obtained 9 rds on BANK F.18.d.	
" -	22/7/18		26 rds were fired in checking Zero Line and on Enemy Outpost Line F.11.d.7.5. I.O.R. from BASE Depot.	

Army Form C. 2118.

Sheet V

WAR DIARY
for
INTELLIGENCE SUMMARY

July 1918

(Erase heading not required.)

Instructions regarding War Diaries and Intelligence Summaries are contained in F. S. Regs., Part II. and the Staff Manual respectively. Title Pages will be prepared in manuscript.

Place	Date	Hour	Summary of Events and Information	Remarks and references to Appendices
ROTTEN RENING F.2.d.08.35	23/7/18	12.30 AM	Fire 290 Rounds MIXED FUZES to support raid by 1st Royal Berks Regt. No 1 Gun fired from Zero to Zero +3. 2, 3 & 4 Guns fired from Zero to Zero + 60 . The hostile artillery fire became very intense from Zero +30 for 1 hour. 3 O.Rs recommended for immediate rewards. 1 M.G. and five prisoners were taken by 1st Royal Berks. Lieut S.V. Upham rejoined from Leave to U.K.	
- do -	24/7/18		Fired 24 rounds at trench F.7.c.2.5 and F.12.c.6.4. also 30 rds at reported T.M. Dump (Ammo) in Comp. at F.17.d.1.1. and dug-outs 10 rds fired in retaliation for E.T.M. firing from F.23.d. 1. O.P. on re-engagement leave to U.K.	
- do -	25/7/18		50 rds fired from No 5 Gun on Enemy Outpost Line F.11.d. Received congratulations through C.R.A. 2nd Divn. from G.O.C. 2nd Division on good work and keenness of batteries.	
- do -	26/7/18		20 rds fired on Ammunition Dump. F.17.d. 11. with good results also 30 rds on Enemy work and trench F.12.c.90.55 and F.12.c.60.50. 1. O.R. to Hospital "Sick".	
- do -	27/7/18		35 rds fired on Ammunition Dump F.11.d. No 2. 3. 4. & 5 Guns fire 13 rds in registration for Raid by 1st Kings	
- do -	28/7/18		70 rds fired on work in F.18.a. with very good results Enemy were	

2449 Wt. W14957/M90 750,000 1/16 J.B.C. & A. Forms/C.2118/12.

Army Form C. 2118.

Sheet VI"

WAR DIARY
INTELLIGENCE SUMMARY
July for 1918

(Erase heading not required.)

Instructions regarding War Diaries and Intelligence Summaries are contained in F. S. Regs., Part II. and the Staff Manual respectively. Title Pages will be prepared in manuscript.

Place	Date	Hour	Summary of Events and Information	Remarks and references to Appendices
ROTTEN (ANNIE) F.2.d. 08.25	28-7-18		observed at work on dug-out at F.18.d.3.6. Several direct hits were obtained on this trench. Six of the enemy running out over the open and disappearing at F.18.d. 45.40. Relief of Forward Section of Guns. 1.O.R. to U.K. (Commissioned) Cpls. Ferguson & Gutteridge & Adamson awarded Military Medals for good work during raid on night of 22nd, 23rd.	
"	29-7-18		28 rds fired in registration for support of raid by 15th King's. Satisfactory registration was obtained 10.40 pm to 11.00 pm fire 185 rounds in support of RAID. No. 1 Gun firing on F.17.b.80.75. No. 3. F.17.b.80.75. No. 4. GWY. No. 2. No. 5. F.11.d. 95.50. for 1 minute afterwards lifting to F.12.c. 65.20. Six prisoners were taken in THIS RAID including 1 German Sergeant Major & Sergeant. Retaliation moderately heavy. The BARRAGE was reported by O.C. 15th King's to have been very effective in that no hostile M.G. opened fire from Zero to Stop although they became very active afterwards.	
"	30-7-18		54 rds fired at Snipers Post and Camouflage trench in F.17.b.5.8. Much damage was done. Enemy retaliated heavily with 4.2's for about 1 hour. Infantry observers report very effective shoot. Capt B.C. TUCKER rejoined from Hospital. 3 O.Rs. posted from No1 Section and 3 O.Rs. from No 2 Section. O.M.C.	

Army Form C. 2118.
Shee-Vi

WAR DIARY
or
INTELLIGENCE SUMMARY
July 1915

(Erase heading not required.)

Instructions regarding War Diaries and Intelligence Summaries are contained in F. S. Regs., Part II. and the Staff Manual respectively. Title Pages will be prepared in manuscript.

Place	Date	Hour	Summary of Events and Information	Remarks and references to Appendices
Potten Ravine F.2.d.6t.25.	31/7/18		31 rds. fired on Enemy Work at F.18.a. 30.85. and F.18.a. 3.6. with Nos 2, 3 & 4 guns. Several direct hits observed but shoot very much hampered by E.M. Observation and afterwards by Balloon.	
			Total No. of Rounds Fired from Present Positions } 2021.	
			Total No. of Rounds Fired During Month of July } 1897.	
			Average No. of Rounds fired Daily in Month of July } 61.	
			2-8-18.	
			Raymond Daniel Lieut. for O/C ½ T.M. Battery	

2nd Divisional Artillery.

X & Y TRENCH MORTAR BATTERIES ::: AUGUST 1918.

Army Form C. 2118.

WAR DIARY
of X/2 T.M. B'y. for AUGUST 1918. R/ MAPS:
INTELLIGENCE SUMMARY.
FRANCE 51cSE,51b SW.
57d NE, 57c NW.

(Erase heading not required.)

Instructions regarding War Diaries and Intelligence Summaries are contained in F. S. Regs., Part II. and the Staff Manual respectively. Title pages will be prepared in manuscript.

Place	Date	Hour	Summary of Events and Information	Remarks and references to Appendices
POMMIER	Aug 1st		Battery in action on the AYETTE - MOYENNEVILLE sector.	
			A shoot of 40 rounds was carried out on targets in MOYBLAIN Trench - good shooting was made on a M.G.E at A8a 90.85 and a suspect grenatenwerfer position at A2d 10.10. Work was continued on the defence position dugout at ADINFER (X27b)	
	2nd		A section relief took place & the positions were inspected by BM. RA. 2nd Div.	
			A shoot of 30 rounds was made from AYETTE position on New work at A7 b 9.4 & on a M.G.E at F12c 95.55 - several good hits obtained on both targets - shoot curtailed owing to bank behind the mortar collapsing with shooting after heavy rain. No shooting took place on the Left Bde sector owing to the O.C. 15th UX + Bucks objection to us shooting while the new American platoons were in the line. The dugout at AX1+2 guns (F5a) was completed.	
	3rd		A shoot of 80 rounds was made on O enemy post in WITH J BEDS at A2c 60.30 - several good hits obtained @ new work at A8a 6.8 - parapet damaged @ M.G. observed shooting at plane from A8a 95.95 - one first round dropped on it @ also heavy fire was thrown ↑ from this point. O + ② were shot up at the request of 2nd 14th Bn. G.O.C 5th Inf Bde consented to our mortars on Left Bde front carrying out daily destructive shoots having regard to O.S.C Battalions wishes as T the time of American company relief.	

A6915 Wt. W14422/M1160 35,000 12/16 D.D. & L. Forms/C./2118/14.

WAR DIARY
of X/2 T.M. Bty. AUG. 1918.
INTELLIGENCE SUMMARY.
(Erase heading not required.)

Army Form C. 2118.

Place	Date	Hour	Summary of Events and Information	Remarks and references to Appendices
POMMIER	Aug 3rd (cont)		Positions for the defence of AERODROME SWITCH were chosen at S25d 20.30	
	4th		43 rounds were fired at the enemy post in WITHY BEDS — several hits were obtained on & around the post — one round threw up a Boby & another strips of camouflage. 16 rds were fired at MOYBLAIN Trench — a man was observed sniping over the parapet & on first rd dropped on the parapet. One rd apparently penetrated to an underground chamber as the debris of wire & material was thrown up & lightly	
	5th		6 shot 134 rds was made on MOYBLAIN Trench & flaming several direct hits on parapet at A.2 at 15.14 — A.x.3 gun went out of action with a faulty bomb jamming in the bore. Enemy harassing fire on & around A.x.3,4+5 position increasing nightly. An RE working party was provided for work on the new AERODROME SWITCH position	
	6th		Section relief carried out. Night firing was arranged to surprise enemy working parties in A11 — our patrols reported that these effectually stopped all enemy work during the night. No firing took place on left Bat front owing to a relief of companies.	
	7th		50 rounds were fired from our AYETTE gun in trench at A.17d.25.50 & flaming 12 direct hits and 88 rounds were fired on MOYBLAIN Trench in A.2.a, A.2.d + A.2.b in a combined shoot with an Artillery - Smoke barrage	

WAR DIARY
of X/12 T.M.B.Y.
INTELLIGENCE SUMMARY.

Army Form C. 2118.

AUG. 1918.

(Erase heading not required.)

Place	Date	Hour	Summary of Events and Information	Remarks and references to Appendices
POMMIER	AUG 7th (Contd)		A additional positions for defence of PURPLE LINE were chosen at X.27.a.9.4., in accordance with VI Corps defence scheme for the preparation of permanent positions for all TM's on the front. 2/Lt F PARTNER (RFA attached 4/2 TMB.) was posted to this battery.	
	8th		A shot of 13H who was made on MOUSBAIN Trench + a good percentage of hits was started chiefly on points in A.2.d. The ammunition wagons going to AX.3.4.T.5 guns had one mule killed. Driver THORP was awarded the Military Medal for his good work + courage in attending to his wounded animal under fire. 2/Lt BOSWORTH relieved Capt GORRIE at Bty HQ. The enemy evacuated part of his outpost line on the Centre Bde front.	2nd DAC
	9th		10 rounds were fired in retaliation at the regimental of 2nd H.L.I on A.8.a. + a night-firing program of 40 rounds from AYETTE position was carried out under heavy fire from 5.9s + MGs. the enemy apparently having located the guns from the flash. Gnr T. EDGE was awarded the Military Medal for his excellent work in carrying through this shoot. A counter fire program 2D is T.M's was started.	
	10th		40 rounds were fired from A.X.35.H guns on the WITH H.BEDS + Trench in A.8.a	

WAR DIARY

of X/2 TMB. AUG. 1918

INTELLIGENCE SUMMARY

Army Form C. 2118.

Place	Date	Hour	Summary of Events and Information	Remarks and references to Appendices
POMMIER	AUG 10th Cont'd		and the enemy retaliated on hard lately by shooting up our position with a 4.2 how battery damaging the sand bag buttresses around AxH gun. Also 12 rounds were fired from the AVETTE gun in a confined short with artillery on enemy outpost line in expectation of attack on this sector. The gun was heavily shelled during the shoot but a misfire interrupted the firing. Bdr BENTLEY was wounded in the cheek but remained at duty.	
	11th		Section relay carried out. 10 R injured in hands & face by accidental explosion of detonator. Forwarded from to packing in transit. No shooting was done on the sector front owing to battalion relief — American battalion now in as R.I. Batt. 2 Sef.B'de.	
	12th		Capt CORRIE relieved 2/Lt BOSWORTH at H.Q. & he in turn relieved 2/Lt PARTNER at the forward position. Pt. SUGDEN returned from special leave & extension owing sickness. 2 O.R's admitted to hospital.	
	13th		38 rds were fired from AVETTE gun on enemy outpost line in F/120 in conjunction with artillery in expectation of enemy attack at dawn. 69 rds were also fired on MOISLAIN trench — good shooting was made & the parapet knocked about. 2/Lt BG HESTER was classified B.ii at Base & struck off the strength. A O.R.'s were posted to the battery from 2nd D.A.C.	

WAR DIARY

of X2 TMB INTELLIGENCE SUMMARY AUG. 1918

Army Form C. 2118.

Place	Date	Hour	Summary of Events and Information	Remarks and references to Appendices
	AUG			
POMMIER	14th	2.30am	150 rds were fired as covering fire for a raid by 1st KINGS & 1st KRRs on enemy posts in F12.c. O/C KINGS reported complete absence of enemy M.G. fire in raided area & 7 prisoners & 2 MGs were captured. Our position was shelled by H2s during this operation. A shoot of 28 rds was made on a suspect T.M.E. at F17.c.90.90. stunning several hits. The enemy evacuated all his forward posts in AVETTE sector putting up AX1+2 & AVETTE guns out of action – all shooting was stopped owing to no daylight patrols being out. Lt SUGDEN relieved Capt GORRIE at HQ. 10R returned from hospital.	
	15th		Shooting was resumed on the 26/11 Bde front – 126 rds were fired on MOUSTAIN Trench & the area from A8 a 90.80 to A3 a 10.10. The shooting was excellent, the detachments working splendidly in carrying out salvoes & battery fire at short intervals. Patrols report MOUSTAIN Trench to be very strongly held.	
	16th		10 ORs attached from DAC for work on new HQ dugout under REs were returned to 2nd AE. 10R was sent to VI Corps signal School for Course. Section relief carried out. 113 rds were fired on MOUSTAIN Trench with excellent results – Trench very much knocked about. There was no retaliation.	
	17th		120 rds were fired on the same targets with good results. Patrols report	

Army Form C. 2118.

WAR DIARY
of X/2 T.M. B'y. AUG. 1918
INTELLIGENCE SUMMARY.
(Erase heading not required.)

Place	Date	Hour	Summary of Events and Information	Remarks and references to Appendices
POMMIER	AUG 17th (cont.)		That MOYBLAIN Trench is now held only by isolated posts.	
	18th		2/Lt. PARDNER relieved 2/Lt. BOSWORTH at forward position.	
			250 rounds were fired on enemy posts in MOYBLAIN Trench – very good effect was obtained as many trench throw up trusting metal sheets. 2 OR's returned to duty. One from hospital + one from duty at H.Q.R.A. as orderly.	
			Work was commenced on 2 positions at the junction of BADEN AVENUE with the AYETTE-BUCQUOY road at F.22.b.47.05 as part of a concentration of 6" TM's to provide a barrage on ABLAINZEVELLE village in the projected attack. Guns & beds for this work were brought from our AX # + 2 positions at night.	
	19th		250 rds were fired at MOYBLAIN Trench slightly in A2 + F.A.8.a with a good percentage of hits.	
			One R.R. Chamberlain was reported to the battery from 298 A.F.A. Bde.	
	20th		All detachments at forward + defence guns returned to POMMIER excepting the detachment for the special shoot who may S/R as guards of the various guns. Work on the BADEN AVENUE position was continued + the guns were registered on a point in ABLAINZEVELLE with 3 rounds each.	
	21st 4.55 am		106 rounds were fired from the two guns in ABLAINZEVELLE CEMETERY	

WAR DIARY
of X/2 TMB? AUG. 1918
INTELLIGENCE SUMMARY
(Erase heading not required.)

Army Form C. 2118.

Place	Date	Hour	Summary of Events and Information	Remarks and references to Appendices
POMMIER	AUG 21st cont'd		during the first 10 minutes of the attack barrelled between MOYENNEVILLE & BUCQUOY. Our fire effectually stopped all enemy M.G. fire in this area.	
	22nd		All guns & beds were withdrawn from their positions to the wagon lines. The relieving thorwhole unit. 1 O.R. returned to duty from the Base.	
	23rd		A working party of 30 men was provided for work in forming a new A.R.P. at DOUCHY. Capt. T. WHITESIDE was reported to this unit from 48th A.F.A. Bde.	
	24th / 31st		That of the battery was employed in providing working parties for salving ammunition from the deserted field battery positions + in manning the A.R.P. which in turn moved forward to DOUCHY, COURCELLES-LE-COMTÉ Railway Embankment + GOMIECOURT as the advance continued.	

RWG Cotter Capt.
O.C. X/2
RWG Cotter Capt RA?S?

Army Form C. 2118.

The Lusk Moli By

SHEET. I.

WAR DIARY
INTELLIGENCE SUMMARY
(Erase heading not required.)

August 1918.

Instructions regarding War Diaries and Intelligence Summaries are contained in F. S. Regs., Part II. and the Staff Manual respectively. Title Pages will be prepared in manuscript.

Place	Date	Hour	Summary of Events and Information	Remarks and references to Appendices
ROTTEN RAVINE F.23.D.25. F.17.b.23.50.	1-8-18.		Capt. S.C. Luckin, 2/Lt. S.V. Upham and 20 O.Rs. in the line. The following targets at: F.17.d.1.0 to F.17.d.1.5. were engaged. also SNIPERS POST at. F.17.b.23.50. with good result. 80 Bombs complete sent forward.	No. of Rounds fired Daily 84.
" "	2nd		The following targets were engaged :- ROBERTS TRENCH. F.11.d.40.20. to F.11.d.60.40. Shoot carried out at request of K.R.R.s who expressed great satisfaction. 160 Bombs complete sent forward.	42.
" "	3rd		The following targets were engaged. Area. F.17.b.4.5. to F.17.b.4.8. M.G. Post at. F.17.d.31.85. also Post at F.12.c.60.60.45 to F.12.c.60.60. at VERY LIGHT DUMP in F.18.d. was blown up. Hostile trench mortars fire neutralised. 80 Bombs complete sent forward. 2/Lieut. J.P. Gunn admitted to Hospital "sick". Lieut. R.J. Daniels awarded "Military Cross" for Gallantry in the field. Night of 23rd-24th July 18. Auth. 3rd Army. R.O. 1798.	84.
" "	4th		2/Lieut. N. Benton relieves 2/Lieut. S.V. Upham. The following targets were engaged. Dug Outs in Sunken Road. F.17.d.2.0 to F.17.b.22.50. Snipers Post and New Work in F.17.b.22.50.	20.6 C.F.

2449 Wt. W14957/M90 750,000 1/16 J.B.C. & A. Forms/C.2118/12.

WAR DIARY

INTELLIGENCE SUMMARY

(Erase heading not required.)

August 1918

Army Form C. 2118. SHEET II.

Place	Date	Hour	Summary of Events and Information	Remarks and references to Appendices
ROTTEN ROW №2			Shoot of regiment of Infantry who expressed his appreciation	No. of Rounds fired daily
F.2.a. of 2.b.				B.F. 206
	5.2		40 Bombs complete sent forward.	105
"			The following targets were engaged. Bank & Enemy Work at F.18.a. 30.60. and SNIPERS POST on F.17.b. 42.50. Direct-hits were obtained.	62
"	6.2		40 Bombs complete sent forward. 2 Gunners pulled from 2nd D.A.C. The following targets were engaged. New Work at F.12.c.6.5. and F.a. 2.5. also Work in F.18.a. 7.4. and F.12.c.6.5. with Excellent results. Two of the enemy were observed to fall.	
"			80 Bombs complete sent forward.	76
"	7.2		The following targets were engaged. N.E. of Copse at F.17.a. & O. 2 Boche were observed bolting from this point. Suspected Snipers T.C. position in F.12.c.90.55. New Work in F.12.c.6.5. and Work at F.18.a. 1.4 to 6.6.B. Work commenced on four new emplacements covering the PURPLE LINE. Sites selected by D.I.M.O. Two in Rotten Avenue and the remaining two in Rotten Ravine. Work was carried on at night by Infantry Working Party supplied by 99th Bde.	6
				B.F. 516

WAR DIARY
INTELLIGENCE SUMMARY

(Erase heading not required.)

AUGUST 1918.

Army Form C. 2118.

Place	Date	Hour	Summary of Events and Information	Remarks and references to Appendices
ROTTEN ROVINE T/k F.2.d.05.25.	7/8	—	Usual supervision of our L.M. Gun from Rear Bullet to Rovereto completed over Sud. Inward. 2/Lt. F. Parkin from Att. 9/12 and posted to 9/12 T.C.B.	No. of Rds FIRED DAILY. B.F. 516.
—	8th	—	The following targets were engaged at request of 1st Royal Berks. SNIPERS POST. in F.11.d. 30.10. and TRENCH. F.11.d.40.20. to " 50.40.	
			ENEMY.WORK. in F.18.d. Two BOSCHE trollies and were engaged by Snipers of C. Company. 1st Royal Berks. from Post. 23.a. Many direct hits were obtained on enemy post. N. Infantry highly pleased. 50 rounds complete sub- forward. Lieut. J.P. Garro returns from Hospital. Work on the PURPLE LINE Defence Scheme continued.	69.
—	9th	—	The following targets were engaged:– TRENCH at. F.11.d.3.4. to " 8.6. Wood work and galvanised iron was thrown into its air. BANK. and work in F.S.a.1.3 to " 3.6. was fired on. 50 Bombs complete with Sud. forward. Work on PURPLE LINE Defence Scheme continued. I.O.R. on 31 days re-engagement. Cont to S.K.	100.
—	10th	—	Reported T.M. Position at. (approx.) F.12.0.7.6. was engaged. During shoot Enemy Very lights were fired. Trench at F.11.d.5.4 to F.12.C.2.7. was also engaged. H.H.	B.F. 735

WAR DIARY
INTELLIGENCE SUMMARY

(Erase heading not required.)

Army Form C. 2118.

SHEET N.

AUGUST 1916.

Instructions regarding War Diaries and Intelligence Summaries are contained in F. S. Regs., Part II. and the Staff Manual respectively. Title Pages will be prepared in manuscript.

Place	Date	Hour	Summary of Events and Information	Remarks and references to Appendices
ROTTEN RAVINE. F.2.d.of.25.10th			40 Bombs completi. Sent. forward. Work on PURPLE LINE Defenses. Schemi continued. Two BEDS for ROTTEN RAVINE Rennor Positions sent. up from Rear Bills.	No. 0-100 Fires Daily 8.7.1/35.
— " —	11th		62 rounds were fired at ENEMY POST. in F.14.c.6.5. in registration. by Balloon Observation. Capt. G.W. Potrib. O.C. (O.T.O.S) being the Observer. 80 Bombs completi. Sent. forward. Lt. J.P. Eame. relieves Lt. S.W. Upham 64.	
— " —	12th		The E. TRENCH at F.12.c.60.55. was engaged. The enemy retaliated with guns of light. calibre. The Suspected PINE APPLE T.M. at F.12.c.F.F. was engaged. Signals of our infantry. (12. Kings)	15.
			160 Bombs completi. were Sent. forward.	
— " —	13th		The following targets were engaged:— F.17.b.65.60 F.18.d. O.C. and F.17.b.65.00 F.18.a.O.O. in registration. also. F.18.C.— F.18.a. & F.12.d.75.00.— F.12.b.75.75. (Night Firing.) by order of RIGHT GROUP. rough for Kings). 160 Bombs completi. sent. forward. Work on the PURPLE LINE Defense Scheme continues. Fire Gunno fired from 2nd O.P.G.	17.
— " —	14th		214 Rounds fired in support of Successful raid by 1st Kings and 10". K.R.Rs. the following targets engaged:— F.17.b.62.15.	C.F. 949

WAR DIARY or INTELLIGENCE SUMMARY

Army Form C. 2118. Sheet V.

August 1918

Place	Date	Hour	Summary of Events and Information	Remarks and references to Appendices
ROTTEN RAVINE F.2.d.05.25.	14th		F.17.b.50.40., F.17.b.50.60., F.18.d.00.00. The C.O. of the 1st King's expressed great appreciation of our co-operation. The following large guns also engaged during the day. F.12.d.93-20. Work on the PURPLE LINE Defence Scheme continued.	No. 9. Mds. Fried Duty 2.7.1949. 245.
"	15th		A. request of our infantry no firing took place owing to repeated evacuation of Posts by the enemy, and patroling of our troops. Same conditions prevailed as in previous day and same remarks apply.	
"	16th		Bus. New Positions reconnoitred by Capt. F.W. Roberts. M.C. (O.C.N.O) Capt. S.E. Tucker and Lieut. J.P. Gunn in 37th Divisional Front. in SUNKEN ROAD at F.22.d. and work commenced Nos 1, 2, 3 and 4 Forward Positions and No.1 and 2 Reserve Po.	
"	17th		Characteristics the 6 Guns, Bros. and Sub-beds being taken to the forementioned new positions. The whole of the Battery was engaged in this work — one half by day and the other half by night. Battery personnel occupied trullis at CIONCHY to escape the work and fatuitive shifts. One Corporal promoted Sergeant. 1 Bar. and 1 Gunner to Bar. 1 Gunner to Bar. and 2 Gunners to Paros.	1194.

Army Form C. 2118.

WAR DIARY
or
INTELLIGENCE SUMMARY

(Erase heading not required.)

Sheet No. VI

HAGOS. 1918.

Instructions regarding War Diaries and Intelligence Summaries are contained in F.S. Regs., Part II. and the Staff Manual respectively. Title Pages will be prepared in manuscript.

Place	Date	Hour	Summary of Events and Information	Remarks and references to Appendices
ROTTEN ROW F.20.6.25	18th		Sec. New Positions in SUNKEN ROAD completed and Guns mounted. 300 Completed Rounds taken from old forward positions and conveyed to Guns. 2 O.R.'s. wounded unit from Base Depot.	No. of Cop. Ing. Daily C.I. 1194
"	19th		Lieut. S.V. Upham relieves Lieut. J.P. Gann. Bombs at new forward positions prepared for action and improvements in positions carried out.	
"	20th		Further improvements in New fwd. Positions 16 Rounds fired for registration purposes. Capt. J.G. Tucker, Lieut. S.V. Upham and 15 O.R.'s. manned the Sec. Guns. Remainder of Personnel sent to Rear Billets at POMMIER. Driver J. Thorpe attached from 2nd D.A.C. awarded MILITARY MEDAL for Gallantry in the field on 12th, 13th inst.	16.
"	21st		254 Rounds fires as per prearranged Artillery Barrage Scheme in support of Infantry Attack the target being selected points in the vicinity of ABLAINZEVILLE. 2 Prisoners rounded up and sent to Divisional P. of W. Cage. Guns were left under charge of 1 N.C.O. and 3 men and Battery N.U. and Personnel returned to rear billets at POMMIER.	254. Total 146.4

WAR DIARY
or
INTELLIGENCE SUMMARY
(Erase heading not required.)

Army Form C. 2118.
SHEET. 1/11.

HOOST. 1916.

Place	Date	Hour	Summary of Events and Information	Remarks and references to Appendices
POMMIER	22nd		Lieut. N. Benton and 15 O.R's dismantled Gun positions and brought back all Guns, Beds, Sub-teds, Stores etc etc. to Builts at POMMIER.	B.F. 1464
"	23rd		1 Gunner reported unfit from Base Depot.	
"	24th		All Ranks on duty overhauling and cleaning Guns & all Battery Stores. Continuation of work commenced on previous day, and Guns mounted in Gun Park. Baths and change of clothing arranged. In all N.C.O's & Men C. working party of 1 Officer (Lt. R.J. Daniels OC) and 30 O.R's supplies to A.R.P. at CLONCHY.	
"	25th		The following working parties were supplied. 1 N.C.O and 13 Men to A.R.P. CLONCHY. 6 Men for salvage work at- D.36. old By positions 9 Men, 18 Mules and 3. G.S. Wagons returned to 2nd D.I.T.E.	
"	26th		Working parties as on 25th continued.	
"	27th		Working Party at A.R.P. CLONCHY returned and 7 O.R's salving Ammunition at- old battery positions. 1 O.R. reported unit- from Base Depot re-engagement. Leave to O.R. 1 O.R. reported unit- from Base Depot 31 days.	
"	28th		Working Party of 6 men salving Ammunition at old battery positions.	G.F. 1464

Army Form C. 2118

WAR DIARY
or
INTELLIGENCE SUMMARY

(Erase heading not required.)

Sheet VIII.

Place	Date	Hour	Summary of Events and Information	Remarks and references to Appendices
POPERINGHE	28th		Remainder of Battery furis received instructions as per programme of training	B.J. 1464
- " -	29th		Working Party at A.R.P. returns. Training continued. 6 New Salving Arms as total	
- " -	30th		Training continued. Usual party of 6 men supplied for salvage.	
- " -	31st		Half of the Working Party at A.R.P. returns. and 6 men attached to 2nd D.A.C.	
			The Battery was actually in Action 16 Days. During which period 1464 rounds were fired making an average of 91.5 rounds per diem.	

Sydney C. Fuller
Capt.
Comdg 1/2 Lancs Motor Battery.

Total 1464 Rds

2nd Divisional Artillery.

X & Y TRENCH MORTAR BATTERIES ::: SEPTEMBER 1918

Army Form C. 2118

WAR DIARY
of X/2 Trench Mortar Battery for SEPTEMBER 1918
INTELLIGENCE SUMMARY.
(Erase heading not required.)

Place	Date	Hour	Summary of Events and Information	Remarks and references to Appendices
POMMIER	1st		15 or.s for duty a H.T.P. and 8 or.s to D.A.C. Mobile Section prepared for action to support 62nd Divn Infantry in Vaulx VRAUCOURT, but the situation changed too quickly to permit of us getting into action.	
	3rd		1 or.s from 1st Section 2nd DAC attached to Battery with 2 G.S. Wagons and 12 Mules for Transport. Lieut. E. Sugden & 2/Lt. H. Bosworth in charge of Mobile Section (3 Guns) proceeded to DAC in order to be nearer the line in case of necessity.	
	4th		Capt T.M. GORRIE proceeded on leave in France.	
	6th		11 or.s attached to H.T.P. for duty.	
	7th		1 or proceeded on Special Leave to U.K. 8/9/18 to 29/9/18	
	8th		D.T.M.O. and Lieut. SUGDEN proceeded to the line to reconnoitre. In the evening Lt SUGDEN 15 or.s and 2 Guns (mobile beds and Go rounds) went into action on the HAPLINCOURT Sector. The detachments at H.T.P. and DAC returned to battery or duty as above.	
	9th		Personnel in the line returned to MORCHIES owing to Infantry attack on and capture of prospective targets. Two Casualties. Corp. Gates. gassed. 8 Bomb. Cates, wounded in right eye by enemy shell fire. Both admitted to hospital. 2 Guns and Mobile Beds remained in the line.	

Army Form C. 2118.

WAR DIARY
or
INTELLIGENCE SUMMARY.   SEPTEMBER 1918

(Erase heading not required.)

Instructions regarding War Diaries and Intelligence Summaries are contained in F. S. Regs., Part II. and the Staff Manual respectively. Title pages will be prepared in manuscript.

Place	Date	Hour	Summary of Events and Information	Remarks and references to Appendices
MORCHIES	10th		Battery moved from POMMIER to MORCHIES in early morning	
	12th		2/Lieut H BOGNOTH & 1 o.r. proceeded to Third Army Artillery School MONCHAUX for Course	
	13th		1 o.r. proceeded to Third Army School of Cookery for Course. 2 o.r's returned from hospital	
	14th		20 o.r's on fatigues mending roads in MORCHIES. 2 Mobile Carriages received from Ordnance	
	15th		1 o.r. proceeded on Special leave to U.K. 14-9-18 to 1/10/18 - 3 o.r's attached from 2" D.T.C. posted to X/2 T.M.B. A considerable quantity of serviceable 18 pdr Ammunition was salved and returned to S.A.R.P. D.T.M.O and Lieut. SUADEN proceeded to the trenches to examine Boache "MINNIE" and report on probability of firing same. This was found impossible, but positions for Two 6" Newtons were reconnoitred.	
	16th		1 o.r. to H.Q.R.A as temporary Orderly. 2 Guns and mobile beds withdrawn from line to Morchies. 18 pdr Ammo salved and returned to S.A.R.P.	
	17th		1 o.r proceeded on leave to U.K. 19/9/18 to 3/10/18. 1 o.r. returned from leave to U.K. Capt. R.M. GORRIE returned from leave in France	
	18th		1 o.r. admitted to hospital. Several cases of slight dysentery caused by local supply of water. Salvaged 77mm Shell Cases, 1 German Machine Gun and German Trench Mortar.	

Army Form C. 2118.

WAR DIARY
or
INTELLIGENCE SUMMARY   SEPTEMBER 1918.
(Erase heading not required.)

Place	Date	Hour	Summary of Events and Information	Remarks and references to Appendices
MOTCHIES	19		1 or proceeded on leave to U.K. 21/9/18 to 5/9/18. Capt T.M GORRIE acting D.T.M.O in absence of Capt H.W.ROBERTS M.C on leave. Salvaged 4.5 H.E. Complete with charges, 18 pdr, and 4.5 Shell Cases, 1 German Trench Mortar, 1 German Range Drum, Stokes Bombs and Buffer Spring.	
	20		Salvaged 16 pdr and 4.5 Shell Cases and German Aeroplane Engine.	
	21		2/Lt F.PATTNER and 1 or attached 28" Batty R.F.A. Salvaged 18 pdr & 4.5 Shell Cases. 4 or's wounded by Enemy Shell Fire. One or admitted to hospital. remainder at duty.	
	22		28 N(C)O and men attached to A.T.P for duty. Serg Helliwell proceeded to VI Corps Gas School for Course.	
	23		Salvaged German 4.2 and small shell cases.	
	24		Lieut E SUGDEN and 1 or attached to 48" Bty. R.F.A. Salvaged 4.2 and 8" shell cases. Machine Gun Belt and Box, 5.9 – 4.2 and 18 pdr Shell Cases.	
	25		1 or proceeded on leave to U.K. 27/9/18 to 11/10/18. All stores & moved to HQTH except Mobile Section of 2 Guns. 2 or's as Guard of Stores.	
	26		Salvaged 4.2 and 4.5 shell Cases.	
	27		1 or returned from leave to U.K. Battery moved from MOTCHIES to HERMIES.	

Army Form C. 2118.

WAR DIARY
or
INTELLIGENCE SUMMARY. SEPTEMBER 1918

(Erase heading not required.)

Instructions regarding War Diaries and Intelligence Summaries are contained in F. S. Regs., Part II. and the Staff Manual respectively. Title pages will be prepared in manuscript.

Place	Date	Hour	Summary of Events and Information	Remarks and references to Appendices
HERMIES	28		1 or proceeded on leave to U/K 30/9/18 to 14/10/18	
	30		Battery moved from HERMIES to No 1 Lock CANAL du NORD.	
			1 or proceeded on leave to UK 2/10/18 to 16/10/18	

R.W. Gorrie
Capt. F.F.A
Cmdg X/2 Trench Mortar Batty.

WAR DIARY
SEPTEMBER, 1918
INTELLIGENCE SUMMARY

Y/2 TRENCH MORTAR BATTERY

Place	Date	Hour	Summary of Events and Information	Remarks and references to Appendices
POMMIER	1-9-18		8 Men attacked 16" 2nd O.A.C. 15 Men return an equal number at	
"	2nd		A.R.P. Remainder of battery general training and fatigues	
"	3rd		Training as per programme 1 O.R. on leave to U.K. 4-9-18 to 18-9-18	
"	4th		" " " " 1 O.R. on leave to U.K. 4-9-18 to 18-9-18	
"	5th		Training as per programme	
"	6th		" " " " N.C.O. & 10 Men attached A.R.P.	
"	7th		" " " "	
"	8th		" " " " 2/Lt J.P. Gane & N. Bevan with Calmar B'n's respectively	
"	9th		attacked 16" 17th and 18th B'n's respectively	
"	10th		Training as per programme	
MORCHIES	11th		Battery moved by 3 Motor Lorries and 2 G.S. Wagons to MORCHIES	
"	12th		Guns cleaned and examined. Construction of Cubb'les etc.	
"	13th		Ap 11th inst. 1 O.R. admitted to Hospital "SCK"	
"	13th		Training as per programme	
"	14th			
"	15th		300 Rounds of 18 Par. Ammunition issue from C. 30, & I.G. and returned to F.R.P. 2nd Div. 2 O.R.s admitted to Hospital "SCK"	

Army Form C. 2118.

WAR DIARY
or
INTELLIGENCE SUMMARY

September 1918

1/2 TRENCH MORTAR BATTERY.

Instructions regarding War Diaries and Intelligence Summaries are contained in F. S. Regs., Part II. and the Staff Manual respectively. Title Pages will be prepared in manuscript.

Place	Date	Hour	Summary of Events and Information	Remarks and references to Appendices
MORCHIES	16th		198 Rounds 1.8 Ptr. Ammunition Salved from Enemy Locality and sent to- 2nd Div. A.R.P. 1 O.R. from Leave to- U.K.	
"	17th		200 Rds 1.8 Ptr. Ammo. Salved and returned to- 2nd Div. A.R.P. 1 O.R. from Leave to- U.K.	
"	18th		4 Loads Salvage collected from MORCHIES - LAGNICOURT area and returned to- 2nd Div. Sal. Dump. 1 O.R. on Leave to- U.K. 1 O.R. returned from hospital	
"	19th		2 Loads of salvage collected & returned to 2nd Div. Salvage Dump.	
"	20th		" " " " " " "	
"	21st		1 O.R. to- 205th Div. Employ. Coy. 2 Loads Salvage collected & taken to- 2nd Div Salvage Dump. 1 O.R. from Leave to- U.K. 26 N.C.Os & Men at- A.R.P. returned try 'X' By. & Men at- 2" D.C.T. returned try 'X' By, Lieut S.V.UPHAM & Robson att. D/36 Battery	
"	22nd		2 Loads salvage collected & Taken to- 2nd Div Salvage Dump. 1 O.R. on Leave to- U.K. Capt. E.J. Ferguson MM. (R.F.A.) Killed by Enemy Shell fire.	
"	23rd		2 O.R's report for Duty at- Canada Division A.R.P.	
"	24th		2 Loads Salvage collected & Taken to- 2nd Div Salvage Dump.	
"	25th		" " " " " " "	

Army Form C. 2118.

WAR DIARY
or
INTELLIGENCE SUMMARY

September 1918

(Erase heading not required.)

 ~~4/3 Trench Mortar~~ Battery

Instructions regarding War Diaries and Intelligence Summaries are contained in F. S. Regs., Part II. and the Staff Manual respectively. Title Pages will be prepared in manuscript.

Place	Date	Hour	Summary of Events and Information	Remarks and references to Appendices
Morchies	26th		3 Loads salvage collected and returned to B" Div. Stores Salvage Dump. 1 O.R. on Leave to U.K. All Guns, surplus kits and stores deposited at.	
-"-	27th		2nd Div. R.A. Rear H.Q. in preparation for advance. Advance commences. Move from Morchies to Hermies with 2 G.S. Wagons. 27 O.R's return from Guards Div. O.R.P. and return to No's 1 & 3 Sections D.A.C. (2nd) 2 O.R's on leave to U.K.	
Hermies	28th		Move from Hermies Village to Quarry South of Hermies Gr. N.E. Sect 8 and 1 O.R. on leave to U.K.	
-"-	30th		Move from Hermies 2 G.S. Wagons to Brickkilns at Lock 7 Canal Du Nord in K. 15. 4.	
Lock 7 Canal-du-Nord				

Raymond Davies
Lieut.
for Offr Cmdg ⁴/₃ T.M. Battery.

1-10-18.

2nd Divisional Artillery.

X & Y TRENCH MORTAR BATTERIES ::: OCTOBER 1918.

WAR DIARY
of X/2 Trench Mortar Battery.
INTELLIGENCE SUMMARY. OCTOBER 1918.
(Erase heading not required.)

Army Form C. 2118.

Place	Date	Hour	Summary of Events and Information	Remarks and references to Appendices
Lock 7, Canal du Nord.	Oct 1st		1 or. returned from 6th Corps Gas School. Trial of new Pattom Guys for 6" Trench Mortar.	
	2		1 or. proceeded on leave to U.K. 4/10/18 to 18/10/18. Detachment from X/2 and Y/2 T.M.B's. proceeded to NOYELLES to get a German 15 cm How. It was brought from NOYELLES Village into action @ L4 B 95.05 and 40 rounds were fired on FONTEN VILLE. Map 57c NE.	
	3		Battery moved from Lock 7 to FLESQUIERES. Detachment at Noyelles fired 30 rounds of 15 cm. on FONTENVILLE and on H2 c.9.3. Map 57 B NW.	
	4		1 or. proceeded on Special leave to U.K. 6/10/18 to 20/10/18. 1 or. returned from Burss at VII Corps Signal School. 1 or. returned from Special leave to U.K. Checked registration of 15 c.m on NIERGNIES - 35 rounds -, by making use of H.V. Rate R.F.A. O.P. at Mont Siur-l'Oeuvre. A second detachment of Trench Mortar men put into action a 10 cm. H.V. Gun found in Nine Wood by replacing a damaged wheel. 3 rounds were fired to test buffer.	
	5		20 rounds 15 cm. on Crossroads in H2 c.70.25 and 40 rounds were fired. 10 cm H.V. brought into action at L10 a.9.1. 40 rounds were fired with Ballon observation on WAMBAIX, HAIT and LA TARGETTE. 23 rounds were fired on FONTENVILLE and QUARRIES in H10 a from a 21 cm "Long Mortar" put into action by Trench Mortar men at L10 c 80 (Quarry in Nine Wood).	

Army Form C. 2118.

WAR DIARY
INTELLIGENCE SUMMARY. OCTOBER 1918

(Erase heading not required.)

Place	Date	Hour	Summary of Events and Information	Remarks and references to Appendices
FLESQUIERES	6th		3 rounds 21 c.m. How. and 24 rounds 10 c.m. H.V. Blue Cross on WAMBAIX. 20 rounds 15.c.m. Hows. on H.2 c.70.25 and H.7 6.70.40. Great difficulty was experienced in mending the 21 c.m. How? in order to reinforce the platform in the soft soil.	
	7th		Arranged for balloon observation with H.1.St. Balloon Section, but found impossible owing to high wind, also arranged for supply of charges for 21 c.m from 3rd Army. 10 c.m H.V. fires 25 rounds Blue Cross on WAMBAIX village and 15 c.m How.? fires 20 rounds on cross roads in H.2.C.	
	8		1 or. returned from leave to U.K. 1 or. returned from Course at 3rd Army School of Cookery. The captured guns (3) were employed during 3 hours barrage for attack on positions NIERGNIES and SERANVILLERS. 21 c.m fires 60 rounds, 15 c.m fires 135 and 10 c.m H.V. fires 160 (Blue Cross and HE) on targets around Wambaix, the Railway and Wambaix Copse. Detachments were withdrawn to FLESQUIERES when the guns were put out of range by the advance.	
	10th		Personnel of Battery on Salvage work - Salvaged 18 pdr Shell Cases, Rifles, Packs and Equipment &c.	

Army Form C. 2118.

WAR DIARY

of X/2 Trench Mortar Battery

INTELLIGENCE SUMMARY. OCTOBER 1918

(Erase heading not required.)

Instructions regarding War Diaries and Intelligence Summaries are contained in F.S. Regs., Part II. and the Staff Manual respectively. Title pages will be prepared in manuscript.

Place	Date	Hour	Summary of Events and Information	Remarks and references to Appendices
	11		Battery moved from FLESQUIERES to NOYELLES	
NOYELLES	13		1 OR proceeded on leave to U.K 15/10/18 to 29/10/18. 1 OR returned from leave to U.K	
	14		2/Lieut. H. BOSWORTH and 1 OR returned from 3rd Army Artillery School. Battery Stores & moved from VAUX VRAUCOURT to VELU and 3 OR detailed as dump Guard.	
	15		1 OR proceeded on leave to U.K 17/10/18 to 31/10/18. 1 OR proceeded on leave to U.K 18/10/18 to 1/11/18	
	16		Salvaged 18 pdr and H.5" Shell cases	
	17		1 OR proceeded on leave to U.K 20/10/18 to 3/11/18 - Salvaged 1 load of German Material &c	
ESTOURMEL	18		Battery moved from NOYELLES to ESTOURMEL. 1 OR from leave from U.K.	
	19		1 OR on leave to U.K 22nd Oct to 5th Nov 1918. Salvaged 1 load 18 pdr Shell Cases	
	20		10 OR returned from D.A.C to prepare ground for Trench Mortar demonstration	
	20		1 OR from leave from U.K	
	21		10 Divisional Supplies Dumps removed from VELU to CARNIERES. Bomb. Bentley Gunner Marsh, awarded 3 days Field Punishment No 2 for being absent from Camp reprimanded for being absent from camp without permission on 19-10-18	

Army Form C. 2118.

WAR DIARY
of X/2 Trench Mortar Battery
INTELLIGENCE SUMMARY.
October 1918

(Erase heading not required.)

Instructions regarding War Diaries and Intelligence Summaries are contained in F. S. Regs., Part II. and the Staff Manual respectively. Title pages will be prepared in manuscript.

Place	Date	Hour	Summary of Events and Information	Remarks and references to Appendices
ESTOURMEL	Oct 22		3.O.R on leave to U.K. 24/10/18 to 7/11/18. Battery moved from ESTOURMEL to ST YAAST.	
			1.O.R from leave from U.K. 2nd Lieut. Bosworth M.O.R. proceeded to Divisional Surplus Dump	
ST YAAST	23		Battery moved from ST YAAST to ST PYTHON.	
ST PYTHON	24		1.O.R from leave from U.K.	
	26		1.O.R on leave to U.K. 28/10/18 to 11/11/18.	
	28		Divisional Surplus Dump removed from St HILAIRE to ST PYTHON	
			Captain R.M. Corris proceeded on leave to U.K.	
	30		2nd Lt. Bosworth with Captain Tucker reconnoitred the line south or near to getting our Trench Mortars in action. Owing to lack of targets the G.O.C. 5th 176th Infantry Brigade stated that no useful purpose could be served by getting the Guns into action at that moment.	
	31		2nd Lt. Bosworth & 1.O.R joined 48th Battery R.F.A.	
			Value of Salvage for month of October £122.	

J.B.Tucker, Captain
for O/C X.2. T.M.B

Army Form C. 2118.

WAR DIARY
of Y.2. Trench Mortar Battery
INTELLIGENCE SUMMARY
October 1918

(Erase heading not required.)

Place	Date	Hour	Summary of Events and Information	Remarks and references to Appendices
Lock 7. Canal du Nord	Oct. 1.		1 O.R. proceeded on leave to U.K. 3/5/17th. Firing test with new pattern spring guns. Satisfactory & easy manipulation.	
	- 2		1 O.R. proceeded on leave to U.K. 4/5 18th. 1 N.C.O + 3 men proceeded to Noyelles to form detachment to fire a captured 5.9 Howitzer at I.4.b 95.06. Gun taken from Noyelles village. 40 rds fired on Inchy village.	
Inchy en Artois	- 3		Moved to Inchy en Artois. 30 rds harassing fire with captured 5.9 How. on to a road behind Iwuy village. Lawn.	
	- 4		1 O.R. proceeded on leave to U.K. 6th to 20th. Fired 35 rds registration with 5.9 How on to Iwuy village from Mont. sur l'Oeuvre. Salvaged wheel of damaged gun and fitted same to a captured 10 c.m. A.V. Gun to Bois de neuf, so as to tow round also to make it fit to fire. Removed to firing position at I.10.d.9.2. Fired 3 rounds on test.	
	- 5		26 rds fired by captured 10 c.m A.V. Gun on a registration with Balloon observation. Good registrations obtained on objects at A.10.c.95.13 & on Cross roads La Targette at A.14.d.90.35. Another detachment prepared a captured 8 inch Howitzer for firing. 14 rounds 10 c.m. Gun fired harassing above targets. Driver Ross wounded.	
	- 6		Fired 24 rds Blue Cross Gas Shells on to Noyelles village in at 16 a with 10 cm A.V. Gun. Driver Echo wounded to hospital.	
	- 7		1 O.R. proceeded on leave to U.K. 9th to 23rd. Received orders to fire on barrage on the Brit. Eleven man proceeded to line 10 mins ago also elements on the Noue. captured guns.	

WAR DIARY
or
INTELLIGENCE SUMMARY

of Y.2 (Spencer) Mortar Battery
October 1915.

Army Form C. 2118.

(Erase heading not required.)

Place	Date	Hour	Summary of Events and Information	Remarks and references to Appendices
Hogueros	Oct. 8		1.O.R on leave to U.K. 10th-24th. 1.O.R. from leave from U.K. Issued 135 rds from captured 5.9 How – 160 rds (50 blue cross gas) from captured A.M. and 60 rds from captured 8 inch Howitzer in the barrage for attack at 4.30 a.m. Various targets H.10.A.7.C.	
	" 9		Detachments – except A.O.R – returned to billets at Hoogezand.	
	" 10		1.O.R relieves 1.O.R at 17th Battery R.F.A. Salvaged 1 load 18 lb cases to Corps Salvage Dump	
	" 11		2nd Lieut Renton proceeded on leave to U.K. 13th–27th. 1.O.R on leave to U.K.	
Abeele	" 12		1.O.R. rejoins from 16th Battery. R.F.A. 1.O.R. on leave to U.K.	
	" 13		Returned Divisional Ordnance Stores to Railhead. 1.O.R. reported from Hospital	
	" 14		1.Cpl. & 5.O.R. proceeded to Yebu Railhead to take charge of 2nd Div. R.A. Dumps	
	" 15		1.O.R from leave from U.K.	
	" 16		1.O.R on leave to U.K. Salvaged 1 load of 18 Pdr Cartridge cases to Corps Salvage Dump.	
	" 17		1.O.R from leave from U.K. Salvaged 2 loads of 18 Pdr Cartridge cases and 1 Gunner Branch Mortar.	
Estamel	" 18		Moved to Estamel. 2.O.R from leave from U.K. 1.O.R on leave to U.K.	
	" 19		1 load of Salvage to Divisional Salvage Dump. 1.O.R on leave to U.K. Capotain S.C. Tucker from leave from U.K.	
	" 20		1 load WD Salvage to Divisional Salvage Dump.	

Army Form C. 2118.

WAR DIARY of Y.2 Heavy Motor Battery

INTELLIGENCE SUMMARY

October 1918.

Place	Date	Hour	Summary of Events and Information	Remarks and references to Appendices
Estourmel	Oct 21		1 OR on leave to U.K. 2 OR from leave from U.K. 2 O.R. returned at Divisional Surplus Dump.	
St Vaast	" 22		2 OR on leave to U.K. Moved to St Vaast. 8 OR attached to D.A.C. 1 OR reported from Divisional Surplus Dump. 2 OR on leave	
	" 23		Lt Daniels and 2 OR returned from Divisional Surplus Dump.	
St Python	" 24		Moved to St Python. 1 OR to R.A. Surplus Dump. Captain S.C. Tucker engaged in locating recently captured Guns.	
	" 25		Captain Tucker engaged on locating recently captured Guns. A list of 19 Guns located handed to D.A.Q.M.G., 2nd Division. 1 OR on leave to U.K. 1 OR from leave from U.K.	
	" 26		2 Captured 77 m.m Guns brought from Riqa & handed to Corps Captured Gun Park. 2 OR on leave to U.K.	
	" 27		2 Captured 4.2 Howitzers brought from W.3 central & handed to Corps Captured Gun Park. 2 OR from leave from U.K.	
	" 28		5 Wagons loaded set out to assist removal of R.A. Surplus Dumps	
	" 29		1 4.1 Captured Gun brought from Q.30.a. 8.2 & handed to Corps Captured Gun Park.	
	" 30		Capt. J.C. Tucker & Lt. Bosworth reconnoitred the line with a view to getting our Heavy Motors into action owing to lack of Targets the G.O.C. 6th T.C. Infantry Brigades stated that no useful purpose could be served by getting the Guns into action at the moment. 2nd Lieut N. Newton from leave from U.K.	

Army Form C. 2118.

WAR DIARY
or
INTELLIGENCE SUMMARY

of Y.2. Trench Mortar Battery

October 1918.

(Erase heading not required.)

Instructions regarding War Diaries and Intelligence Summaries are contained in F. S. Regs., Part II. and the Staff Manual respectively. Title Pages will be prepared in manuscript.

Place	Date	Hour	Summary of Events and Information	Remarks and references to Appendices
St. Python	Oct 30		Sending German Salvage returned to Corps Salvage Dump.	
	31		2 OR on leave to U.K.	
			Value of Salvage returned for the month of October = £191 – 9 – 0.	

Sydney H Luker
Captain
o/c Y.2. T.M.B.

2nd Divisional Artillery.

X & Y TRENCH MORTAR BATTERIES ::: NOVEMBER 1918.

Army Form C. 2118.

WAR DIARY of X/2 T.M.Bty. NOVEMBER 1918.
INTELLIGENCE SUMMARY.
(Erase heading not required.)

Place	Date Nov	Hour	Summary of Events and Information	Remarks and references to Appendices
ST PYTHON	1st/4th	-	Battery in billets in ST PYTHON with majority of personnel attached for duty to sections of 2nd D.A.C.	
RUESNES	5th	-	Battery moved from ST PYTHON to RUESNES. 2/Lt Parker proceeded on leave.	
VILLERS-POL	10th	-	Battery moved from RUESNES to VILLERS-POL, where party on A.R.P. duty rejoined battery.	
	11th	-	Armistice signed. Hostilities ceased at 11.00 hours.	
	13th	-	2/Lt Bowith proceeded on leave.	
	14th	-	Orders received for all personnel to be attached to D.A.C. units & remaining guns & stores to be handed in to D.A.D.O.S.	
	15th	-	Orders received to reassemble personnel & stores. Capt Gorrie returned from leave.	
ST PYTHON	16th	-	Battery moved from VILLERS-POL to ST PYTHON & became attached for rations & discipline to 2nd Div. Reception Camp. Lieut Sugden returned to duty from A8-Bty. R.F.A.	
	19th	-	Remainder of personnel returned to duty from 2nd D.A.C.	

Army Form C. 2118.

WAR DIARY
of X/27 M.B/5
INTELLIGENCE SUMMARY. NOVEMBER 1918.
(Erase heading not required.)

Instructions regarding War Diaries and Intelligence Summaries are contained in F. S. Regs., Part II. and the Staff Manual respectively. Title pages will be prepared in manuscript.

Place	Date	Hour	Summary of Events and Information	Remarks and references to Appendices
ST PYTHON	NOV 20th		Training carried out daily on a program of rifle drill, physical training, route marches + football.	
	30th		2/Lieut Parker returned from leave.	
	20th			
	26th		All guns + stores returned from Surplus Dump at CARNIERES.	

R.M.Gorrie Capt. M.B.
O.C.
25.

Army Form C. 2118.

WAR DIARY
1/2 T.M. Battery
INTELLIGENCE SUMMARY.
November 1918.

(Erase heading not required.)

Instructions regarding War Diaries and Intelligence Summaries are contained in F. S. Regs., Part II. and the Staff Manual respectively. Title pages will be prepared in manuscript.

Place	Date	Hour	Summary of Events and Information	Remarks and references to Appendices
St Python	1st		Battery Personnel mostly attached to Sections of D.A.C. and Divnl. Arty.	
-- --	2nd		A.R.P. 1 O.R. rejoined from Leave to U.K.	
-- --	5th		Lieut. R.J. Davis M.C. proceeded on Leave to U.K.	
Ruesnes	6th		Battery H.Qs. move from St Python to Ruesnes.	
-- --	7th		1 N.C.O. rejoined from Leave to U.K.	
-- --	8th		1 Man " " " " "	
-- --	9th		Battery Hd. Qrs. move from Ruesnes to Villers-Pol.	
Villers-Pol	10th		All Battery personnel at A.R.P. rejoin and 1 N.C.O. rejoin from Leave to U.K.	
-- --	11th		1 N.C.O. from Leave to U.K.	
-- --	12th		3 Men " " " "	
-- --	13th		1 " proceed on Leave to U.K.	
-- --	14th		18 O.Rs. under Lieut. Roberts 2/DAC proceed to Railhead for Divnl. Reception Camp at St Python.	
-- --	15th		Battery Officer and Clerks join 2nd Divnl. Reception Camp at St Python in accordance with Divnl. Movement Order	

Army Form C. 2118.

V/o J.M. Baston

WAR DIARY
INTELLIGENCE SUMMARY

November 1918

(Erase heading not required.)

Instructions regarding War Diaries and Intelligence Summaries are contained in F.S. Regs., Part II. and the Staff Manual respectively. Title Pages will be prepared in manuscript.

Place	Date	Hour	Summary of Events and Information	Remarks and references to Appendices
VILLERS-POL	15.	A.M.	Guns, Equipment and Stores handed over to D.A.D.O.S. 2. Div.	
			2 O.R.s on leave to U.K. and 2 O.R.s from leave to U.K.	
" "	16.		Battery Hq. Qrs. move to St. Python. Leaving Capt. S.G. Tucker and Stores at VILLERS-POL. Guns, equipment and part of stores handed to D.A.D.O.S. 1 N.E.O. return from leave to U.K. 1 N.E.O. return from leave to U.K.	
ST. PYTHON	17.		The whole of the Battery reserved reassembles (including Recovered Party)	
			3. G.S. Wagons and 13. Mules returned to 8" P.A.C.	
" "	18.		Lieut. N. Boston with Return return from St. Bettey.	
" "	19.		Capt. Jo. Tucker with Stores return unit. 1 O.R. from leave to U.K. 1 O.R. Rambles to hospital "Sick"	
" "	20.		Lieut R.J. Daniels M.C. return unit from leave to U.K. A programme of training consisting of Drill (Rifle and Foot) Route Marching Physical Training and Football was commenced and continued daily.	
" "	21.		Training Continued. 2 U.R.s from leave to U.K. 1 U.R. to hospital Sick.	
" "	22.		Guns and Equipment of CARNIERES Surplus Amp. Group to Bty. Hq. Qrs.	

Army Form C. 2118.

WAR DIARY
or
INTELLIGENCE SUMMARY

(Erase heading not required.)

Instructions regarding War Diaries and Intelligence Summaries are contained in F. S. Regs., Part II. and the Staff Manual respectively. Title Pages will be prepared in manuscript.

Place	Date	Hour	Summary of Events and Information	Remarks and references to Appendices
Sth Python	22nd		1 O.R. to Hospital "Sick". Training etc. continues.	
"	23rd		1 " " on Leave to U.K. — " — " —	
"	24th		Training, Physical Drill etc. etc. continues. 1 O.R. to Hospital "Sick" 1 O.R. from Leave to U.K. 1 O.R. to Hospital "Sick".	
"	25th		Training etc. etc. continues	
"	26th		— " — " — " — " — " —	
"	27th		— " — " — " — " — " —	
"	28th		— " — " — " — " — 1 O.R. Discharged from Hospital to Duty.	
"	29th		Training continues	
"	30th		— " — " —	

Cowdrey ½ Lieut Nota Bully
Capt

2449 Wt. W14957/M90 750,000 1/16 J.B.C. & A. Forms/C.2118/12.

2nd Divisional Artillery.

X & Y TRENCH MORTAR BATTERIES ::: DECEMBER 1918.

Army Form C. 2118.

WAR DIARY

of X/2 T.M.B. for DEC. 1918.

INTELLIGENCE SUMMARY.

(Erase heading not required.)

Place	Date	Hour	Summary of Events and Information	Remarks and references to Appendices
	DEC.			
ST PYTHON	1st/27th		Battery in billets & attached to 2nd Div. Reception Camp for discipline. Parades & training carried out as per program of training in rifle drill, gun drill, physical training, football & tug of war	
	28th		Battery entrained at SOLESMES for Germany.	
	29th		Battery detrained at DÜREN & proceeded to billets in Cinemas Hall in BIRKESDORF.	
	30th		Battery marched to MARIA WEILER & took over billets there	
	31st		I.O.R. proceeded to England as a WATFORD DETAIL.	

R.M. Gottie
Capt R.F.A.
O.C. X/2 T.M.B.

Army Form C. 2118.

WAR DIARY
or
INTELLIGENCE SUMMARY

(Erase heading not required.)

H₂ J.M.B

Instructions regarding War Diaries and Intelligence Summaries are contained in F. S. Regs., Part II. and the Staff Manual respectively. Title Pages will be prepared in manuscript.

Place	Date	Hour	Summary of Events and Information	Remarks and references to Appendices
R. Python	1		The Battery paraded at 9.30 a.m. the daily lining consisting of Rifle Exercise, drill, marching drill, football etc.	
	2		do	
	3		do	
	4		do	
	5		do	
	6		do	
	7		do	
	8		"D" Battery signaller from bere left	
	9		do Lt J.P.Williams " " " "	
	10		do	
	11		do	
	12		do	
	13		do	
	14		1 O.R. on leave to U.K.	
	15		do	
	16		do	
	17		do	
	18		do	
	19		do 1 O.R. 6 to 8 U.K.	
	20		do	

Army Form C. 2118.

WAR DIARY
or
INTELLIGENCE SUMMARY

(Erase heading not required.)

Place	Date	Hour	Summary of Events and Information	Remarks and references to Appendices
	21		Training as per program	
	22		"	
	23		"	
	24		"	
	25		"	
	26		"	
	27		" " till the Brigade	
			The Battery paraded at 9am and entrained at Stump for	
	29		Dover. Arrived and into temporary billets at the Priory	
	30		and 6 Biggin at Lower Wales.	

[signatures]

Army Form C. 2118.

WAR DIARY
or
INTELLIGENCE SUMMARY

SEPT. 1918
41st L.T.M.B.

Sheet 1

(Erase heading not required.)

Instructions regarding War Diaries and Intelligence Summaries are contained in F.S. Regs., Part II. and the Staff Manual respectively. Title pages will be prepared in manuscript.

Place	Date	Hour	Summary of Events and Information	Remarks and references to Appendices
YPRES SECTOR	1		8 GUNS in defensive position in YPRES SECTOR	
	2		Work done:- Improving position. Carrying new ammunition to guns and retiring old Pistol Head ammunition	
	3		No firing war carried out in this sector	
	4			
	5		Battery relieved by 42nd L.T.M.B.	
NIGHT 5/6	6		Moved to billets at BRAKE CAMP 28/A 30.c 85.	
	7		Training. Cleaning of guns and equipment. One man taken on strength	
	8		2/Lt. R.V. ATKINS taken on strength officially and struck off strength of 2/9th D.L.I. Authority 14 Division A.2/175 of 7/9/18	
	9		Training	
	10		Training. 2 men struck off strength (hospital)	
	11		Training. 1 man struck off strength (hospital)	
	12		Training	
NIGHT 13/14			Battery relieved 42nd L.T.M.B. in YPRES SECTOR	
	14			
	15		2/Lt. R.V. ATKINS, 1 N.C.O. and 3 men proceeded to MINKAM 2nd Corps L.T.M. School	
	16		1 man struck off strength (hospital)	

Army Form C. 2118.

WAR DIARY
or
INTELLIGENCE SUMMARY.

(Erase heading not required.)

SEPT 1918
4/1 L.T.M.B.

Place	Date	Hour	Summary of Events and Information	Remarks and references to Appendices
YPRES SECTOR	17		3 men struck off strength (hospital)	
	18		2 men struck off strength (hospital)	
	19		Work done in sector during last 6 days:- CONS ENGAGEMENTS in more forward advanced outpost line moved forward.	
MCHT	19/20		Battery relieved by 26th L.T.M.B. 9th Divn.	
	20.		Battery proceeded by train to CRIBBAGE HOUSE 27.N.E I.18.c.5.8. Cleaning guns and equipment	
	21.		Training. BGC visited Battery in lining area	
	22		Training A/Battery S.M. and A/Battery Sergt. returned to their Units	
	23		Training 1 N.C.O and 4 men Orderly Room H.Q.rs	
	24.		Training	
	25.		Training 7 men attached to Battery. 1 Sergt taken on strength from 29th O.B.L.I.	
	26.		Training 1 N.C.O. and 1 man struck off strength, proceeded to 25th Divn for duty with a L.T.M.B.	

WAR DIARY
or
INTELLIGENCE SUMMARY.

Army Form C. 2118.

SEPT. 1918
D.A.L.T. H.B.
Sheet III

Place	Date	Hour	Summary of Events and Information	Remarks and references to Appendices
	27		One Segt. taken on strength from 18th Yr L's. One man proceeded to his Base Depot.	
			Battery moved by train to RENNING HELST acting as DIV RES. arriving at 9.0 p.m. 28/G.34.A.1.2.	
	28		Battery moved from RENNINGHEAST to MEDOC FM. 28/C.28.a.u.9. at 7.30 am	A
	29		Salvage work.	
	30		Salvage work.	

J.S Heskeye
O/C 410e-TMB.
30/9/18.

CONFIDENTIAL.

WAR DIARY

- of -

41st TRENCH MORTAR BATTERY (LIGHT).

From: 1st October, 1918.
To: 31st October, 1918.

VOLUME V.

Army Form C. 2118.

WAR DIARY
or
INTELLIGENCE SUMMARY
(Erase heading not required.)

SHEET I OCTOBER 1918
 41st L.T.M.B

Instructions regarding War Diaries and Intelligence Summaries are contained in I.S. Regs., Part II. and the Staff Manual respectively. Title Pages will be prepared in manuscript.

Place	Date	Hour	Summary of Events and Information	Remarks and references to Appendices
MEROC FARM	1		Battery to proceed by march route to MESSINES AREA taking over from 90th L.T.M.B	
MESSINES	2		2 guns in defensive position at KINGSCHERE. 1 officer's caused out from the position (P35.c.30.95)	1 man struck strength (hospital) 1 shea wounded by shell fire near Bn H.Qrs
	3		1 man admitted hospital 1 man struck off strength Capt. J.O. FLECK admitted hospital. Lt Fleck taken over command. Cpl Dean 18th appointed A/Sgt. 2/Lt Soderskim + 1 O.R. proceeded to XIX Corps L.T.M. School.	
	4		2 Guns in position at MAWELL PARK. 1 shot fired on BLANCHE FARM. 5 men returned from hospital.	
	5		2 men struck off strength. 2 N.C.Os + 5 men taken on strength. 1 men struck off strength, 2 men taken on strength, 3 men admitted hospital. Battery H.Qrs moved to Q6.c.30.95. HOUTHEM CANAL.	
(Q6.c.30.95)			4 men taken on strength.	
	6		2 guns at MAWELL PARK fired to enemy T.Ms + M.Gs. 1 man admitted hospital 2 guns transferred from KINGSCHERE to positions near GOOSHUIS & fired on enemy M.G at P35.a.00.1 which was eventually silenced. 2 guns fired from T.Ms + P35.d.9.9. + DISTILLERY & fired on enemy T.Ms + M.Gs in positions near GOOSHUIS.	
	11		Shot carried out on 2 ts ISTULEBY lay guns in position near GOOSHUIS	

Army Form C. 2118.

WAR DIARY
or
INTELLIGENCE SUMMARY

(Erase heading not required.)

OCTOBER 1918
A/151 A.T.M.B.
SHEET 1

Instructions regarding War Diaries and Intelligence Summaries are contained in F. S. Regs., Part II. and the Staff Manual respectively. Title Pages will be prepared in manuscript.

Place	Date	Hour	Summary of Events and Information	Remarks and references to Appendices
P. de C. 30/45	12		2/Lt Rocker & H.D. proceeded to IV Army Rest Camp	
	13		1 man admitted to hospital	
	14		1 man admitted hospital	
NIGHT	15		Battery withdrew from line on relief by H3RP Lng Bde.	
WOLVERGHEM	16		Battery arrived WOLVERGHEM area. 1 man admitted to hospital	
	17			
COMINES	18		Battery moved & marched into to area SOUTH OF COMINES.	
RONCQ	19		Battery moved & marched to RONCQ area. 1 man struck off strength (hospital)	
HERSEAUX	20		Battery split up into 2 sections. 2 guns & teams complete with each section & two guns & teams with H.Q & 2 Bde. H.Qrs. March to HERSEAUX by march route	
	21		Training (actual)	
	22		Capt J.D. FIELK struck off strength, authority list N° 1285. D.A.G. G.H.Q.	
	23		2/Lt. J. CARSTAIRS & 1.O.R. returned from H.T.M. course at XIX Corps School	

WAR DIARY
or
INTELLIGENCE SUMMARY

Army Form C. 2118.

OCTOBER 1916
41st L.T.M.B.

SHEET VII

Place	Date	Hour	Summary of Events and Information	Remarks and references to Appendices
HERSEAUX	24		Training, 1 man returns from hospital.	
	25		" "	
	26		" "	
	27		" "	
	28		" "	
	29		" "	
	30		N.C.O. to DOTTIGNIES	
	31			

Mulenbeen CAPT
COMMANDING 41 LTM. BTY.

C O N F I D E N T I A L.

W A R   D I A R Y

- of -

41st TRENCH MORTAR BATTERY (LIGHT).

From: 1st November, 1918.
To: 30th November, 1918.

VOLUME VI.

41st

LIGHT TRENCH Form C. 2118.
MORTAR BATTERY.

41st L.T.M.B.

WAR DIARY
or
INTELLIGENCE SUMMARY
NOVEMBER 1918

(Erase heading not required.)

Place	Date	Hour	Summary of Events and Information	Remarks and references to Appendices
DOTTIGNIES	1/11		Took over from 42nd Bde. L.T.M.B. Co. Been promoted to Sergt. with pay from Oct 1st 1918	
	6/11		A/Cpl Hopkins promoted to Cpl with pay from Oct 1st 1918	A.M.S.
	7/11		Dvr. BROOK wounded at HELCHIN	A.M.S
	8/11		1 man admitted to hospital	A.M.S
	9/11		Battery left DOTTIGNIES for HERSEAUX by march route	A.M.S
			1 man admitted into hospital	A.M.S.
	11/11		N/Cpl Saddler 32nd London Regt. section promoted to Cpl with pay from 11.11.18.	A.M.S.
	13/11		One man struck off strength (wounded.) One man returned to duty from hospital	A.M.S
			Cpl Hopkins proceeded on L.T.M. Course G.H.Q. School	
	14/11		Battery proceeded to BONDUES by march route	A.M.S.
	15/11		One man struck off strength (hospital)	A.M.S.
	16/11		Cpl Hopkins recalled from L.T.M. Course G.H.Q. School	A.M.S.

WAR DIARY
or
INTELLIGENCE SUMMARY

(Erase heading not required.)

41st LIGHT TRENCH MORTAR BATTERY

Army Form C. 2118.

No. ....
Date ..30.11.19......

41st L.T.M.B. NOVEMBER 1919

Instructions regarding War Diaries and Intelligence Summaries are contained in F.S. Regs., Part II. and the Staff Manual respectively. Title Pages will be prepared in manuscript.

Place	Date	Hour	Summary of Events and Information	Remarks and references to Appendices
BONQUES	18/11/19		One man admitted to hospital. One man returned to duty from hospital	AAS
	20/11/19		Rfn. Rowe returned to duty (unpaid). One man admitted into hospital.	AAS
	26/11/19		One man admitted into hospital. One man returned to duty from hospital	AAS
	29/11/19		Coy. Bed. proceeded to Rest Camp with truant	AAS

W. Burke Lt for CAPT.
COMMANDING 41 LTM. BTY.

CONFIDENTIAL.

WAR DIARY

- of -

41st LIGHT TRENCH MORTAR BATTERY.

From: 1st December, 1918.
To: 31st December, 1918.

VOLUME VII.

Army Form C. 2118.

WAR DIARY
or
INTELLIGENCE SUMMARY

(Erase heading not required.)

41ST T.M.B. DECEMBER 1918

Instructions regarding War Diaries and Intelligence Summaries are contained in F. S. Regs., Part II. and the Staff Manual respectively. Title Pages will be prepared in manuscript.

Place	Date	Hour	Summary of Events and Information	Remarks and references to Appendices
BONNIERES	1st		SUNDAY. One man returned from hospital	69.
	2nd		Recreation & training	69.
	3rd		"	69.
	4th		" One man returned from hospital	69.
	5th		"	69.
	6th		"	69.
	7th		" One man admitted hospital, one man returned from leave	69.
	8th		Capt. Pick & servant returned from Officers' Rest Hotel, Hardelot Plage	69.
	9th		Recreation & training. One man returned from leave, all ammunition returned	69.
	10th		"	69.
	11th		" One man admitted hospital	69.
	12th		"	69.
	13th		" One man admitted hospital	69.
			49208606 Pte Sawyer O. 18th Yorks & Lancs Regt. ex appointed Acting Lance Corporal from this date	69.
	14th		Recreation & training. Surplus attached strength having proceeded to Divisional Concentration Camp for demobilization, in accordance with Demobilization Circular Memorandum No 1. One man returned from hospital	69.
	15th		SUNDAY	69.
	16th		Recreation & training. One man proceeded to Divisional Concentration Camp for demobilization & attached strength in accordance with Demobilization Circular Memorandum No 1. 2/Lt A.W. Cooper proceeded to U.K. on leave.	69.

Army Form C. 2118.

WAR DIARY 41st L.T.M.B.
INTELLIGENCE SUMMARY. December 1918

(Erase heading not required.)

Place	Date	Hour	Summary of Events and Information	Remarks and references to Appendices
BONDUES	17th		Recreation & Training. One man struck by enemy having proceeded to Divisional Concentration Camp for Demobilization, in accordance with Demobilization Circular Memorandum No. 1.	
	18th		Recreation & Training	
	19th		"	
	20th		"	
	21st		"	
	22nd		SUNDAY. One man returned from hospital.	
	23rd		Recreation & Training. One man admitted hospital	
	24th		"	
	25th		Christmas Day	
	26th		Boxing Day	
	27th		Recreation + Training	
	28th		" One man returned from hospital & one man admitted hospital	
	29th		SUNDAY	
	30th		Recreation Training. One man returned from hospital	
	31st		" 2/Lt. G.A. Crabtree proceeded on leave to U.K.	

J.M. Mean CAPT.
COMMANDING 41 L.T.M. BTY.

stray/wo/as/u

www.ingramcontent.com/pod-product-compliance
Lightning Source LLC
Chambersburg PA
CBHW080918230426
43668CB00014B/2152